HYDROCARBON HUCKSTERS

HYDROCARBON HUCKSTERS

Lessons from Louisiana on Oil, Politics, and Environmental Justice

Ernest Zebrowski and **Mariah Zebrowski Leach**

University Press of Mississippi / Jackson

www.upress.state.ms.us

The University Press of Mississippi is a member
of the Association of American University Presses.

Copyright © 2014 by University Press of Mississippi
All rights reserved
Manufactured in the United States of America

First printing 2014

∞

Library of Congress Cataloging-in-Publication Data

Zebrowski, Ernest.
Hydrocarbon hucksters : lessons from Louisiana on oil, politics, and
environmental justice / Ernest Zebrowski and Mariah Zebrowski Leach.
    pages cm
Includes bibliographical references and index.
ISBN 978-1-61703-899-0 (hardback) — ISBN 978-1-61703-900-3 (ebook)
1. Petroleum industry and trade—Political aspects—Louisiana. 2. Petroleum industry
and trade—Environmental aspects—Louisiana. 3. Louisiana—Politics and government—1951– 4. Louisiana—Economic conditions. I. Zebrowski Leach, Mariah. II. Title.
HD9567.L8Z43 2014
338.2'72809763—dc23   2013018796

British Library Cataloging-in-Publication Data available

To Owen Zachary Leach,

born May 30, 2012,

and to all the men

and women of his generation

CONTENTS

PREFACE

This is the saga of the oil industry's takeover of the state of Louisiana—its leaders, its laws, its environment, and the critical thinking skills of so many of its voters. It is a story of mind-boggling scientific and technological triumphs sharing the same public stew with imaginative myths and bald-faced lies, to the point where even many critical thinkers can't quite be sure of what they're digesting. It's a chronicle of money and power, greed and corruption, jingoism and exploitation, pollution and disease, and the bewilderment and resignation of too many of the powerless. Most importantly, it is an exemplary case study of what happens when the oil and petrochemical industries are uncritically handed everything they ask for.

As authors, we are not so foolish as to propose that the whole oil industry be slaughtered and buried. Not only would that be uncharitable, but such an industrial demise would also be disastrous to our society, insofar as petroleum is the prime ingredient in a huge number of modern products—including fertilizers, insecticides, paints, plastics, inks, soaps, synthetic rubber, roofing, paving materials, lubricants, and even some pharmaceuticals. What we do suggest in our later chapters, to the contrary, is that our society should value petroleum *more* highly and quit squandering so much of it by simply burning it. After all, there now exist practical alternatives to sending so much of it up in smoke. Why not leave some behind for future generations so they can concoct even more clever and environmentally friendly uses for this valuable gift from Mother Nature, which she herself took so many millions of years to brew?

We also hope to set to rest the myth that the oil-and-gas industries are major job creators. They are not. They indeed do generate huge amounts of private wealth, but not for a whole lot of ordinary Americans. The relatively small number of workers who indeed depend on Big Oil for their weekly paychecks could just as gainfully be employed in other parts of a restructured energy sector that is less hydrocarbon dependent.

As for us, the coauthors, we are uncle and niece, a generation apart, who have melded these conclusions from two different tracks. The elder of us (Ernest, aka "Zeb") is a former physics professor who taught in

Louisiana for seven years and has visited most of the nooks and crannies of the state while conducting the research for this and several of his previous books. The younger (Mariah) holds a degree in environmental law and has made firsthand environmental observations in each of the fifty states as well as several foreign countries. Together, we have attempted to weave together the science, the legal history, the economic issues, and the national and global contexts of what has happened in Louisiana over the past century—and to critically examine the possibility that other parts of the United States may be at risk of repeating Louisiana's follies.

Yet, as parents as well as authors, we have written this book with a hopeful spirit. Oil is a dwindling resource, and no amount of rhetoric will reverse that. Meanwhile, the present batch of lawmakers and oil executives will gradually be replaced by younger ones, and that also is a fact of life. The time is ripe to forge a connection between these two inevitable processes. Hopefully, our efforts will help set the stage for the next generation, properly educated, of course, to make better-informed decisions that will lead to a less hydrocarbon-dependent world.

LOUISIANA BY THE NUMBERS

Different sources disagree slightly about some of the statistics listed below. The two main reasons for such discrepancies are (1) many of the data change over time, so the published figures depend on when they are collected (yes, even the state's land area is changing continuously due to erosion), and (2) different sources may use slightly different criteria regarding what to include or exclude within a given statistical category. The following, therefore, should not be considered to be an exact description (*exact* being theoretically impossible), but rather a general statistical picture of the state of Louisiana at the time of this writing.

Total surface area of Louisiana: 51,843 sq. mi. (31st of 50 states)
Area of inland waters: 8,639 sq. mi. (17.7% water)
Land area, exclusive of inland waters: 43,204 sq. mi.
Rate of land loss per year: 25 to 35 sq. mi.

Number of Louisiana parishes: 64
Number of parishes with active oil or gas wells: 64
Total number of active oil and gas wells on land in Louisiana: 39,960
Number of oil/gas wells drilled on land in Louisiana since 1901:   185,000
Number of derelict oil and gas wells on land in Louisiana: 60,000[1]
Number of active offshore production platforms in entire United States,
    exclusive of rigs engaged in drilling: 3,959[2]
Average number of wells per offshore platform: 12 to 13
Approximate total active offshore wells in US waters: 50,000

---

1. The relevant state offices do not have a precise figure for the number of orphaned or otherwise derelict wells. It is likely that our estimate of 60,000 errs on the low side, given the huge number of wells that have been drilled in Louisiana over the past century. Some news sources have reported a number as high as 220,000.
2. In addition to these production platforms, there are several hundred offshore exploration (drilling) rigs active at any given time.

Portion of US offshore oil production from waters off the coast of
        Louisiana: 81.6%[3]
Average lifetime of an offshore well: 17 years
Total abandoned wells offshore: 27,000
Number of offshore production platforms already removed: 3,816
Number of offshore platforms awaiting removal: 700

Louisiana population (2010 census):   4,533,372 (25th of 50 states)
Size of civilian labor force: 2,023,976
Total workers actually employed: 1,894,163 (93.6%)
Workers employed in the oil/gas industry:
According to state government sources: 47,900 to 55,900[4]
        (2.5% to 3.0% of workers)
According to industry sources: 81,893 (4.3% of workers)
According to industry sources, minus marketing and consumer
        utilities: 62,322 (3.3% of workers)
Job multiplier factor (Economic Policy Institute):   2.02[5]
Maximum likely number of Louisiana jobs dependent on the
        oil/gas industries: 127,910 (6.8 % of workers)

State gross domestic product (GDP): $213.6 billion
State gross domestic product per capita: $49,400[6]
Total economic impact of oil/gas on the state's economy, according
        to industry sources: $65 billion (30.4% of GDP)
State budget: $26 billion
State budget per capita: $5,735
Louisiana median household income: $42,492[7] (41st of 50)

---

3. Based on data from the Louisiana Department of Natural Resources.
4. In this category, the Louisiana Workforce Commission includes some jobs related to
   other extraction industries, including sulfur mining.
5. In some of its promotional material, the Louisiana Oil and Gas industry claims a job multiplier factor of 4.5, but without any explanation of how that figure was arrived at. The same
   industry sources then seem to apply this multiplier to jobs that are *already* in the spin-off
   category (marketing, for instance). The Economic Policy Institute's lower figure of 2.02 is
   in line with that organization's computations for other sectors of the economy; the highest
   job multiplier factor they report for any job sector is 2.71, for automobile manufacturing.
6. US Census Bureau.
7. Half of Louisiana's households have an annual income greater than this figure; the other
   half have an income lower than this figure.

Average household size: 2.74
Median income per capita: $15,508[8]

Life expectancy at birth: 74.2 years (49th out of 50)
High school graduation rate: 82.2% (46th out of 50)
Residents with bachelor's degree or better: 21.4% (46th out of 50)
Poverty rate: 18.8% (2nd out of 50)
Children living in poverty: 31% (3rd out of 50)
Violent crime rate, per 100,000 population: 730 (4th out of 50)
      (159% of national average)
Property crime rate, per 100,000 population: 4,076 (4th out of 50)
      (156% of national average)
Average pollution, per sq. mile per year: 1,800 pounds
Average pollution nationwide, per sq. mile per year: 570 pounds
Louisiana cancer deaths per 100,000 per year: 196.2
Cancer deaths nationally per 100,000 per year: 178.1
Excess annual cancer deaths in Louisiana per year: 820

Number of US senators: 2
Number of US representatives: 6 (down from 7)
Number of state senators: 39
Number of state representatives: 105

---

8. This figure was arrived at by taking the ratio of the two previous figures. Some sources
   claim, without explanation, that the state's median income per capita is actually closer to
   $20,000. These figures are per man, woman, and child, whether working or not.

HYDROCARBON HUCKSTERS

Chapter 1

THE WELL FROM HELL

April 20, 2010, Transocean's $560 million offshore rig *Deepwater Horizon* is barely two days from completing its part of the project. The exploratory drill (monikered "Macondo") has successfully tapped an enormous reservoir of oil 13,293 feet beneath the seabed at the bottom of the mile-deep Mississippi Canyon, about forty-two nautical miles from the Louisiana coastline. The tasks remaining are to temporarily seal the well, offload the drilling fluid (aka "mud"), and tow the giant rig to the coordinates of its next exploration job. On some future date, the owner of this particular offshore lease, BP (formerly British Petroleum), will tow in a "production" platform to begin extracting its bonanza.

BP's public relations office is preparing a news release for a day hence, heralding the company's discovery of up to 100 million barrels of commercially extractable oil. That particular announcement, however, will never reach the press.

Shortly before the 11:00 p.m. work-shift change that night, the drilling crew is startled by a "kick"—a burst of drilling fluid surging up the drill pipe. This is cause for concern because it signals that the upward pressure of the undersea petroleum is greater than the downward pressure exerted by the weight of the three-mile-high column of drilling mud. Clearly, the problem needs to be resolved quickly, because the event that must be prevented at all costs is an uncontrolled gusher. Yet, for quite some time thereafter (the estimates vary, but it was apparently more than a hour), there is more discussion than action.

The well signals its imminent misbehavior with two additional burps, then throws a tantrum and ejects a powerful fountain of mud high into the rig's superstructure. Ominously, this torrent appears to be squirting out of both the central drill pipe and the annular pipe encasing it—which by that time was supposed to have been properly plugged with cement by personnel from Halliburton, one of BP's subcontractors.

3

During training sessions, a shout of "blowout!" is a signal for all floor hands to spring into frenzied action to hoist a heavy emergency shutoff valve into position, then quickly bolt it in place so the surge can be controlled. Unfortunately, because the twelve-hour work shift is now in the process of changing over, the rig's drill deck is temporarily undermanned. Compounding matters, it is after dark and visibility is further curtailed by the rain of goo that quickly engulfs everything, including the floodlights. The few oil-soaked workers manning the machinery frantically call for assistance.

In a control room on the bridge, a twenty-three-year-old technician is shocked by the sight of twenty warning lights flashing simultaneously. Although she is fully aware of her duty to trigger a gas alarm if even a single red light flashes, so many warnings all at once stymie her. Surely, this must be an instrument malfunction of some sort. She takes no decisive action for at least six minutes, possibly as many as nine. Others on the bridge at the time are equally aware of all those warning lights but offer her no guidance.

Modest discharges of natural gas, while serious matters, seldom cause explosions. The electrical equipment on every drilling rig is specifically designed to prevent spark-ignited flare-ups, and all sorts of other work-zone fire precautions are strictly enforced on every platform. If, however, combustible gases mushroom to the surface uncontrolled, then all such safety measures are for naught. Sooner or later, there will be a miniscule spark from *something*—even static electricity—and that's all it will take to trigger a disaster.

Two of the *Deepwater Horizon*'s six huge diesel engines are operating that night. Their function is not just to supply electricity, but also to keep the floating rig accurately centered above the borehole on the seafloor a mile below. One of those engines disobeys its controls and accelerates. The second quickly follows suit, over-revving the main electrical generator. Lights throughout the rig glow brighter and brighter, then begin to pop. Computers and other electronics are fried by the overvoltage. The cause—not apparent to the engine-room technicians at the time—is that those engines' intakes are sucking in not just air, but also natural gas. Who would consider such an event, given that there is a gas warning system in place and there has been no warning?

Diesel engines are not designed to ingest natural gas for very long or to run at very high speeds. As the engines destroy themselves, the lights flicker and go out. Emergency lighting blinks on in a few critical places, but the main emergency generator does not start, which plunges all the bunkrooms into darkness. With no motive power, the *Deepwater Horizon*

1.1. The *Deepwater Horizon* during its last hours. *Courtesy of the US Department of Energy.*

is now adrift, straining the riser pipe that connects it to the wellhead a mile below.

Then, as if matters couldn't get worse, an explosion rocks the platform, followed by a second. Sirens finally wail. A voice blares through the loudspeakers: "This is not a drill! Repeat, this is not a drill!" The 115 workers who survive the two blasts dash to the lifeboats. One boat deploys before it is full to capacity. Some of the stragglers revert to an inflatable raft, which they launch with considerable difficulty during the mayhem. At least seven of the survivors climb over the sides and scamper down the platform's steel ladders—some falling a portion or even most of the way—ultimately to find themselves spending anxious minutes treading water in a blossoming oil slick with an inferno roaring above them. Injuries range from bruises and lacerations to broken bones and serious burns.

As for actuating the shear ram—the well's seafloor fail-safe against an uncontrolled gusher—it's unclear whether anyone tries to do that before evacuating. If they do, the device doesn't work. (If it *had* worked, the fire would have been deprived of fuel and would have quickly burned itself out.)

A 260-foot workboat, the *Damon Bankston*, is nearby to offload drilling mud and other materials the following morning. The *Bankston's* crew rescues the survivors they can find, then backs off about a mile, everyone onboard watching in horror as flames engulf the giant platform. Seventeen of the rescued crew require medical attention. Another eleven workers remain missing and will never be found.

Within eighty minutes, Coast Guard helicopters are buzzing about the inferno, which is now a billowing mass of sooty flames fifty stories high. Their crews radio for the fireboats, then begin to airlift the injured from the *Damon Bankston*'s deck to hospitals on the mainland.

The ninety-eight uninjured survivors are sequestered on the rescue ship until everyone is debriefed. For approximately forty hours, none are permitted to even contact their loved ones. Transocean, BP, and their subcontractors have all had experiences with major accidents before, and their company lawyers know they'll soon be involved in a flurry of lawsuits—some of which may even be filed against one other. It's not only essential to get your own employees' experiences documented before they become contaminated, but also equally important that nobody encourage the news media to conduct a kangaroo trial in the court of public opinion. Blabbermouths, as every corporate lawyer knows, are guarantees of trouble down the road.

All of the employees on the platform at the time of the accident are "encouraged" to sign statements for their own companies (and there are several different outfits involved) regarding what they did or did not witness, as well as to formally pledge that they won't make unauthorized statements to the press.

News reporters scramble for information, but in this tightly controlled environment the pickings are slim. The staff at BP, Transocean, Halliburton (the cementing contractor), the US Coast Guard, the US Minerals Management Service, and virtually everyone else in a position to know something are all essentially mum. For the first two days, there aren't even any photos of the disaster to publish—even though everyone knows it would be impossible for such photos to *not* exist.

Fighting the blaze itself is a lost cause. Weakened by the extreme heat, the huge platform twists and folds into an unrecognizable mass of junk. And then, slowly, around 10:00 a.m. on April 22 (about thirty-six hours after the explosions), it capsizes and sinks into the depths. During its plummet to the seafloor, the giant rig's mile-long riser pipe fails to disengage from the still-unactuated blowout preventer at the seafloor. The pipe kinks and ruptures in three places, and as it bends it places additional strain on the still-open valves at the wellhead. Oil continues to gush unabated from the well. A huge gooey slick blooms on the surface of the sea.

Over the next few days, BP's damage-control engineers use tethered ROVs (remotely-operated vehicles) in a series of futile attempts to actuate the unresponsive blowout preventer. Confusingly, a major section of that 450-ton, six-story-high stack of valves, rams, and control pods doesn't look exactly like the engineering drawings. The prospect that there may have been undocumented changes to the equipment design or installation will be an issue to be investigated later. Regardless, the engineers conclude that the failure of the riser pipe to disconnect as it descended inflicted so much damage on the blowout preventer as to render futile any further efforts to shut those seafloor valves.

With that, a lengthy series of other efforts are initiated to siphon off or otherwise contain the spill. A huge "top hat" fails, clogged by methane hydrate crystals, which form under the extreme pressure and low temperature at the five-thousand-foot depth. A "straw" inserted on May 16 draws off no more than 20 percent of the leak. A "top kill" effort of injecting mud and solid materials into the wellhead becomes a lost cause on May 28, although it isn't actually pronounced a failure until two days later.

And so, week after week, the nation watches in horror as a monstrous oil slick balloons in the Gulf of Mexico, closing down fisheries and ultimately polluting more than five hundred miles of US coastline. Gradually, the reality dawns on everyone that the decisive solution still lies several months in the future—when one of two relief wells will hopefully intersect the original drill pipe at a point deep beneath the seabed, allowing cement to be pumped in to forever seal off the wild well from the bottom.

On July 16—eighty-six days after the blowout—BP engineers succeed in temporarily plugging the gusher from the top. It is not until September 19, however, after a "bottom kill" via one of the relief wells, that the Macondo well is officially declared dead.

The unheralded heroes are the dozens of engineers and technicians who worked night and day to accomplish this feat (unheralded because their employment contracts prohibit them from giving interviews). During the five-month ordeal, a total of at least 4.9 million barrels of crude oil escaped into the Gulf of Mexico. Arguments about how much was recovered, how much was burned at the surface, how much was eaten by bacteria, and how much remains in the environment will probably never be fully resolved.

Eventually, of course, someone is bound to drill a new well in the same general area. After all, there's no question that there's still a lot of oil down there, for which BP still owns the lease. Nor is there any question, as we shall see, that Louisiana's politicians remain fully supportive of more deepwater drilling, in spite of the ever-more-demonstrable risks exemplified by the *Deepwater Horizon* disaster.

◆ ◆ ◆

How could such a catastrophe have happened in the first place? Here was a pair of highly experienced companies (BP and Transocean), plus several equally experienced subcontractors (including the already controversial and therefore presumably attentive Halliburton)—all with access to the finest petroleum engineers in the world, the best-trained offshore workers, and the best technologies. The procedures used were not untried; in fact, the *Deepwater Horizon* itself had already successfully drilled considerably deeper than at the Macondo site.

Numerous *ifs, buts, yeses,* and *maybes* rattled around in millions of people's heads as the nation and much of the world watched the disaster unfold in the news media.

Hadn't fail-safes and backup fail-safes been engineered into BP's Macondo project?

Indeed they had. Hmm. Well yeah, there might be a few questions about that, but, after all, don't such questions always arise after any disaster?

And wasn't this drilling approved by the appropriate oversight agencies of the US government?

Yes, it was—by the Minerals Management Service (MMS).[1] Hmm. Are there really walruses in the Gulf of Mexico, as some of applicants' paperwork suggested?

By law, shouldn't the Environmental Protection Agency (EPA) have reviewed the environmental impact part of BP's drilling permit application?

Hmm. Then why didn't the EPA ask for it?

As the oversight agency, didn't the MMS make any on-site inspections as the drilling proceeded?

Of course it did. And it documented those inspections on all the right government forms, no less. Everything was hunky-dory. Hmm.

---

1. On the heels of the *Deepwater Horizon* disaster, the MMS was reorganized and renamed the Bureau of Ocean Energy Management, Regulation, and Enforcement (BOEMRE). As of October 1, 2011, the duties of the BOEMRE were split into the Bureau of Ocean Energy Management and the Bureau of Safety and Environmental Enforcement. More about these agencies later.

And so it went. Nobody, including those in government and the news media, had any meaningful understanding of how this disaster had been allowed to happen.

◆   ◆   ◆

The first shoreline to be affected, of course, was the closest one: Plaquemines Parish, Louisiana. By May 13, 2010 (about three weeks after the explosions), squishy brown gobs of "meuse" the size of golf balls were washing up on its barrier islands. There was little doubt that tidal currents would soon sweep this goop around and past those little ribbons of sand and into Louisiana's coastal wetlands.

Piyush ("Bobby") Jindal—who had held Louisiana's governorship since January of 2008—awkwardly expressed deep concern about the prospective environmental impacts. Surely he remembered that he himself had played a considerable role in setting the stage for the disaster. Now he was getting tangled up in a thorny and embarrassing series of self-contradictions.

Back in 2003, during his first (unsuccessful) campaign for governor, Jindal had actually promoted renewable energy. After his loss at the polls that fall, he apparently decided that representing himself as anything less than pro fossil fuel wasn't the way to get elected to office in Louisiana. When he campaigned for a congressional seat the following year, Jindal was fully on the side of the gas and oil industries, and this time he won. Two years later, his congressional district reelected him in a landslide, awarding him a remarkable 88 percent of the popular vote.

That same year, 2006, Jindal sponsored H.R. 4761 in the US Congress: the Deep Ocean Energy Resources Act, which proposed to eliminate the then-existing partial moratorium on new outer continental shelf (OCS) oil and gas drilling.[2] As he pointed out to his constituents, 30 to 40 percent of all US oil reserves lie near the Louisiana coast, and he argued that they

---

2. The partial moratorium operational in 2006 dated back to June 1990, when President George H. W. Bush issued a directive to the Interior Department to limit outer continental shelf (OCS) drilling in parts of the Gulf where it was not already being done. In 1998, President Clinton extended Bush's order through 2012. The 2006 Energy Security Act negated Clinton's extended date. In March of 2010, President Obama announced that he would extend deepwater drilling to other regions, including parts of the Atlantic seaboard. After the *Deepwater Horizon* disaster a month later, Obama backtracked on that idea.

should be fully exploited. Jindal's original bill was replaced by S. 3711—the Domenici-Landrieu Gulf of Mexico Energy Security Act (Mary Landrieu being the Democratic senator from Louisiana)—which accomplished essentially the same goal and which, after passing in both houses by overwhelming majorities, was signed into law by President George W. Bush on December 20, 2006. Meanwhile, Jindal's unabashed pro-drilling stance prompted several environmental groups to rate his environmental record as one of the worst in Congress.

Economically, the enacted legislation promised to be helpful to Louisiana, which was reeling (and in some regions still is) from the devastating blows of Hurricanes Katrina and Rita in 2005. The 2006 Energy Security Act opened 8.3 million acres of offshore seabed to new oil and gas production, with provisions to ultimately return 37.5 percent of the public revenues to the states of Louisiana, Texas, Mississippi, and Alabama. The press release issued by Senator Landrieu's office stated:

> The . . . plan [S. 3711] allows for increased domestic energy production for the first time in 25 years, and geologists expect to find significant new oil and natural gas reserves. The area is projected to produce enough natural gas to sustain more than 1,000 chemical plants for 40 years, and enough oil to keep 2.7 million cars running and 1.2 million homes heated for more than 15 years.

Yes, this was the bill that authorized the drilling that led to the *Deepwater Horizon* disaster of April 20, 2010. And yep, it was actually proposed and promoted, successfully, by the two most prominent politicians from the state of Louisiana: Bobby Jindal and Mary Landrieu, the former a Republican, the latter a Democrat.

To be fair, we should mention that the same act simultaneously promised Louisiana increased federal funding for hurricane protection, coastal erosion mitigation, wetlands restoration, and "navigation projects" (a subject to which we will return later). Such public works ventures, however, require years of planning, and as of this writing, not much has yet been accomplished along those lines.   *2014*

Now nobody—and that includes companies—can just go ahead and punch a hole in the continental shelf without specific approvals. If you're within two hundred miles of the coastline of any sovereign nation (a region referred to in the 1982 United Nations Convention on the Law of the Sea as a nation's "Exclusive Economic Zone," or EEZ), you need

1.2. Senator Mary Landrieu and Representative (later Governor) Bobby Jindal introduced the initial legislation in the US Senate and House, respectively, to open the Gulf of Mexico's outer continental shelf to deepwater drilling. *Courtesy of Senator Mary Landrieu and Governor Bobby Jindal, Louisiana.*

that government's authorization to drill an offshore well. So it is with the United States. Furthermore, between the time drilling-related legislation is signed into law and when it is actually operational, a fair amount of work needs to be done to develop the relevant procedures and to hire the staff to implement them. In the case of S. 3711 of 2006, more than a year passed before the Department of the Interior began to auction off the mineral rights for the regions specified in that legislation.

One of the first auctions, held on March 19, 2008, was for Block 252 of the offshore region known as the Mississippi Canyon. The multinational British-based corporation BP outbid eight rival companies and was awarded lease OCS-G 32306 for a price of $34,003,428—which works out to about $5,900 per acre. The oil giant (BP is the fourth most profitable company in the world) immediately announced its plans to drill five exploratory wells at the site, to be named Macondo (and presumably later to be numbered 1 thru 5). If one or more of these wells became productive, BP would be expected to pay additional royalties to the federal treasury; and according to S. 3711, a full 37.5 percent of that cash flow would be divided up among the states of Louisiana, Texas, Mississippi, and Alabama.

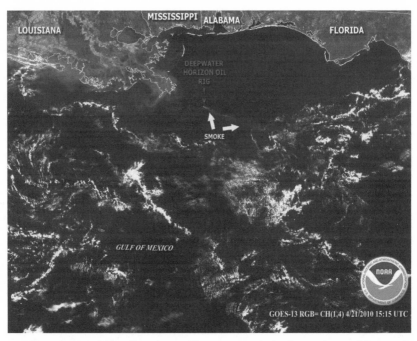

1.3. BP's rogue Macondo well was located forty-two nautical miles southeast of the mouth of the Mississippi River. This satellite photograph, taken on April 21, 2010, shows smoke from the flaming well. *Courtesy of the National Oceanic and Atmospheric Administration.*

Having a lease, however, doesn't mean you have an oil well. To create a well, you need to drill. And to drill, you need to go through another procedure to get a permit.

On March 10, 2009, BP filed a fifty-two-page application with the MMS for a permit to drill and temporarily cap the first of two exploration wells under its Mississippi Canyon lease. Each of these bores would require an estimated one hundred days of drilling. According to that application, the project was to commence on April 15, 2009.

That's right. BP was proposing to begin the actual drilling barely a month after the date it *filed its application* for the permit. Industry sources, meanwhile, were advising drillers to expect the permitting process for OCS wells to take a year or more. Could it be that the folks at BP already knew that the MMS wouldn't question anything in its application? Could it be that they knew that nobody at the MMS would even read it?

Under the 1990 Oil Pollution Act, prospective drillers are required to prove their ability to handle a worst-case spill. And indeed, as part of its

2009 drilling permit application, BP included an assurance that it was fully prepared to deal with any accident that might release up to a phenomenal 160,000 barrels per day. As for the possible environmental impacts of an uncontrolled gusher of that magnitude, the application's few paragraphs on the subject are chillingly brief, vague, and smack of "boilerplate" writing, for instance:

> *14.2.3.2 Wetlands*—An accidental oil spill from the proposed activities could cause impacts to wetlands. However, due to the distance to shore (48 miles) and the response capabilities that would be implemented, no significant adverse impacts are expected. Both the historical spill data and the combined trajectory risk calculations referenced in the publication OCS EIS/EA MMS 2002-052 indicate there is little risk of contact or impact to the coastline and associated environmental resources. The activities proposed in the plan will be covered by our regional OSRP (refer to information submitted in Section 7.0 of this plan).

Yes, that's the complete text of BP's paragraph relating to wetlands. It's virtually the same wording as appeared in other BP drilling permit applications, and it's not a great deal different than corresponding chunks of text one finds in drilling applications filed by at least five other companies around the same time. (Is it mere coincidence that multiple oil companies happen to use the identical Louisiana- and Texas-based consulting firms to prepare their applications?)

Because the above-quoted language fails to mention any *specific* wetlands, of course it can't address the practical matters of how they'd be accessed (some are quite difficult to get to, even by boat). Nor does this text mention how the personnel for a response would be mobilized, let alone hired and trained. It doesn't say how the spilled oil will be captured, at what rate, nor what will be done with it, and so on. Instead, it refers to a "regional OSRP, or Oil Spill Response Plan," which is not appended (nor is its date clear), and it cites an MMS document that had been published nine years earlier—before deepwater leases were even granted in this region—as evidence that everything about this proposed project had already been properly thought out.

One might think that such glaring omissions and unsubstantiated claims would be grounds for the federal government to return the application to BP, scolding the company to revise it. Nope. Instead, the MMS waived the requirement for a focused environmental impact study (which

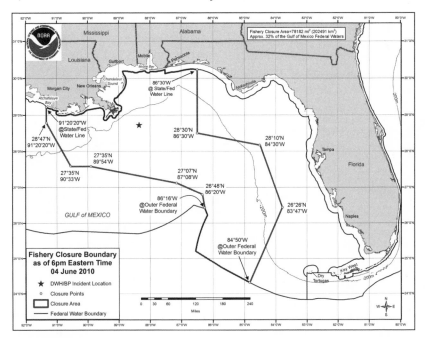

1.4. The geographical region affected by the Macondo well's oil spill. *Courtesy of the National Oceanic and Atmospheric Administration.*

presumably should then have been sent to the folks at the EPA for review). On April 6, 2009, the MMS signed off on BP's drilling plan—just twenty-six days after it was submitted (and only fourteen business days). If there was any other arm of the US government more efficient at processing its paperwork, the MMS surely didn't lag far behind. Yes, it might be said that the MMS ran like a well-oiled machine.

Then something and probably multiple somethings go terribly wrong. During the first ten weeks or so after the disaster, BP's highest recovery rate for the spilled oil is no more than a few thousand barrels per day. In other words, after assuring the American public, via its own documents filed with the MMS, that it is fully prepared to handle a "worst-case" spill of 160,000 barrels per day, BP proves to be incapable of containing even a tiny fraction of that amount. During the first eighty-six days of the disaster, as much as 60,000 barrels per day spew uncontrolled into Gulf waters. The total spill from the gusher eventually adds up to about 4.9 million barrels.

• • •

But back to Bobby Jindal. One of his populist pitches had always been to keep federal meddling out of Louisiana. Now he desperately needed the federal government's assistance in limiting the scope of the BP disaster.

Jindal is certainly a smart man—one of a small minority of Louisianans with an ivy-league education (having graduated from Brown University in 1991). On matters of abortion rights, gun control, same-sex marriages, regulation of business activities, single-payer health care, and immigration policies (despite his own parents being immigrants from India), his negative postures appealed to a broad conservative constituency in his home state. Some of those stances, however, did create a few backlashes. Several national scientific organizations, for instance, rejected Louisiana as a possible site for their future conventions after Jindal signed into law the Louisiana Academic Freedom Act of 2008, which permitted teachers to introduce political and religious ideologies into the state's public school science curriculum.

BP's big spill initially caught Jindal flatfooted. For the first few weeks he acted as if he expected the problem to go away on its own (for which he was criticized by a small but vocal minority of Louisiana lawmakers). Ultimately, however, he decided he had little choice: he needed to act like a leader. One newscast after another began showing him scooting around on a boat with his sleeves rolled up, or tramping through one or another marsh with a coterie of locals in tow. Jindal then teamed up with Billy Nungesser, the Republican president of Plaquemines Parish (the outcropping of marshy land straddling the mouth of the Mississippi River, and the first region affected by the spill). Together, Jindal and Nungesser forwarded a three-page proposal to the US Army Corps of Engineers.

Their idea was this: a crash program of dredging sand from the offshore shallows and dumping it into the gaps between the string of barrier islands in the threatened region, starting around Sandy Point at the east and running along a 101-mile arc as far west as Timbalier Island. The objective: this line of berms was to prevent the expanding oil slick from entering the marshland homes and/or spawning grounds of millions of waterfowl, fish, shrimp, oysters, crawfish, alligators, and other marine- and swamp-dependent life.

When Jindal and Nungesser announced their proposal, most coastal scientists and environmentalists shrieked. Their objections were numerous, but the main complaint was that a project on such a scale needed "adult supervision" and should be implemented only after considerable study and planning. Not willy-nilly.

Breaking events often have their ironies, and this was one. On May 19, while Jindal and Nungesser were still waiting for a response from the Army Corps of Engineers, a civil hearing began in federal court in Baton Rouge. The plaintiff, Dr. Ivor van Heerden, was suing Louisiana State University (LSU) to get back his job as a research professor in civil and environmental engineering after he'd been fired about a year earlier for (he claimed) being too critical of the US Army Corps of Engineers in the wake of the Hurricane Katrina disaster. Shortly thereafter, on May 28, the presiding judge ruled against van Heerden's petition for the injunction that would have saved his job.

That the court ruled in favor of LSU surprised few who knew much about the case. The university administrators who had fired van Heerden were closely linked to the George W. Bush administration; in fact, they had invited President Bush to deliver the commencement address at LSU on May 21, 2004. The resulting speech had brimmed with so much political ideology that it left many faculty members aghast. Then, at the end of the following summer, along came the Hurricane Katrina debacle—hardly a high point of Mr. Bush's presidency. Dr. van Heerden harshly criticized the Bush administration for aggravating that awful disaster through its numerous ineptitudes.

Other than just being vocal to the press, however, van Heerden had also written a book (published by Penguin Press in 2006) that included sketches and maps illustrating his ideas for protecting New Orleans, its environs, and the coastline from the ravages of future tropical storms. The diagrams in that publication are clearly a conceptual scenario rather than a formal proposal (in fact, they're actually reproductions of the author's freehand pencil drawings). They illustrate how an integrated system of new levees and tide gates might, if properly designed and managed, not only safeguard southern Louisiana communities from storm surges, but also encourage the disappearing wetlands to rebuild themselves over time. As the outermost line of defense, van Heerden's sketches also suggest how offshore sand might be dredged and relocated to recreate some long-gone barrier islands at critical locations. Although it would ultimately turn out that this latter part of van Heerden's proposal was flawed, the idea was now out there in print.

Given the amount of news attention van Heerden had received over the previous several years, it's unimaginable that Governor Jindal wouldn't have known about him. Although Jindal himself probably didn't have time to read van Heerden's book, surely someone in his office would have picked up a copy and at least flipped through its pages. When that person did so, the author's pencil sketches could not have failed to jump out at him or her.

Yes, Jindal and Nungesser's proposal to build berms linking the existing barrier islands appears remarkably similar to some of van Heerden's drawings in his 2006 book. The main difference is that van Heerden advocates a more time-consuming engineering approach to integrating all of the design elements, whereas four years later, Jindal and Nungesser sped ahead full blast without so much as an environmental impact study.

◆ ◆ ◆

Past governors of Louisiana, from both parties, have never elevated emergency planning to a high priority. Even after the devastation wrought by Hurricane Katrina in 2005, Bobby Jindal's administration continued this same pattern of neglecting most aspects of disaster management. Billy Nungesser and his cronies, on the other hand, were considerably more conscientious—at least in the matter of public safety. In fact, ever since the late 1950s, Plaquemines Parish has sported an exemplary track record of safely evacuating its population in the face of oncoming hurricanes—which have struck here, on average, every 2.5 years. (In fact, the main reason Plaquemines Parish never makes national news after a big hurricane is that so few lives are ever lost there.) As for safeguarding that region's wetlands, however, the actual projects have been paltry in number and scope, and the oil and gas industries' activities have continued to wreak environmental damage at a rate much greater than the pitifully slow pace of environmental restoration.

In early 2006, roughly six months after Hurricane Katrina had devastated New Orleans, Billy Nungesser graciously invited one of us (Ernest), along with another colleague, to visit him at his home to discuss the aftereffects of that awful disaster. He apologized for the condition of his place; much of the fencing on his multi-acre estate was still damaged or missing, downed tree limbs and other debris still littered some of the gardens and lawns, and the ground floor of his upscale residence had suffered water damage even though it was perched on the highest spot around.

Sequestered in a fenced area surrounding a gazebo that commands a grand vista of a bend in the Mississippi River were at least two dozen lost or abandoned dogs. "I need to get those guys back to their owners or else find new homes for them," Billy explained with a winsome smile. "I just haven't found the time yet." When we went indoors, three other hounds pattered over and curled up at our feet. The man clearly has a soft spot for dogs. And reciprocally, all those dogs clearly love him back.

Most of Plaquemines Parish remained in shambles from the failures of several levees, and that's mostly what we talked about. Billy's sincere concern for the welfare of the locals was unquestionable. Even then, in 2006, he was a man of grand ideas—who talked fast in the manner of someone whose words have a hard time keeping up with his agile mind. To prosper, he told us, Plaquemines Parish not only had to recover from the recent flooding, but also needed to go farther and expand its economic base. How? His proposal: a deep ship canal that would cut across the parish from Port Fourchon to points east in the Gulf of Mexico.

And how would such a canal traverse the Mississippi River, which is higher here than the surrounding land? There will be locks, Billy explained, the operation of which will create permanent jobs. But wouldn't such a canal increase the risk of flooding from future hurricanes? "Naw," he said. "It'll run east and west, and everyone knows that hurricane surges come from the south." Although his logic sounded a lot like the kind of erroneous reasoning that led to the folly of the MRGO (the Mississippi River Gulf Outlet canal, or "Mr. Go," completed in 1965 and now abandoned but yet to be restored), arguing about something like that wasn't the reason for our visit. We thanked him for filling us in on the status of his parish's recovery, and we expressed our gratitude for his kind hospitality.

Now, five years later, Billy Nungesser is appearing on a whole string of national news programs. Governor Bobby Jindal joins him on the first few. After that, Jindal moves on to other (undoubtedly important) matters, and the scheme to connect the barrier islands with berms is left to Billy to pretty much pursue on his own.

On Tuesday, June 1, 2010, Billy attends a meeting to discuss and debate his plan for the 101 miles of berms. In attendance are officials from the US Coast Guard, the Army Corps of Engineers, and various outside consultants. That evening, Billy once again appears on national television (Cooper Anderson's show on CNN), and his fatigue and frustration clearly show. He suggests that BP president Tony Hayward, who is still claiming that the entire spill is confined to the surface, be dunked ten feet down in the Gulf, to see what he looks like when he comes up. Billy also accuses the federal government of criticizing alleged shortcomings in his plan when nobody is coming forward with an alternative plan.

On June 3, at the direction of President Barack Obama (who is undoubtedly anxious to appear more involved than former President Bush), and despite the shrieks of dozens of regional coastal scientists, part of Billy Nungesser's plan to link Louisiana's barrier islands with sand berms is approved. Five berms are to be built, in addition to the one Billy is already bootlegging in, for a total of 39.5 miles of protection (rather than Billy's proposed roughly 100 miles). In the interest of expediency, work will begin without environmental impact reviews. The $360 million price tag will be paid by BP.

On that same day, the expanding oil slick begins to goo up the sparkling white sands of Pensacola Beach, Florida.

◆ ◆ ◆

Despite the BP disaster, neither Bobby Jindal nor Mary Landrieu ever waver in their worship at the hydrocarbon altar. Nor, according to some polls, do as many as 70 percent of Louisiana's other 4.492 million residents. In fact, when President Obama imposes a six-month moratorium on new OCS drilling, pending review and possible revision of the safety and environmental protocols, he is immediately met with howling objections from virtually every Louisiana politician and business leader. Senator Landrieu sends the president a letter advising him that he will get no support from her even on unrelated matters until he lifts his ban, and, in fact, she actually manages to hold up the confirmation of one presidential appointment. This, despite the fact that only thirty-three (out of more than three thousand) offshore rigs are adversely affected by the specific language of the temporary ban, and all of their permit applications are every bit as questionable as was BP's Macondo paperwork. Meanwhile, a group of Louisiana businessmen files a lawsuit to have the Obama moratorium declared unconstitutional, and they get a federal district judge in Louisiana to agree. On October 12 (forty-nine days before it was due to expire anyway) the administration backs off and lifts its temporary OCS drilling ban.

BP had already terminated its cleanup program on September 22, 2010. Not that there is no oil remaining in the environment; in fact, there's plenty of it. At this point, however, the spill has become so dispersed that

1.5. A portion of the sand berm project promoted by Governor Bobby Jindal and Billy Nungesser. Designed to protect the Louisiana wetlands from the *Deepwater Horizon* spill, the berms began to erode away even as they were being built. *Courtesy of the US Department of Defense.*

further recovery will be monumentally difficult. Much of the unrecovered goo lies on the seafloor or swirls in huge plumes deep beneath the surface. The only practical recourse, according to BP, is to simply abandon this remainder to the armies of oil-eating microbes that have blossomed in the affected regions. How long it will take those little chompers to return the Gulf to its pre-spill condition is anybody's guess.

As for Billy Nungesser's sand berms, they did indeed prevent a bit of oil from entering the wetlands: about one thousand barrels by most estimates. Meanwhile, storms eroded away some of the work in progress, simultaneously destroying a considerable amount of expensive construction equipment. Although the wild well had been capped and the initial objective of capturing BP's surface spill was no longer a concern, the berm project temporarily acquired a life of its own. By the end of 2010, approximately $195 million was spent (or committed by contract) to complete about 14 miles of the approved 39.5 miles of berms. The cost per foot was about $2,600. The cost per barrel of crude oil collected was about $200,000.

As of November 2011, on the advice of the Presidential Commission investigating the BP spill, and with allegations of overcharging by at least one Louisiana-based contractor, the berm project was officially terminated. An additional $25 million was nevertheless spent, even as the total length of the berms actually shrank. The final tally was $220 million of the allocated $360 million spent to get about 10 miles of the approved 39.5 miles of berms in place, out of a project that was originally going to stretch about 101 miles.

Meanwhile, most coastal engineers estimate that the lifetime of this remaining 10 miles of artificial sand berms is no more than a couple of years.

Chapter 2

BLACK GOLD

It's actually not black when it first sees the light of day. Usually it's a reddish brown or sometimes a pale dishwater yellow or even a pastel greenish-brown. There are numerous places in the world where it seeps from the ground naturally. When that happens, the lighter chemical components soon evaporate away, and what's left behind is a dark, sticky tar. An example can be seen today at the La Brea Tar Pits in downtown Los Angeles, where scientists have recovered the bones of thousands of prehistoric animals that unwittingly got trapped in the ooze, including wooly mammoths, saber-toothed cats, dire wolves, short-faced bears, ground sloths, and vultures that tried to feed on the mired victims only to get stuck in the goo and become fossils themselves.

Even in ancient times, humans discovered a wide variety of practical uses for these natural seeps of petroleum. Ancient Greeks used it to lubricate the axles of wheeled vehicles and to set fire to enemy ships. Native Americans employed it to seal canoes and to make war paint and medicines. Others, including the Babylonians, recognized its value as an illuminant and a fuel. The Chinese were recovering it in quantity by 500 BCE, and by AD 350 they were digging underground to get to it. In 1264, Marco Polo saw petroleum being "mined" in Persia. In the 1500s, seep oil collected in the Carpathian Mountains was used to fuel street lamps in several towns in Poland. Around 1735, the French begin extracting it from oil sands in the Alsace region.

During the many centuries before the light bulb was invented, an oil lamp was a great item to have around at night, provided, that is, that you were in an economic bracket where you could afford to buy the oil—much of which came from whales in those days and was fairly expensive. Then, in the early 1800s, several chemists independently discovered that if they distilled seep oil properly, they could extract a high-quality illuminant, which they referred to as "paraffin oil" or "kerosene." The commercial challenge was that crude oil from natural seeps just wasn't plentiful enough to justify building industrial-scale distilleries. Thus, for several additional decades, kerosene remained little more than a laboratory curiosity.

To remedy the supply problem for this commercially promising substance, several visionaries hit on the idea of trying to extract it from the ground. The Russian engineer F. N. Semyenov succeeded in drilling a producing well in 1848. Beginning in 1854, the Polish chemist Jan Ignaci Łukasiewicz, who had already invented a kerosene residential lamp and a street lamp, bored a series of successful wells in Poland. In the United States, the credit for the first oil well usually goes to "Colonel" Edwin Drake, who in 1859 drilled near Titusville, Pennsylvania, and for a while extracted about twenty barrels of petroleum per day from a depth of 69.5 feet. A few months after that success, however, a fire destroyed the facility along with its machinery. Having proven to his investors that he wasn't quite as nutty as many folks had thought, Drake proceeded to bore another well, where fire-prevention measures were taken more seriously.

Most of these early wells were not "drilled" in today's sense of rapidly twisting a cutting tool. Their chisel-like bits did not rotate much; instead, they were essentially hammered down into the bedrock to create the borehole. This process later came to be called "cable drilling," and it is effective only for fairly shallow wells, initially less than a few hundred feet but eventually, with some improvements, as deep as a thousand feet or so.

And why wouldn't those petroleum pioneers choose to use a rotary drill bit right from the start? Because neither the electric motor nor gasoline or diesel engines had been invented yet, and there was no easy way to attach a cumbersome steam engine to a rotary drilling rig. Steam power could, however, be harnessed to raise and drop a guided weight that hammered a helical drill rod into the ground.

The oil extracted from those wells was—just as the pioneer drillers expected—vastly superior to oil collected from natural seeps. It was less viscous, cleaner, and more predictable in its chemistry. Accordingly, it was also more valuable. A barrel of Pennsylvania crude from a well in the 1860s sold for up to forty dollars, or nearly a dollar a gallon, which was quite a bit of money in those days. An economic incentive like that was bound to trigger an oil rush, and indeed it did. Soon, drilling derricks were sprouting up all over western Pennsylvania and northern West Virginia.

Along with those wells came the distilleries, or refineries, as they eventually came to be called. They were typically located along waterways, not only because water was needed as a coolant in the distillation process, but also because that's where most of the rail lines ran. Streams that were already being polluted by other industries (e.g., steel factories) soon began to be further contaminated by petroleum byproducts—and not just the streams, but the air as well.

Initially, the most commercially important petroleum product was the kerosene. The viscous sludge left behind, although less valuable, could be sold as a roofing material or used for road maintenance (dirt roads at that time were often "oiled" to waterproof them and inhibit erosion). There was, however, another byproduct of the distillation process: gasoline, or "petrol" as it was sometimes called. It was dangerously flammable and had no practical use. The early petroleum distillers either dumped it into pits or flushed it into the nearest stream.

For a while, that is. And then someone did find a use for it. That person was the German inventor Nicolaus Otto, who in 1876 built a small engine that was fueled by gasoline vapor. He used it to power an experimental motorcycle-like vehicle.

As with most earthshaking ideas, Otto's wasn't completely original. As early as 1807, the French inventor Joseph Nicéphore Niépce had demonstrated a working model of an engine where the combustion took place inside the mechanism rather than in a separate boiler (as in the then-familiar steam engine). Niépce, however, had chosen as his fuel lycopodium dust (then commonly used to prevent fleas), and nobody took his "flea-powder engine" seriously enough to develop it further. In 1863, another Frenchman, Jean Lenoir, used a small, gasoline-powered engine to propel a carriage. It was not an impressive demonstration compared with the capabilities of the steam engines of that time, and Lenoir gave up.

Otto's 1876 engine was different in this respect: it put out a great deal of power for its small size and weight. Moreover, as other inventors began to tinker with Otto's design, that power-to-weight ratio was improved even further.

In Germany in 1885, Karl Friedrich Benz built a three-wheeled carriage propelled by an internal-combustion gasoline engine similar to Otto's. The following year, Gottlieb Wilhelm Daimler, another German, built an even better petrol-powered vehicle with four wheels. In 1893, Charles and Frank Duryea set up the first American automobile manufacturing company. By 1904, there were at least thirty-five companies building and selling gasoline-powered cars in the United States alone.

Never again would petroleum refiners dump gasoline into rivers just to get rid of it. Now there was money to be made from the stuff.

♦   ♦   ♦

On January 10, 1901, a crew of drillers struck oil near a salt dome called Spindletop Hill in southeastern Texas, just thirty miles west of the Louisiana border. The investors had reason to gamble on this particular spot because flammable gas was already bubbling out of the ground. To reach the underlying oil, however, the workers needed to bore to a depth of 1,139 feet—a feat that would have been technologically impossible a mere decade earlier.

When they did succeed, they were totally unprepared for Mother Earth's violent reaction. Propelled by the subterranean pressure and the expansion of its own dissolved gases, the deposit of crude oil blew all of the drilling fluid out of the drill pipe and gushed to a height of more than 150 feet. The initial flow was estimated by the site engineer to be eighty thousand barrels per day (although the figure of one hundred thousand was also widely quoted). It took nine days for the gusher to calm down enough to allow the well to be brought under control, and by then the whole area was an oily mess.

The news spread, and within three months the population of nearby Beaumont, Texas, tripled, from ten thousand to about thirty thousand. By the end of that year, 285 active wells were poking into the ground in the vicinity of Spindletop.

Meanwhile, near Jennings, Louisiana—about eighty-eight miles east of Spindletop Hill—the news of the Texas discovery piqued the curiosity of a rural rice farmer. Jules Clement, who had often noticed gas gurgling up in one of his own fields, rummaged around in his barn for an old stovepipe, tramped out to that peculiar spot, collected some of the fumes, and lit a match. The resulting explosion knocked him on his butt.

Clement told his amusing story to some friends, they laughed and told others, and before long the word reached five local businessmen who quickly got together and created the S. A. Spencer Company. That organization's first order of business was to buy up two thousand acres of mineral leases near the region's known gas seepages. They then sent a representative to Beaumont to find someone who knew how to drill an oil well.

The man the company settled on was twenty-nine-year-old W. Scott Heywood. That young man visited the Louisiana site and confirmed that the terrain, which included a bulge in one of Mr. Clement's fields, looked awfully similar to Spindletop, only slightly flatter. Sure, he said. He'd take the job. He'd drill.

Unfortunately, that was going to require more money than any of the principals had. The owners of the Spencer Company cooked up a new corporation, the Jennings Oil Company, and peddled enough stock to raise sufficient cash for the project. They experienced no problem whatsoever in attracting investors. People from all over thronged to buy up the shares.

Jules Clement, however, was less than enthusiastic. He had no interest whatsoever in oil; after all, he farmed with mules, not tractors, and in the winter he heated his home with a wood stove. He also didn't want a mess created on his farm, and he didn't want any of his cattle to get injured. He padlocked his gates and hired an attorney. The ensuing negotiations, however, didn't take very long. Clement accepted some sort of a deal (whose documentation and details no longer exist), and the drilling began on June 15, 1901—five months after the Spindletop gusher just across the Texas border.

The initial plan was to bore two wells on Clement's property, each to a depth of 1,000 feet. With the help of his brothers and several hired helpers, Heywood began to drill. It was the worst possible time of the year to be engaging in that kind of labor, with the mud and heat and humidity and the relentless hordes of mosquitoes. When they reached 400 feet, the drill pipe broke. They were forced to abandon the initial hole, move over, and start again.

The second time, they made it to 1,000 feet, but still there was no sign of oil. Heywood insisted that they drill deeper. Yes, he admitted to the investors, his contract indeed said that he would drill two 1,000-foot wells. But, he argued, it did not specify that the second well had to start at the surface. All he wanted to do was to start his second well at the bottom of his first one.

Jennings Oil's board of directors nervously agreed. None of them, of course, knew anything about drilling. Whether they realized at the time how much the cost per foot increases with depth is doubtful.

At 1,500 feet, Heywood ran out of pipe and there was a hiatus as more was brought in. Everyone was getting itchy. Stockholders began to bail out, some selling their one-dollar shares for twenty-five cents. Heywood continued to 1,700 feet. Still no oil. But the last four feet had penetrated oily sand, which was promising. Unfortunately, they were out of pipe again, and there was another wait.

Then, on the evening of September 21, 1901 (less than nine months after the Spindletop discovery in Texas), a local farmer on horseback delivered the exciting news to the town of Jennings: oil had been struck on Jules Clement's farm!

As fate would have it, however, this first Louisiana well was a bust. After gushing for about seven hours and ruining several acres of Mr. Clement's rice fields, the well clogged itself up with sand. Various efforts were made to reopen it, some partially successful, but ultimately it became a losing battle. The hole had to be abandoned. Jules Clement returned to his rice farming and cattle raising—minus several hopelessly polluted acres and no monetary compensation in return—cursing himself that he should have stuck to his guns about prohibiting the drilling in the first place.

With their equipment now sitting in that area, Heywood and his team of drillers moved on to other sites in southwestern Louisiana. Despite their disappointment with the initial bore, they found oil almost everywhere else they poked a hole.

On the Louisiana Office of Conservation website's update of April 22, 2010 (two days after the *Deepwater Horizon* explosion), some unknown public servant ended the agency's account of the Jennings oil discovery with the comment: "It is this first well which changed the history of our State forever." Whether intentional or not, that chilling statement is certainly true. From 1901 on, Louisiana has indeed been a pawn in a high-stakes game played by oil investors, drillers, refiners, and oil-worshipping politicians.

Economists use the term "petro-state" to describe nations whose governments are dominated by oil interests—Venezuela, Nigeria, and prewar Iraq, for instance. Such countries are often prone to a curious economic paradox: despite their richness in petroleum, their populations tend to have *lower* living standards than otherwise-comparable places on the globe. Although Louisiana is not a sovereign nation, the concept seems to apply here as well. Despite its treasure of oil and gas, which has generated huge cash flows for more than a century now, Louisiana today ranks forty-ninth among the fifty states in life expectancy, has the second-highest rate of infant mortality, is fourth in violent crime, ranks forty-sixth in the percentage of people with college degrees, is forty-seventh in per-capita income, is tied for second in the percentage of people living below the poverty level, and fluctuates between forty-ninth and fiftieth in all of the kindergarten through twelfth-grade educational performance measures.

As for environmental quality, that too isn't much of a priority for Louisiana's leaders. Greenhouse gas emissions in the state are consistently about double the national average. Airborne carcinogens from chemical plants, refineries, and power plants spew into many residential neighborhoods (particularly the poorer ones). Sewers in low-lying areas commonly overflow during rainstorms. Officials usually look the other way when an industry contaminates a stream; after all, the pollutants will soon wash away, right? Oil and gas wells are drilled willy-nilly in suburban neighborhoods, next to churches, and near schools, resulting in continuous noise pollution from compressors and other equipment. And so on.

◆ ◆ ◆

Yes, petroleum was also discovered in several other states and territories circa 1900. Only in Louisiana, however, did those bonanzas lead to such an overwhelming political obsession with oil. Nor did other states continue to worship at the altar of petroleum long after production began to decline. Louisiana's production, on the other hand, peaked around 1970—yet still today the state government is dominated by petrochemical interests.

In Oklahoma, by contrast, the first shallow well drilled in 1889 produced about a half-barrel per day, which was bottled and sold as a tick preventative for cattle. After the Spindletop gusher in Texas, a couple of drillers near Tulsa decided to probe deeper; and in 1905, at just under 1,500 feet, they hit a reservoir that produced seventy-five barrels per day. By the time statehood became official in 1907, the Oklahoma Territory had dozens of profitable oil wells.

Oklahoma's crude oil production, however, peaked in 1927, and since then (despite several booms and busts) the overall trend line has been downward. The fraction of Oklahoma's workforce employed by the oil and gas industries maxed out at about 5 percent around 1930. In their 1943 hit musical *Oklahoma!* Richard Rogers and Oscar Hammerstein wove a lighthearted story of human conflicts between cowboys, farmers, and a Persian traveling salesman just as the Oklahoma Territory was about to achieve statehood. That script did not, however, include any oil workers. There just weren't enough of them to be worth including.

In fact, for most of its history, Oklahoma has been predominantly an agricultural state. Although petroleum has indeed played (and still plays) a relevant role in the state's economy, it has never been the main driver. Moreover, with a few localized exceptions, such as the Tar Creek

Superfund Site, Oklahoma's overall environmental quality has always been quite good.

Another oil-producing state, of course, is California. There, the history of petroleum followed the same general pattern. Long before the Spaniards arrived, Native Americans had already found numerous uses for seepages of crude oil. Later, pioneers would stop at natural oil pits to lubricate the axles of their wagons. As early as 1856, a San Francisco company began distilling lighting oil from the tar pits at La Brea Ranch, several hundred miles to the south in Los Angeles.

Then, around 1861, several individuals in California began to drill. None had much success until 1866, when Thomas R. Bard (later to become a US senator) was able to extract 15 to 20 barrels per day from a well he'd bored to a depth of 550 feet near Ventura. With that success, more distilleries sprang up, which in turn incentivized the drilling of more wells. Most of those ventures, however, produced no more than a few hundred barrels per day for only a short time before they were depleted. Oil, in other words, was not a particularly lucrative business to be in at that time.

Finally, in February 1892 while exploring near Santa Paula, drillers for the Union Oil Company hit the first big gusher—1,500 barrels per day. No provision had been made to store oil in such quantities, and over the next month about 40,000 barrels ran down the Santa Clara River and out into the Pacific Ocean. Of course, there were no environmental regulations at that time. No local residents even attempted to complain about the unholy mess from that spill.

The fledgling oil companies were not particularly concerned about such spillages. After all, the oil itself was essentially free, so why should they care if some of it spilled? Their costs lay in the equipment, labor, transportation, processing, and distribution of the final products—not in the crude oil itself. Before long, California drillers were hitting one gusher after another, each creating its own environmental mess.

One of the worst California spills came from a well that was begun near Maricopa in 1909. The original driller, Lakeview Oil Company, ran out of money when the borehole reached 1,655 feet, and Union Oil of California took over the rights (yes, the same company that sixty years later would create the big Santa Barbara oil spill). On March 15, 1910, at a depth of about 2,225 feet, the well went out of control. For the next *eighteen months*—until September 9, 1911—it continued to gush, ultimately releasing about 8.2 million barrels of oil into the environment. A portion of that historic "Lakeview Gusher" was impounded by sandbags and eventually recovered, but most of it was not.

By the 1930s, however, oil production in California was on a decline. Yes, from time to time, here and there, there was indeed a new discovery. Overall, however, most Californians found other ways to make money. As in Oklahoma, Pennsylvania, and even (albeit to a lesser extent) in Texas and Alaska, the oil and gas interests would never grow powerful enough to fully dominate the state governments. Unlike in Louisiana.

•   •   •

And what drove all of that demand for petroleum circa 1900?

No, it wasn't passenger cars; those were still a rarity at the time and they wouldn't fully replace horses until several decades later. And because most of the nation's cities had been electrified (or at least were well on their way to having electricity), the demand for kerosene for lighting surely wasn't increasing. Yes, clever chemists were learning how to transform petroleum into dyes, the first plastics, paints, and various other products—but none of those were consumable in large quantities. So, where was all that oil going?

There was something else that began to swallow up oil. Diesel engines.

No, they were never used much in cars, and initially not even in trucks. From the get-go, diesels were installed in ships, in heavy excavating equipment, and in stationary power plants. Unlike the gasoline engine, which started off small and stayed that way, the diesel engine started off big: many of the earliest ones stood two stories tall and weighed as much as a herd of elephants.

Rudolph Diesel patented the device in 1892. By 1897, it was commercially practical—due partially to the efforts of some other developers who never bothered to acknowledge Diesel's original invention. The main engineering challenge was how it would be fueled. Experimenters tried peanut oil, which worked fairly well (and still works), but which was hardly in great supply. Diesel himself tried coal dust, which was so difficult to regulate that a prototype engine exploded and almost killed him. And no, crude oil wouldn't work either, because its chemical composition was too variable to allow the combustion process to be controlled properly. With some crude oils, the engine wouldn't even start, while with others, it would quickly speed up and destroy itself. Furthermore, under even the best circumstances, crude oil would gum up the mechanism, which would then call for a major overhaul. Clearly, what needed to be done was to match the mechanical features of Diesel's engine (in particular, its compression ratio and its cooling arrangements) with a consistent formula for the chemistry of the fuel it would be fed.

Today, that formulated mixture of hydrocarbons is referred to as number 2 fuel oil. It is slightly oilier than kerosene and considerably less volatile than gasoline. It results from fractionally distilling crude oil within a controlled range of temperatures.

By the early 1900s, then, there arose this additional demand for petroleum: fueling the diesel engines that powered many of the newer ships and submarines, drove heavy excavation machinery, and was being used to generate electricity at numerous electric power plants.

Yes, many industrialists and shippers continued to prefer steam, particularly after the 1884 invention of the steam turbine engine (which replaced reciprocating pistons with a more efficient arrangement of rotating blades). Steam turbines, however, still had to burn a fuel to create the steam. Why not burn something that was less clumsy to handle than coal? That something was obviously fuel oil.

By the end of World War I (1918), virtually every nation of the world had come to view petroleum as a natural resource of strategic importance. After all, hydrocarbon products had been used to power and lubricate a wide variety of the tools of that war, from surface ships and tanks to submarines and aircraft. Totalitarian nations like the Soviet Union quickly imposed full state control over all the oil fields within their boundaries.

The United States, however, actually relaxed its strategic concerns about petroleum, leaving it to its captains of industry and its public servants to jointly work out what was best for the nation. That laissez-faire policy, in turn, led directly to the "Teapot Dome Scandal" of 1922-1923, which remains a case study of the political fallacy of expecting corporate America to act in the best public interests.

On the heels of the Great War, the large navies of the world began to downsize. In fact, the British Navy shrank to the point where for a while it actually had more admirals than ships. At that time, the US Navy controlled several deposits of petroleum, including one at Teapot Dome, an oil field on public land in Wyoming. In March of 1921, President Warren G. Harding appointed a Republican senator, Albert B. Fall of New Mexico, as his secretary of the interior. Simultaneously, control of the Teapot Dome and two other naval petroleum reserve sites in California were transferred to Fall's Interior Department, which was directed to open them up to commercial development.

Mere months after this jurisdictional transfer, Secretary Fall granted a lease for the Teapot Dome oil field to Harry F. Sinclair (founder of Sinclair Oil), and the oil field at Elk Hills, California, was leased to Edward L. Doheny (a Los Angeles oilman who also started an outfit in Mexico that would eventually become the Mexican Petroleum Company, or Pemex). Fall handed out those two leases without soliciting competitive bidding.

The *Wall Street Journal* smelled something fishy and began to poke around. On April 14, 1922, it broke the story. Remarkably, there was nothing illegal about Fall's granting noncompetitive mineral leases to two of his friends. But personally accepting money in return for those favors granted while holding public office *was* illegal. A Senate committee investigated and uncovered compelling evidence of the crime. In 1929, Fall was tried and convicted, sentenced to a year in prison, and fined $100,000 (which by some accounts was less than a quarter of the total value of the bribes he'd received). Sinclair was also fined $100,000 and received a short sentence for contempt of court and jury tampering. In 1930, Doheny was acquitted of bribing Fall.

By then, in two separate decisions (in February and October of 1927), the US Supreme Court ruled that the oil leases granted by Fall were invalid and ordered them returned to the US government.

Thus, no long-term harm was done. Or was there?

• • •

In those days, there were three ways you could make money from oil exploration. First, you could engage physically in the sweaty and backbreaking labor of working at a drilling site. Secondly, you could invest your money in a drilling operation, which always carried the risks that a given project might result in a worthless "dry hole." And then there was a third way: you could finagle around with mineral leases in such a way that money poured into your bank account without your doing anything socially useful at all.

Alfred B. Fall had tried the third tactic, but he'd been stupid about it. It took some good ol' boys in Louisiana to elevate oil lease manipulation to a high art, and to do it successfully beyond the reach of the law. Governor (and later, US senator) Huey Long (1893–1935), for instance, with the involvement of his family and close friends, formed the Win or Lose

Corporation, whose sole function was to buy up public mineral leases and resell them at a healthy profit. The scheme was so cleverly designed that it would never be completely unraveled.

The Louisianan who benefited most extravagantly by fiddling with leases, however, was "Judge" Leander Perez (1891–1969) of Plaquemines Parish. Although he never earned more than $7,000 per year as a public servant, at the time of his death his estate was worth about $100 million (some $500 million in today's dollars). This in a parish where even in the 2010 census the average per capita income was just $15,937 and 18 percent of the population lived below the poverty line.

Perez was a lawyer, district attorney, parish commissioner, former judge, and a vicious white supremacist. During his short tenure on the bench, he so perniciously overstepped his judicial bounds that in 1924 he was impeached for a long list of misbehaviors. After several days of brutal testimony before the Louisiana Supreme Court, a closed-door deal was worked out and Perez resigned from the judiciary. He would nevertheless continue to use the title "Judge" for the rest of his life.

In 1928, the parade of wells marching across Louisiana's southern wetlands reached Plaquemines Parish, and almost immediately oil was discovered there as well. Leander Perez smelled a golden opportunity, and he was not the kind of fellow to let it slip away.

There is a lot of public land in Louisiana: real estate controlled by dozens of different levee boards, school boards, and other public authorities. Much of this property is under water (in Plaquemines Parish, close to one-third of it is), and therefore it is not privately owned. So who owns the minerals under it? The public does, of course.

Ah, but that could be changed.

Leander Perez cooked up a deal with then Governor Huey Long. In the 1928 election, Perez had delivered numerous votes to Long (the number was actually higher than the number of voters in Plaquemines Parish—some of the "registered" voters having included "Babe Ruth," "Charlie Chaplin," and "Herbert Hoover"). Now Long owed Perez a return favor. With some arm-twisting from the governor, the Louisiana legislature passed a constitutional amendment allowing the Plaquemines Parish police jury (the official parish governing body) to take over the bonded indebtedness of any levee district located wholly or partly within that parish and to hold the assets of such levee districts *as long as they remained in debt*.

Initially, the eight levee boards involved were legitimately in the red financially due to the ravages of the great flood of 1927. Now, however,

Perez had the power to keep them perpetually in debt by manipulating the appointments of their commissioners (whose signed but undated resignations the "Judge" kept in a locked file cabinet). Perez also had friends in the State Land Office who, at his request, acquired federal swamplands whose ownership was then transferred to the levee boards. By manipulating his parish's school board elections, Perez also gained power over that body and thereby got control over the mineral wealth that lay beneath the school district's property. Eventually, he even used the levee boards' powers of public domain to acquire the mineral rights under swaths of some privately owned property. Royalties from oil and gas poured into the parish coffers, the windfall income far exceeding the small amounts the parish was required to return to the levee boards to pay the interest on their bonds.

But if Perez indeed profited personally from publicly held mineral rights, how the heck did he pull that off? Yes, he certainly controlled various public boards, but that alone didn't allow him to legally reach into their tills.

What Perez did was this: As their legal counsel, he "persuaded" all those public entities to lease out their mineral rights. There was no legal requirement that they hold out for any particular price; generally they sold those leases for around ten cents per acre. The companies that bought the leases were not outfits anyone had heard of before. They were incorporated in Texas or Delaware or elsewhere rather than in Louisiana, and because they were privately owned there were very few public records available about them. Moreover, none of those outfits ever conducted any actual drilling. All they did was buy up mineral leases, then immediately resell those leases to legitimate oil companies at an extravagant profit.

It so happened that those dummy companies were all owned by close friends and relatives of Leander Perez. Not only did those outfits make huge profits by reselling their leases to legitimate oil companies (which were happy to pay a dollar or two per acre), but beyond that, they also collected royalties on every barrel of oil ultimately produced.

The final step was simple. Perez forged ironclad lifelong contracts to provide legal services to those shell companies he himself had set up. He regularly sent them exorbitant bills for his services, and of course they always paid. After all, "they" were none other than Leander Perez himself.

After Perez died in early 1969, Plaquemines Parish sued his heirs for the restitution of $87 million. Much of the evidence in that litigation related to one particular shell organization, the Delta Development

Company. Also cited (with skimpier evidence) were the Creole Oil Company, the Louisiana Land and Exploration Company, and a string of outfits curiously appearing in the court records only under aliases, including Mandrake and Houdini. In 1987, the parish finally settled with the Perez family for $12 million.

Today, a parish park established as a memorial to Judge Perez stands locked up and overgrown. Perez's legacy, however, still lingers in the region in the form of a highway and a lake that bear his name.

With some variations, Leander Perez's general scheme was copied by other individuals in other parts of Louisiana. By the mid-1930s, a huge quantity of oil and gas was flowing out of the state, and a great deal of money was streaming back in return. Almost all of that wealth was ending up in a small number of private bank accounts. Very little of it ever dribbled down to the state's common citizens—the *real* owners of all that mineral wealth.

This, regardless of the exact mechanism, is also what happens in Third World petro-states.

Chapter 3

ONTO THE SHELVES

Unlike most other industries, oil producers have little flexibility in choosing their sites of operation. The oil is where it is, and that can include some pretty challenging places: the frozen Arctic, sweltering deserts, and, of course, beneath the seas. In fact, geologists tell us that *all* of our planet's petroleum started out in sea or lake beds tens of millions of years ago. Today's drillers find oil under solid land only because some seafloors happened to heave upward over the ages.

Terra firma is a misnomer; our Earth's crust is anything but stable. On a human-scale timeline, we have earthquakes, rockslides, soil erosion, volcanic eruptions, and silting at the mouths of streams. Extend the timeline to tens of millions of years, and an even more dramatic process is underway: virtually every segment of Earth's crust is in a slow-motion transition: sliding, bending, heaving, and/or twisting. In some regions, this motion is mainly upward, creating mountains as high as Everest. In other places, the land is sinking, creating deep canyons beneath the oceans. The overall process is a zero-sum game: land lifted in one place is always balanced by the same volume subsiding somewhere else. As noted by Eastern thinkers of many centuries ago, it's impossible to have mountains without valleys, and vice versa.

Never are these movements uniform; that is, there are always spots here and there that move more or less quickly than the adjacent regions. Not only that, but sometimes places that have subsided in the past reverse their motion and begin to lift over the course of geological time. And again, vice versa.

Now as soon as you create differences in vertical elevation, something else starts to happen on our watery planet: surface material from the higher places gets washed down to the lower spots. So, even as the mountains are growing, they are also being eroded away. And even as valleys are subsiding, they are also being filled in.

Meanwhile, something else is going on as well. Our planet has teemed with life for at least four billion years, and all of those living creatures have had a carbon-based chemistry. Moreover (with the exception of some one-celled animals), all life eventually dies. The resulting millions of megatons of dead plants and animals, most of them individually quite small, amount to huge stockpiles of chemical compounds consisting mostly of carbon, hydrogen, and oxygen atoms.

And where does all of this deceased biomass end up? Most of it is simply eaten by other organisms (including bacteria) and works its way up the food chain to be recycled into new life-forms. Here and there, however, kilotons or even megatons of such dead organisms accumulate at the lowest elevations—generally underwater (which, after all, is where the very lowest spots are located). There, those carcasses decay under bacterial action until the oxygen in the immediate region is depleted. At that point, this dead gunk has been effectively removed from the higher levels of the food chain.

But that still doesn't turn that slop into oil. To make oil, and particularly an oil *reservoir*, this decomposed biomass must be further acted on by anaerobic bacteria, capped over by natural geological processes, and then subjected to huge pressures for tens of millions of years. It takes a rather unlikely combination of conditions to accomplish that.

First, the seabed needs to continue to subside tectonically for a very long time—millions of years. Secondly, there needs to be some natural mechanism to cover the dead stuff over with deposits that are permeable enough to allow the resulting petroleum to migrate and coalesce. Thirdly, over the eons, this permeable layer needs to be overlaid with a hard and impermeable layer of rock that prevents the oil from immediately oozing to the surface as it is formed. And finally, there must be irregularities in the regional tectonic movements that squeeze the emerging petroleum into some spots (reservoirs) rather than others.

A few natural oil reservoirs have resulted from sedimentation in lakebeds, but not on a significant scale—the most notable exceptions being in China. The limestone of ancient coral reefs, on the other hand, is clearly capable of holding huge amounts of oil; this, for instance, is the origin of most of the Persian Gulf oil fields. Then there are the mouths of the world's major river systems, many of which provide the right kind of sediment to eventually solidify into porous sandstone, which can hold oil. This has happened (again, over geological time spans) in the North Sea, off the coast of Nigeria, at some of the Venezuelan deposits, and, yes, off the US Gulf Coast, where for eons the Mississippi River watershed has been dumping silt into the Gulf of Mexico.

There are also a number of ways that nonporous overlying rock can trap an oil reservoir, but here we'll mention just two. In earthquake-prone regions, reservoirs can be capped over by the slippage of a geological fault (as in California and Alaska). Petroleum can also be confined under an anticline: an upward bulge of impermeable rock (common in Louisiana and Texas, for instance), which often results in a telltale hump on the surface.

That, then, is the general process: dead organic material accumulates in low places, those spots subside further and get covered over by sediment, a layer of impermeable rock forms above that, then the crust bends and twists and bulges in such a way that the oil migrates and accumulates in a geologically sealed reservoir.

This sequence of natural processes is quite hit-or-miss. Over the course of Earth's history, immense quantities of biomass have cycled through the environment, yet Mother Nature has transformed only a miniscule fraction of it into oil.

And, yes, that amount is finite.

◆   ◆   ◆

Even before geology became an analytical science, drillers couldn't help but notice that wells near coastlines tended to be more productive than those farther inland. Soon, drilling rigs were sprouting up not just along seashores, but also beyond them. In 1896, several successful wells were bored in the seabed of the Santa Barbara Channel (California) by mounting the equipment on timber piers extending out over the water. A decade later, wells were being bored in some of the shallows on the Canadian side of Lake Erie. In 1911, the Gulf Refining Company built the world's first overwater platform in Caddo Lake, Louisiana; that well was drilled to a depth of 2,185 feet and for a while it produced 450 barrels per day. Within the next few years, numerous wells were drilled from similar fixed platforms in the tidal regions of southeastern Texas and southwestern Louisiana.

Although it's logistically more difficult, and expensive, to explore for oil underwater than on dry land, the success of many of these early ventures made the efforts worthwhile. Soon the beaches, wetlands, and shallow lakes of much of the central Gulf Coast were peppered with oil rigs.

In 1937, Pure Oil partnered with Superior Oil to build a fixed platform in fourteen feet of water a mile out in the Gulf of Mexico, offshore of Calcasieu Parish, Louisiana. Successful ideas foster imitation, and within a year or so, there were seven offshore wells producing in that same area. Then came a hiatus in drilling innovation, as virtually all of the available engineers became involved in various aspects of the war effort.

After World War II, however, the rate of offshore exploration mushroomed. In 1946, Magnolia Petroleum audaciously erected a platform in about twenty feet of water a full eighteen miles off the coast of St. Mary's Parish. The following year, Superior Oil built one about the same distance off Vermilion Parish, and Kerr-McGee erected one eleven miles off the shoreline of Terrebonne Parish. For the first time ever, wells were being drilled out of sight of land. Not only that, but all of those wells were turning out to be quite profitable.

This technological development, however, added an order of magnitude of complexity to the drilling operations. Because it was no longer practical for laborers to show up for work in the morning and head home or to a hotel in the evening, the platforms themselves had to include living quarters. That, in turn, meant that they also needed to have their own fresh water systems, cooking galleys, and sewerage systems. Different companies handled the workers' schedules differently, but generally it was something like seven consecutive twelve-hour days on duty followed by seven off, or maybe two weeks on, then two weeks off. Meanwhile, hundreds of new businesses sprang up to serve this budding offshore industry—ferrying workers, provisions, food, fuel, equipment, and drilling supplies out to the platforms. With the commercialization of civilian helicopters after World War II, and aided by the availability of pilots trained by the military and now mustered out, entrepreneurs began constructing heliports to shuttle personnel to and from the offshore rigs. Consequently, the rigs also needed to be equipped with helipads and staffed with flight-control personnel.

Prior to a series of US Supreme Court decisions between 1947 and 1950, there was no clear precedent about who controlled offshore oil—the states or the federal government. Louisiana raced forward like a runaway locomotive and leased out millions of offshore acres before anyone could put on the brakes. (Texas also conducted some such offshore leasing at the time, but with considerably more restraint.) Eventually, via the Supreme Court, the federal government gained jurisdiction over all oil and mineral extraction beyond about three miles from the nearest shore.

By then, Louisiana had already consummated scores of lease sales outside that three-mile limit. As usual, however, very little of the resulting cash flow accrued to the state's government. Most of the money went to dummy leasing companies, which had purchased the offshore leases from the state for nickels, then resold them to authentic oil companies at an obscene markup. No in-depth investigation was ever conducted, and given how cleverly Louisiana politicians had learned to cover their tracks, no investigation may have even been possible. All we will ever know is that during those immediate postwar years, legitimate oil companies paid significant amounts of money for leases on offshore submerged lands, yet no more than a miniscule fraction of those payments ever reached the Louisiana or federal governments.

Farther offshore, of course, the continental shelf gets deeper. Because of the difficulty of installing structural cross-bracing underwater, the earliest fixed platforms reached their practical limit at a water depth of about one hundred feet (although today there are fixed designs that can perch above the waves in a thousand feet or more). In 1955, the depth limitation led to the development of an alternative technology: the jack-up rig, which is constructed on shore, then is towed to the drill site. The first of these, the *Scorpion*, was constructed in Vicksburg, Mississippi, then floated downriver to the Gulf. Once positioned, such jack-up rigs extend three or four long supporting legs to the seabed, then the platform is hydraulically jacked up above the water surface to isolate it from wave action. This design can be used in up to about four hundred feet of water, although some jack-up rigs have been designed for even deeper seas.

Another alternative was the "submersible rig," which is a bit of a misnomer. The idea is similar to that of the jack-up rig, except that a huge barge with a slot down its middle is flooded until it settles on the seabed, where it provides a base for the steel legs that support the drilling platform above the water's surface. Submersibles could be built bigger than conventional jack-ups, and then when the drilling was done, they too could be refloated and moved.

There are distinct advantages to being able to tow a rig from one location to another. For one thing, it takes a larger crew and different types of machinery to drill a well than to later extract the oil. Once oil is struck, a dedicated drilling rig can be floated to its next job while a simpler production platform is towed in to take over. In fact, some small production platforms (called "toadstools") are not even manned full time; all they do is collect and store oil, which is then offloaded from time to time. Another advantage of movable rigs is that it's cheaper and easier to build a big plat-form at a shipyard—even a temporary onshore shipyard—than out on the open sea.

Then came a big advance—a result of a failed experiment that actu-ally had nothing to do with oil. Project Mohole, conceived in 1957, was a scientific attempt to drill all the way through Earth's crust into its mantle, for the purpose of analyzing the mineral samples extracted along the way. The moniker was derived from the Mohorovičić discontinuity, the postu-lated geological boundary at the bottom of Earth's crust. The experimental drilling would take place offshore, at a spot where the crust seemed to be thinnest. The surface platform would be a floating drillship.

In 1961, the Project Mohole team bored five shafts off the coast of Guadalupe, Mexico, in a region where everyone was pretty sure they would *not* hit oil. (If they had done so, it would have been a major disas-ter.) The water depth there was a record-setting 11,680 feet. To keep the drill ship *CUSS I* within a radius of 600 feet above the borehole regardless of wind and waves, a system of dynamic positioning was invented. And indeed, that part worked. The scientific project, however, failed for other reasons, including management squabbles and cost overruns.

In 1961, Shell Oil converted a submersible rig, *Bluewater I*, into a new experimental design, which it dubbed a "semi-submersible." The platform was supported high above the sea on four cylindrical columns, but those legs did not extend to anywhere near the seafloor. Instead, they rested on a set of submerged air chambers that were tethered to the sea bot-tom but, other than that, were floating with no solid support below them. Skeptics who thought such an arrangement would be inherently unstable soon became believers; the platform hardly pitched or tipped at all even in choppy waters. Another company, Odeco, immediately built two rigs of its own on this same principle, and they were launched in 1963. By 1974—just over a decade later—there were 117 operational semi-submersible drill-ing rigs in the world, most of them in the Gulf of Mexico, and all of them capable of drilling in 1,000 feet of water.

From that point on, more technical advances came quickly. In the 1980s, third-generation semi-submersibles could operate in 1,500 feet of water. In the 1990s, the fourth generation could reach to 3,000 feet. From about 1998 to 2004, the fifth generation could function at 8,000 feet. Since then, there is a sixth generation that can drill in up to 10,000 feet of water.

That's about as deep as anyone is likely to need to go in the foreseeable future. About 38 percent of the Gulf of Mexico consists of water less than

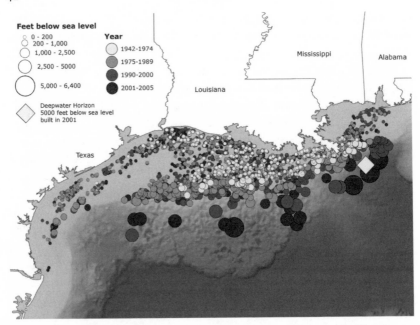

3.1. Locations of the approximately 3,900 active production platforms in the US waters of the Gulf of Mexico. Most of these facilities serve multiple undersea wells, for a total of nearly 50,000 wellheads. More than 80 percent of them are off the coast of Louisiana. *Courtesy of the US Department of Energy.*

3.2. The Gulf of Mexico from Grand Isle, Louisiana. The vista here is confettied with offshore oil equipment. *Courtesy of the US Environmental Protection Agency.*

60 feet deep. The rest of the continental shelf, with depths of up to about 600 feet (excluding the underwater canyons), accounts for about an additional 22 percent. After that comes the continental slope, which plunges to 10,000 feet and covers about 20 percent of the Gulf floor. The final 20 percent of the Gulf consists of the abyssal regions, which run as deep as 14,000 feet, but where no oil has yet been found.

As shown in figure 3.1, most of today's 3,959 active offshore production platforms are on the continental shelf near Louisiana. Figure 3.2 shows a typical view from a vantage point on one of Louisiana's few beaches. No, nobody has ever claimed that the sight is pretty.

• • •

At the time of its demise in April 2010, the *Deepwater Horizon* was 1 of 139 offshore *drilling* rigs (as opposed to production platforms) owned by the Swiss-based company Transocean Ltd. Transocean actually started out as a US corporation registered in Delaware, but in 1999 for tax reasons it moved to the Cayman Islands, and then, in 2008, to Zug, Switzerland. As of this writing, the company has only 12 employees working at its Zug international headquarters (out of a total of 26,300 employees overall). Clearly, the outfit's Switzerland connection is no more than a scheme to dodge US taxes.

Switzerland, being a landlocked nation, of course has no merchant marine fleet of its own. So what flag was the *Deepwater Horizon* flying at the time of the disaster? The same one as all of Transocean's other vessels: the Marshall Islands. The port of registry was Majuro: a seaport that none of the fleet of platforms had ever visited, nor would they ever do so— because there isn't so much as a drop of crude oil anywhere near there. Which also tells the tale, of course, that none of Transocean's platforms were ever physically inspected by officials from their nation of registry, let alone by anyone from the state of Louisiana.

The *Deepwater Horizon* was nevertheless a marvel of modern engineering. Completed in 2001 by Hyundai Heavy Industries of Ulsan, South Korea, this fifth-generation semi-submersible included a complex system of dynamic positioning that used computer-controlled thrusters to keep it centered over the borehole, regardless of wind, waves, or currents. It had berths for 130 workers. The main platform measured 396 feet by 256 feet, minus a rectangular "moonpool" (the opening for the drill pipe) of 21 feet by 93 feet. It could operate in winds of up to 60 knots (65 miles per hour) and waves of up to 29 feet. In shutdown (nondrilling) mode, it could withstand winds of 103 knots (almost 120 miles per hour) without damage, and wave heights of up to 41 feet. It could drill in up to 8,000 feet of water. Its cost was $560 million. Transocean leased it to BP at a rate of $496,800 per day.

The companies involved stood to make a lot of money by drilling on the outer continental shelf. The vast majority of ordinary American citizens, however, did not stand to benefit much at all. Nor did most of the residents of the state of Louisiana.

• • •

The challenges of drilling offshore aren't limited to having an appropriate rig, nor even the logistical wherewithal to staff and supply it. There is also another problem: blowout and spill prevention. And the deeper the water, the more difficult that becomes.

In the early years of *inland* drilling, wild wells occurred with alarming frequency, and they resulted in numerous injuries and deaths. In a few instances, as much as a thousand feet of steel drill pipe was blown out of the borehole. Yet until the 1920s, there wasn't much anyone could do to tame such gushers (explosives could be used to snuff out a well fire by depriving it of oxygen, but this seldom stopped the flow of oil itself). Generally, a wild well would continue to gush until it poohed out on its own as its reservoir pressure declined, much as a pressurized squirt gun shoots only so long on one pumping. Sometimes it took weeks for a gusher to subside; occasionally it took many months.

Then in 1924, the Cameron blowout preventer (BOP) came on the market. This was a heavy-duty valve (weighing 1,380 pounds in its original version) that was set in place before drilling began, and the drill pipe and bit were inserted through its center. It could be used to shut off a well from a safe distance, so as not to endanger the drilling crew if well control was lost. Over the following decades, such BOPs became bigger, heavier, and more sophisticated, eventually evolving into a multi-story stack of valves and rams.

From the onset, however, everyone realized that it was not a good idea to mount a BOP on an offshore platform. First, the devices are extremely cumbersome and heavy and, secondly, that would leave vulnerable the exposed section of pipe (the "riser") that runs between the platform and the seabed. If the riser were to be damaged, say in a storm or from a ship colliding with the rig, a platform-mounted BOP would be in the wrong place to prevent a spill. Clearly, the correct place for blowout prevention is underwater, right smack on the wellhead.

The deeper the water, however, the more difficult it is to design a reliable device that will function in that environment. There are issues of saltwater corrosion, assuring that the hydraulic seals won't deteriorate and eventually leak, and making sure that the mechanicals can handle the pressures—both internal and external. There are other technical issues as well, such has how to actuate a submerged BOP in case of a major accident or some other malfunction up on the platform. Nor is it a simple matter to inspect and/or test these devices once they are situated on the seafloor.

After an exploratory well strikes oil and the wellhead is temporarily sealed with cement, the BOP is removed and replaced by a different system of valves and pressure regulators—commonly referred to as a "Christmas tree." This device allows the extracted oil and gas to be separated and piped to a production platform. Generally speaking, the Christmas tree assembly doesn't need to deal with big surprises; by the time it is in place, all of the operating parameters (fluid pressure, flow rate, viscosity, gas content, etc.) are known fairly accurately. Like the BOP, a Christmas tree also allows the oil and gas flow to be shut off at the seafloor in case of an emergency.

From the onset, offshore drillers took contingency planning quite seriously. The Gulf of Mexico is a breeding area for violent tropical storms and hurricanes, and every offshore rig is 100 percent certain to experience at least a few such tempests during its lifetime. In the event of a big storm, drillers needed to be able to shut down their operations quickly and efficiently.

The first major trial came way back in 1957. At that time, there were 102 offshore platforms and rigs operating in US waters: 96 of them off Louisiana, 5 off Texas, and 1 off California. On the morning of June 26, the New Orleans Weather Bureau announced that a hurricane had developed 317 miles south of the Texas-Louisiana border and was expected to make landfall somewhere in eastern Texas in about thirty-six hours, possibly generating storm tides of five to eight feet. The offshore companies immediately shut down their operations and evacuated the workers. This was before the advent of satellite telemetry, and the region didn't even have any ground-based radar to track the storm, so it was certainly best to err on the side of caution. Meanwhile, very few residents of the coast got flustered; they all seem to have thought they had plenty of time to leave if or when they needed to.

The official forecasts, however, turned out to be tragically wrong in several respects. Hurricane Audrey escalated in intensity as well as forward speed. At about 6:00 a.m. the next morning, the storm tore into the small oil and fishing port of Cameron (pronounced Cam'run) in southwestern Louisiana, with sustained winds of 145 miles per hour punctuated by higher gusts. The flood was twelve to thirteen feet deep, and it surged inland as far as twenty-five miles. Audrey would be retroactively classified as a category-4 event (the system of hurricane categories itself didn't debut until 1971). More than 500 people died, including 395 in Cameron alone—about one-third of that small town's population at the time. Every structure in the entire region was heavily damaged, if not destroyed.

And yes, there were some oil spills. But only from onshore facilities such as storage tanks and pipelines, and those were all relatively small. Offshore, no spills at all were reported. All of those seafloor wellhead valves had functioned exactly as they were designed to!

The offshore platforms themselves, however, didn't fair that well. Of the fifty or so that were in Audrey's direct path, the only rig to escape serious damage was one of the two earliest jack-ups. A seventy-eight-ton fishing boat was tossed onto one fixed platform, wrecking it and killing several of the vessel's crew. Another platform vanished without a trace. Four dozen others were badly battered and needed major repairs. A few required complete replacement.

One of Audrey's lessons was this: if all those offshore wells hadn't been shut down ahead of time, dozens of them would undoubtedly have gone out of control during the storm. Fixing a problem like that would have been monumentally difficult and mind-bogglingly expensive. The oil companies had indeed done it right, and now every new employee who had anything to do with offshore rigs would be briefed about that 1957 disaster, which easily could have been orders of magnitude worse. The message: Don't take chances with hurricanes.

As drilling expanded to ever-deeper water, the precautions initially kept pace. One of the most remarkable successes came in 1969 during Hurricane Camille—the most violent hurricane to ever strike the US mainland (and the storm that would give rise to the current scale of hurricane categories). After sideswiping the mouth of the Mississippi River, Camille made landfall just slightly east of the Louisiana-Mississippi border with a storm surge of a whopping twenty-eight feet and sustained winds of at least 172 miles per hour (measured by automated instrumentation on an evacuated offshore rig before the storm destroyed its wind-sensor).

Extrapolations from measurements on Hurricane Hunter aircraft, however, suggested that in some places the winds at ground level may have actually reached a sustained 201 miles per hour.

Camille also happened to be the first hurricane in history to be tracked continuously by satellite. To the horror of the meteorologists at the National Hurricane Center, its projected storm path threatened hundreds of offshore oil rigs. It turned out, however, that the oil companies were again on top of matters. All those offshore wells were shut down in a timely manner, equipment was secured, and the crews were ferried by chopper to inland sites in Louisiana, which promised to be on the milder left front quadrant of that hefty storm.

Camille wreaked incredible devastation in Plaquemines Parish and on the Mississippi Gulf Coast. More than a hundred ships and barges went aground or sank, including three huge freighters stranded on the beach in Gulfport. Hundreds of smaller fishing boats and workboats were destroyed. The storm was so violent that the lower 120 miles of the mighty Mississippi River actually reversed and flowed backward for several hours.

At daybreak on August 18, 1969, the oil companies sent out airborne observers to radio back preliminary damage assessments. Of the roughly six hundred platforms potentially affected by Camille, it turned out that about a hundred had been mutilated badly enough that the damage was obvious even from the air. Two rigs had vanished completely—sunk. Several others had been scoured of every piece of surface equipment. One had been wrecked in a collision with an errant Japanese freighter, whose captain then ran his damaged ship aground to prevent it from sinking. At least four service ships were also seriously damaged, and one was clearly taking on water. And yes, there was an oil slick. One well was reported to be out of control.

That report, however, turned out to be erroneous. Later in the day, when a repair crew reached the site, it found a relatively small leak, and only about five hundred barrels of oil needed to be mopped up. None of it ever reached shore.

· · ·

Over the following decades, the population of offshore platforms continued to swell, providing ever-increasing opportunities for blowouts and spills. Yet the offshore oil industry's track record continued to be quite good all the way through 2005—the record-setting year of twenty-eight named storms and fifteen hurricanes.

Two of that season's hurricanes, Katrina and Rita, were particularly devastating to Louisiana. Together, they destroyed a total of 113 offshore platforms, either sunken or damaged beyond repair. BP alone lost fourteen rigs (ten during Katrina and four in Rita), the deepest in 153 feet of water and the shallowest in just 40 feet.

Yet (according to the Minerals Management Service, MMS), those two violent hurricanes and all those wrecked platforms resulted in no loss of life and a total of just 6 offshore spills of more than a thousand barrels each and 146 spills of more than one barrel. None of those spills reached shore. (Those hurricanes did, however, cause quite a few *onshore* pipeline and storage tank spills, a subject we'll return to later.)

And that's where matters stood when, in 2006, Representative Bobby Jindal and Senator Mary Landrieu stampeded the Gulf of Mexico Energy Security Act through Congress. The offshore industry at that time indeed *did* have an admirable track record of preventing oil spills during the worst imaginable hazard: hurricanes. And to calm everyone's fears before the first big OCS (outer continental shelf) lease auction under the act, the Bush administration directed the National Marine Fisheries Service to conduct an environmental impact study. The resulting report, which was disseminated by the MMS in June of 2007, concluded that over the next forty years the *total* spillage from the expanded OCS drilling would be within the range of 60,000 barrels to 300,000 barrels. (The actual numbers in the report refer to each of the eleven new lease areas; the figures we quote here are the approximate totals.) That same optimistic document further claimed that *none* of such spillage would ever have any environmental impact whatsoever on the coasts.

Yes, at the low end, the *total* estimated OCS spillage for the next forty years was projected to be about what the *Deepwater Horizon* well would actually release into the Gulf *per day,*—and which it continued to do at that rate for eighty-six days.

So why were there such huge discrepancies between the offshore industry's past performance and its present performance and between the official projections and the ultimate realities?

When the water is only a few hundred feet deep, it's possible for properly trained divers to disassemble underwater equipment, conduct inspections, and even do welding. With the right diving equipment, this working depth can be extended to around one thousand feet—but that strains the human limit. The only way to maneuver hardware at greater depths is with remotely operated vehicles (ROVs), which are guided from a control room on a surface ship. Many of these devices have human-like arms and hand-like grabbing mechanisms, with the added capability of wrists that can rotate continuously like a drill. ROVs perform reasonably well for straightforward, lightweight tasks. They cannot, however, disassemble an inoperable BOP on the seafloor to get at its failed hydraulic system and repair it. Nor can they perform any tasks that involve free-lifting heavy objects.

To drill in water deeper than one thousand feet, in other words, you need to be extra certain that your seafloor equipment is up to the task ahead of time. To use a BOP that has been tested only in shallower water, and which was designed with limited functional redundancy, is to beg for a *very* bad surprise.

· · ·

The *Deepwater Horizon*'s BOP was the same age as the rig itself—dating from 2001 and now long overdue for its five-year inspection and overhaul. Standing fifty-four feet tall and weighing 450 tons, it had four blind rams that could close off the well, but only if the drill pipe was first removed. It also had two annular valves that could seal the space between the drill pipe and the well casing or in an emergency might crimp the pipe to reduce (but not fully stop) the flow. At its top was a flexible connection that permitted the drilling mud to circulate down and up from the surface platform a mile above. But for all of its marvelous mechanicals, hydraulics, and controls, this huge contraption had just one component that could actually prevent a blowout. Referred to as a "shear ram," it was designed to slice and seal off the drill pipe in case of a serious emergency.

That shear ram was controlled by a single valve that admitted hydraulic fluid to the opposing cylinders that drove a pair of shears, sometimes referred to as "pincers." In other words, in this ultimate fail-safe, functional redundancy was nonexistent. If any single component of the shear ram system failed, then the entire arrangement was guaranteed to malfunction.

Regardless of what additional information comes out in the years ahead, it's clear that the design of the *Deepwater Horizon*'s BOP was inadequate. That blueprint was not created by BP's engineers; it was done by the boys at the Cameron Company, headquartered in Houston (yes, the same outfit that built and marketed the world's first BOP back in 1924). But did that mean the failure was Cameron's fault? After all, BP's engineers chose and approved that particular product's installation at their

Macondo well, when there were alternative devices available. And Transocean concurred in the decision.

It's possible that the shear ram's hydraulic fluid leaked (and indeed there were reports suggesting a leak shortly before the disaster). If that's true, then certainly the drilling should have been shut down until such a problem was corrected. But underpinning such a prospect is still a design shortcoming, because even the cars in our driveways all have *dual* hydraulic braking systems. Maybe the single shuttle valve that controlled the system failed, but again, why weren't there at a least a pair of them? Maybe the ram did actuate, but the pincers happened to strike one of the thick steel collars that connected the sections of drill pipe. That prospect is so obvious that it's virtually impossible that a competent engineer wouldn't think about it ahead of time. Then there is the possibility that some violent event took place deep beneath the wellhead, which drove something upward that jammed the shears. It doesn't matter what that something was, because a backup shear ram at a different height would probably have still been functional.

So why didn't the various engineers anticipate such possible failure modes? No doubt they did. But engineers don't always get their way; they operate under economic constraints, and the purse strings are always held by higher-ups in the corporate pecking order: managers, in other words, who often lack engineering credentials. The only possible explanation for not using a different BOP—one with redundancy in its shear ram system— was cost control. And no, considering what was at risk that was not a valid reason. In fact, an old and often-quoted engineering dictum says, "Don't blame machinery for bad management decisions."

In fact, other BOPs had failed before. In 1999, the MMS reported that there had been 117 failures in the previous two years—none of which, fortunately, caused major spills. That was not the case, however, in 2009 when a BOP off northwestern Australia failed to control a blowout and 210,000 barrels of crude spilled into the Timor Sea. That well was under only 250 feet of water, yet the gusher continued for seventy-four days until, on the fifth attempt, cement pumped in through a relief well succeeded in sealing it.

In one series of independent laboratory tests under simulated deepwater conditions, two out of a sample of seven BOPs malfunctioned. Onsite (underwater) testing, however, is essentially limited to measurements of hydraulic pressure, which usually results in a passing grade. In 2009, for instance, the MMS reported that 89,189 such tests resulted in just sixty-two failures—a finding that led industry leaders to request a relaxation of the thirty-day testing cycle for critical hydraulic systems to just once every seventy-seven days. Two months after the *Deepwater Horizon* disaster, however, a BP internal document came to light admitting that when used at a depth of 5,000 feet, current BOPs may have reliabilities of only 45 percent.

The MMS recorded thirty-nine actual blowouts in US waters between 1992 and 2006, but all were not necessarily BOP failures. Actuating a shear ram is not a deed a drilling engineer does on a whim, because doing so means a costly setback of at least several days and, in very deep water, possibly weeks. Some of the reported accidents may have simply been a matter of a crew having waited too long before taking such drastic action.

Several conclusions, however, became apparent long before the Macondo well was finally killed. First, blowout preventers needed to have more redundancy built in, including at least two independent sets of shear rams. (In fact, many companies were already doing this voluntarily; obviously, BP was not.) Second, there needed to be another mode of activating a BOP in cases where a whole platform had to be abandoned. (Again, a few other outfits were doing this with "dead-man" switches and acoustical activators, which can shut a well via a properly coded ultrasonic signal.) Third, an alternative needs to be developed to the expensive and time-consuming procedure of drilling a relief well to conduct a "bottom kill." Yes, there have been some suggestions along this line (including a proposal by one of the present authors), and with enough research and the proper engineering, someone's alternative tactic may eventually prove to be practical.

Ultimately, however, drilling in deeper and deeper water promises to get increasingly difficult and dangerous before it grows safer. Yes, good engineering can often accomplish marvels, but it cannot routinely perform miracles.

Chapter 4

OOPS—1980

November 21, 1980.

The official hurricane season is almost over, with no major storms striking anywhere in the United States this year. An exploratory drill into the bed of Lake Peigneur, in south-central Louisiana, is right on schedule. The owner of the lease is Texaco.

Until now, it's been a small lake, lima-bean shaped, covering about 1,300 acres at an average depth of just three feet and plunging to barely eleven feet at its deepest. In most respects it's an unremarkable body of water, comparable to at least a hundred other unremarkable shallow freshwater lakes in Louisiana's coastal parishes.

This particular little bowl has grown popular with local sport fishers who on a typical outing snag dozens of bream (pronounced *brim* and often spelled that way in those parts) with no limit on their catch. Breaded with cornmeal, deep fried, and sprinkled with Tabasco sauce from the nearby Avery Island plantation, there are few fish meats that tickle the taste buds better with beer and fried potatoes than filleted Louisiana bream.

On the morning of the accident, Texaco's derrick towered 150 feet above the lake surface—roughly fifteen stories. None of the locals seem to have objected to the visual onslaught, or if they did, they mainly grumbled to one another rather than to anyone in the state government. The assumption was that Texaco knew what it was doing and that the bureaucrats in Baton Rouge knew what they were doing. As for the Feds, they weren't even remotely part of the equation.

At a depth of 1,230 feet, the drill suddenly seized up. As the workers struggled to free the bit, they heard a series of popping noises. The derrick started to lean and the tilt alarms went off.

Normally, a drill bit stuck at this depth is not particularly difficult to work free. Nor is a slightly tilting rig usually much of a problem; hydraulic mechanisms are built into such platforms to quickly correct such a happenstance. This time, however, the derrick continued to lean farther and farther despite the efforts of the leveling machinery, which was functioning exactly as it was designed to.

Then came the unimaginable. A whirlpool developed beneath the structure, centered on the fourteen-inch drill pipe. The dozen workers onboard quickly evacuated into a small barge and motored it to the nearest shore, where they watched in astonishment as their entire rig—including the steel tower 150 feet tall—sank nearly vertically into a lake they knew to be just 11 feet deep at its deepest.

Only one fisherman was on the lake that morning—Leonce Viator Jr. Although he heard the drillers' shouts and watched the disaster unfold, from his vantage point nearly a thousand feet away, the whirlpool wasn't immediately apparent. Only when a weird current began sucking his own tiny boat into an inward spiral did he realize he needed to get to shore, and quickly. Barely making headway against the accelerating water even at full throttle, he reached the bank, hopped to the grass, and tossed his mooring line over a tree branch. His heart pounding, he gazed in awe as a sizeable barge disappeared down the vortex. And then, too late to stop it, he realized that his own boat had drifted loose and was also being sucked into the maelstrom. A minute or so later, it too was gone forever.

Most of Louisiana's lakes are drained by bayous, and those whose egresses or inlets are not naturally navigable are commonly interlinked by man-made canals. So it was with Lake Peigneur: as early as 1906, its natural egress (Bayou Carlin) was dredged and renamed the Delcambre Canal (pronounced *Del'kum*). This twelve-mile channel links the lake to the Gulf of Mexico via Vermilion Bay. In the 1940s it was also intersected by the Intracoastal Waterway.

The banks of most of the navigable southern Louisiana waterways are lined with all imaginable pieces of floating equipment: dredges, shrimp trawlers, oyster boats, jack-up workboats, floating pile drivers, tank barges, towboats, oil equipment barges, and so on. So it was with the Delcambre Canal that November morning in 1980. Because the current here was normally so gentle as to be virtually undetectable, even the largest of these vessels had been moored in an extremely casual manner.

Water, as everyone knows, seeks its own level, and this particular morning Lake Peigneur's level inexplicably began to drop. Rapidly so. In accordance with the laws of physics, the Delcambre Canal started flowing backwards—slowly at first, then with unmistakably increasing velocity. Some folks noticed and secured their boats and those of their absent friends before asking what the heck was happening. Others were slower to respond. At least eleven barges broke loose and were swept north toward the lake. One towboat was caught in the accelerating current and its captain found it impossible to motor against it; as the boat skidded along a dock, he and his crew successfully abandoned the vessel, relegating it to what turned out to be a cruel fate.

It took no more than three hours for all of Lake Peigneur—about 3.5 billion gallons of water—to disappear down the whirlpool created by Texaco's drilling rig. By noon, seawater from the Gulf was rushing north through the twelve-mile canal at fifteen to twenty miles per hour, then pouring over a waterfall into the lake basin. Anyone slipping into this torrent would face certain death. Yet, amazingly, nobody fell in. All along the canal, people simply stood around watching in horror and amazement.

Louisiana doesn't have many waterfalls, and the few it does have are mere trickles in the north, near the Arkansas border. In fact, a canoeing group in Baton Rouge, with typical Cajun humor, calls itself the "Louisiana Haystackers," "haystack" being paddler jargon for the monstrous standing waves one often encounters in whitewater streams, of which Louisiana has exactly none. But for three full days, November 21 through 24, 1980, as the Gulf of Mexico gushed up the Delcambre Canal and into the basin of Lake Peigneur, southern Louisiana sported a powerful 30-foot waterfall.

In fact, some reporters would claim that the waterfall was actually 150 feet in height (comparable, in other words, to Niagara Falls), or even 164 feet, or 180 feet, or some other figure. Such higher numbers were justified on the basis that, before the whole event was over, the bottom of the former lake collapsed and seawater poured unimpeded into the abyss. And so, if you stretch the definition only slightly, maybe Louisiana did indeed have a 164-foot waterfall for a few days in November of 1980.

•   •   •

Louisiana's coastal parishes include thousands of conventional islands— the kind grade-schoolers learn about—clumps of dry land completely surrounded by water. But this particular state also sports two other kinds of "islands": cheniers and salt domes.

A chenier (from French, a place of oaks) is a region of modestly higher ground surrounded by squishy marshlands. Cheniers are visually easy to spot, insofar as they are populated by trees (often live oaks) in regions otherwise dominated by shrubs and grasses. Examine a map of southern Louisiana, and you'll find place-names like Cow Island, North Island,

Forked Island, Grand Cheniere, Cheniere au Tigre, Chenier Caminada, and so on. (Yes, sometimes there's a trailing *e* to *chenier*, sometimes not.) In any case, the geological interpretation is that these ribbons of slightly higher ground are ancient Gulf beaches stabilized by vegetation growing on silt from the Mississippi River as it repeatedly changed its course over the eons.

And then there are the Louisiana salt domes, about 150 of them on land (and many more offshore). The five largest, curiously, are almost equally spaced along a forty-five-mile straight line from northwest to southeast near the town of New Iberia. Their names are Jefferson Island, Avery Island, Weeks Island, Cote Blanche Island, and Belle Island. They too are unmistakable, for in this otherwise-flat terrain they bulge upwards seventy feet or more above sea level. Exactly how they were created, and why they arose in a straight line, remains a matter of geological specu-lation. The scientific consensus, however, is that they are all about 100 million years old. Each consists of a huge plug of salt (mostly sodium chlo-ride) thrust upward from deep in the Earth's crust. Today, their bulging tops are encased in thick layers of vegetated soil.

Surrounding each of these salt domes is a layer of upthrust oil-bearing rock. In other words, if you want to find oil without drilling any deeper than you need to, your best bet is to drill near a salt dome, where Mother Nature has already pushed the oil nearer to the surface.

That, in fact, is exactly what Texaco was doing at Lake Peigneur in November of 1980. The lake happened to be adjacent to the northwestern-most salt dome of the major five-dome string, the one known as Jefferson Island. In 1869, that dome (then called Orange Island) and the surrounding land were purchased by the actor Joseph Jefferson, whose claim to fame was having played the part of Rip Van Winkle thousands of times during his long stage career. Jefferson built a mansion on the site, which is now listed in the National Register of Historic Places. Later owners added botanical gardens, a restaurant, a bed-and-breakfast establishment, and another large home on the lakeshore. A salt mine was first excavated at the dome in 1919, and in 1957, that operation was bought by the Diamond Crystal Salt com-pany. By 1980, the mine consisted of several huge subterranean caverns, the deepest one bottoming out at 1,500 feet below the surface.

As the twelve drillers watched the lake disappear from their vantage point on shore, none had any doubts about where all that water was going. Yep, they'd screwed up big-time. They'd punctured the roof of one of the levels of the salt mine.

• ◆ •

Inside the mine, fifty-five men were on the job that morning—most of them at the 1,500-foot level. An electrician, Junius Gaddison, heard clanging noises coming from a nearby corridor. When he investigated, he was startled to find a knee-deep torrent of muddy water. The clanging was from fuel drums being swept along in the current.

The one thing you never want to see in a salt mine is water. The only way the dome had survived for 100 million years is that in all that time this salt had never gotten wet. Now it wasn't just getting moist—there was a small river gushing through it. Moreover, the flow volume was clearly increasing. Gaddison ran to the nearest alarm box. Throughout the facility, lights flashed and sirens wailed.

The miners instantly scrambled toward the eight-person elevator at the 1,300-foot level. The water quickly rose, inundating bulldozers and other excavating machinery. A foreman, Randy LaSalle, heroically drove a buggy into several remote horizontal shafts that lacked alarms, shouting to assure that nobody was left behind.

The elevator made seven excruciatingly slow round-trips to the surface as the floodwaters rose. Ultimately, however, all fifty-five members of the work crew made it out. During the next three days, most of them spent hour after hour just sitting on the lakeshore, watching the remarkable topside scene in amazement.

Although the initial borehole had been just fourteen inches in diameter, erosion quickly enlarged that. All sorts of debris cascaded over the waterfall, down the foot-rapids, and into the ever-growing whirlpool. And not just floating trash and shrubs, but also large trees and the abandoned towboat and eleven barges—one carrying four flatbed trucks. With the entire Gulf of Mexico providing an endless supply of water to the canal, it was clear that this event wasn't going to end until the mine was completely filled. By the second day, helicopters were circling overhead to film the bizarre event. Today, one can easily find some of that video footage online.

Could it get worse? Yes.

Every underground mine, whether it be salt, coal, silver, or whatever, needs something to support its roof. The usual practice is to simply to leave thick columns of unmined material in place at strategic points as the mine is expanded. And indeed that's what was done at the Jefferson Island salt mine.

4.2. Lake Peigneur today. The structure jutting from the water is a residential chimney, all that remains of a home destroyed during the 1980 disaster. *Courtesy of Michael Richard of Rip Van Winkle Gardens, Louisiana.*

Sodium chloride, however, is extremely soluble in water. It didn't take long for all those supporting salt pillars to dissolve away. When that happened, the excavated caverns began to collapse—along with the ground above them.

At least sixty-five acres of surface land subsided to below sea level, along with vehicles, trees, and an entire parking lot. Today, a residential chimney juts eerily from the now-placid water a short distance offshore—the only remainder of what was once a fine home with a wonderful view (fig. 4.1). Locals like to tell the story of how the distraught owner had to hire a diver to recover the contents of his wine cellar. Rip Van Winkle Gardens, however, and the 1870 Jefferson mansion survived and can still be visited today.

By the end of the third day, the mine was fully flooded and the lake filled up again to the level of the canal. As the turbulence died down, nine of the eleven sunken barges popped back to the surface like corks. Simultaneously, air trapped and pressurized in various shafts of the mine created a curious display: geysers, one of which temporarily squirted to a height of 400 feet.

The disaster not only expanded the area of Lake Peigneur, but also increased its maximum depth from the original 11 feet to 1,300 feet, making it today the deepest body of inland water in any of the southern states. (Even Lake Mead, impounded behind Hoover Dam in southern Nevada, has a maximum depth of just 500 feet). Of course, Lake Peigneur is now salty rather than fresh. Today, fishers catch redfish (red drum) and saltwater catfish rather than bream.

Remarkably, nobody died. That probably explains why the disaster didn't get much attention in the national media. Texaco and Wilson Brothers (owner of the drilling rig) paid an out-of-court settlement of $32 million to Diamond Crystal Salt and $12.8 million to the owners of the Joseph Jefferson complex. The drillers could hardly argue that they weren't at fault—after all, they could actually *see* the mine entrance from their rig.

No official blame was ever pronounced for the drilling miscalculation, on the rationale that all the evidence had been sucked down the drain. As for why state officials never raised any red flags before the disaster, that question was never investigated nor answered either. The Louisiana legislature did, however, eventually respond by banning future drilling in the state's freshwater lakes. If you wanted to drill beneath a lake, you henceforth needed to set up your rig somewhere on its periphery and drill in at an angle. It was but a minor hand slap to the oil industry, while satisfying most of the public that the legislature had been responsive. As for more intensive oversight of drilling operations—no, that never happened. After all, the state had only one active salt mine, and most of that one had already been destroyed, so surely there was no need to worry that there might be another similar disaster.

•   •   •

Crystal Diamond Salt continued to mine an unflooded portion of the Jefferson Island dome for the next few years, then abandoned that operation in 1986. In 1994, the Equitable Storage Company of Pennsylvania obtained a mining lease from the State of Louisiana to create two new salt caverns to store natural gas at the site. (Their procedure used high-pressure jets of water to dissolve the salt, which was then flushed out into the Gulf.) Equitable Storage, in turn, sold its lease to American Electric Power, which in turn, in 2004, sold it to the Atlanta-based AGL Resources, Inc. In 2006, AGL announced its intention to expand the storage facility further to ultimately sequester 9.4 billion cubic feet of gas there at pressures ranging from

700 to 2,700 pounds per square inch (psi). At the upper end of this range, the pressure is equivalent to that under about six thousand feet of seawater.

A local grassroots movement arose to oppose this plan (Save Lake Peigneur). One of that group's gripes is that the people of the state of Louisiana will benefit little, if at all, from the facility. In fact, as of this writing, AGL has no customers at all in Louisiana; its six corporate branches serve consumers in Georgia, New Jersey, Virginia, Florida, Tennessee, and Maryland. And, of course, there are historically based reasons not to trust the safety assurances of the fossil fuel industry—particularly when they conduct operations in Louisiana.

The project, nevertheless, is going forward. Nothing, after all, can possibly go wrong. Right?

◆ ◆ ◆

Are there any legitimate links between the *Deepwater Horizon* disaster of 2010 and the Lake Peigneur event of 1980? After all, they took place three decades apart. One was on an inland lake, the other in offshore federal waters. Different people, different companies, and different governmental jurisdictions were involved. The technology was considerably different. And the disastrous outcomes differed by several orders of magnitude.

Nevertheless, there are indeed some provocative similarities. Both events were driven by America's insatiable demand for petroleum. Both involved a business's reckless faith in the fidelity of its technology. Both were approved by bureaucrats who were ill prepared to assess the risks. Both resulted in totally unanticipated consequences. Both disasters were caused by a fourteen-inch drill bit. And both victimized many innocent people—and a lot of fish.

Chapter 5

MORE OOPS—
1969, 1979, AND 1989

It's not clear who decided to name BP's Mississippi Canyon well "Macondo," but it was definitely an inspired choice. (And yes, that name was used even on the original drilling application.) In a 1967 novel by the Colombian Nobel laureate Gabriel Garcia Marquez, *One Hundred Years of Solitude*, "Macondo" is a mythical jungle town where for seven generations the residents repeatedly forget their past and are doomed to make the same mistakes over and again. Marquez's allegory, of course, relates to the history and future of Latin America. By the end of his novel, the city of Macondo evaporates into a mirage.

In BP's parlance, Macondo could just as easily be a metaphor for the state of Louisiana, which likewise seems to be plagued by a disease that erases everyone's memory. Replace the lure of gold that repeatedly seduced the people of Marquez's Macondo with the lust for "black gold" in Louisiana, and the novel's themes are essentially unchanged. Was someone at BP just engaging in a bit of private amusement by assigning that particular name to its well? Or was that strange choice of moniker really the act of cynicism that it appears to be?

Like the townspeople of the fictional Macondo, most of the lawmakers in Louisiana behave as if they've forgotten the not-so-distant past. Listen to their speeches, visit their websites, or look up their "fact sheets" (as posted by the Political Action Committee of the Louisiana Oil and Gas Association, for instance), and you'll find a majority of those public servants to be overtly oblivious to the lessons of history regarding the oil and gas industry. In fact, even before BP's rogue well was permanently plugged, many of those lawmakers were already clamoring for *more* offshore drilling—and for *weakening* the existing regulations.

So, are there any specific past episodes that Louisiana lawmakers and citizens ought to ponder? One, of course, is the 1980 Lake Peigneur disaster we treated in chapter 4. But there are also a few others that, although they did not happen in Louisiana, had the effect of waking up a lot of other people throughout the nation. No regulator or energy policymaker anywhere has the moral right to make decisions relating to the oil and gas industry without being knowledgeable about the three big "impossible" spills that happened in 1969, 1979, and 1989.

• • •

January 29, 1969.

"I am amazed at the publicity for the loss of a few birds." Those unfortunate words were spoken publicly by Fred L. Hartley, president of Union Oil, on the heels of his company's disaster near Santa Barbara. As he went on to point out, no human lives had been lost. In fact, the only negative things that happened were that a few hundred thousand barrels of crude oil had escaped, winds had spread that ooze into a slick covering about eight hundred square miles, and thirty-five miles of pristine California shoreline got polluted by a thick, sticky tar.

If there was any event that would draw Californians into the nascent environmental movement of that time, this was it. The national news networks ran clips of scruffy, longhaired hippies scouring the beaches to rescue thousands of mired feathered creatures. Three animal emergency treatment centers, including one at the Santa Barbara Zoo, made for sobering video footage. Even multimillionaires were filmed transporting tar-covered grebes in their luxury cars. Contrary to Mr. Hartley's claim that a "few" birds were lost, the number was 3,686 according to an actual census of carcasses and upwards of 11,000 according to scientists who estimated that about two out of every three had been swept out to sea and were never recovered. As for the numerous seals and dolphins that washed ashore on the tides, they were also quite dead. Donations to environmental organizations soared. Dozens of lawsuits against Union Oil were filed in California courts.

And how had this spill happened?

Union Oil was drilling an exploratory well 5.8 miles offshore (in other words, still barely in sight of land). This initiative was not much of a gamble, given that four successful production platforms were already operating in the same general vicinity. Clearly, there was a lot more oil down there, so it was simply a matter of tapping it.

At a depth of about 3,500 feet, and closer to striking oil than anyone realized at the time, Union's drilling crew began to retrieve their drill bit to replace it. They then noticed that the drilling mud was disappearing—evidence of a casing or bore failure somewhere. Before they could correct the problem, they had a blowout. Fortunately, there was no fire.

Although the crew quickly capped the wellhead, the actual problem lay deeper. The leaking oil found five other ways to get out—through fractures created by its own upward pressure acting on an adjacent geological fault line. Fortunately, these Santa Barbara leaks were in "just" 188 feet of water (compared to the 5,067 feet for the *Deepwater Horizon* disaster). Although it was still a challenging task, all five leaks were plugged within twelve days of the initial incident. Yet for months thereafter, oil and gas continued to ooze slowly from the sea bottom.

Union Oil sent out skimmers to scoop oil from the deeper water and aircraft to drop detergents near the shorelines to dissolve it. On beaches and in the harbors, workers spread straw to soak up the spill, then raked it up and carted it away to be incinerated. Rocky sections of the shoreline were steam cleaned, which had the unfortunate effect of cooking billions of mollusks and other small shoreline creatures. Union Oil spent millions on the cleanup and millions more in settling damage claims.

Even as the spill was still fouling the region's waters and coasts, other drilling in the area continued. On February 24 (twenty-six days after the disaster began) another well in the same area had a blowout, which, although quickly capped, added to the spill. That event prompted Secretary of the Interior Walter Hickel to order all offshore drilling suspended pending review and revision of the regulations.

Because it was outside of California's three-mile territorial waters, Union Oil's operation in the Santa Barbara Channel did not need to comply with California drilling standards, which at the time were actually more rigorous than federal standards. Nor was there a Minerals Management Service to enforce the existing federal regulations; that agency wouldn't be established until 1982 (it would be reorganized and renamed in 2010). It was the US Geological Survey that gave Union Oil the blessing to use drill pipe that didn't meet California standards, nor even (it would turn out) the federal standards that were in place as of the date the drilling began.

Ever since that 1969 environmental disaster, the state of California has taken a highly cautious approach to offshore drilling. No, nobody was so rash as to advocate shutting down any production wells; after all, it wasn't a production well that caused the disaster, it was an exploration drill. In fact, the oil and gas industry is fond of quoting the fact that, since 1969, about 1 billion barrels of crude have been extracted from beneath California waters, with total spills amounting to just 840 barrels. An interesting and impressive statistic, but irrelevant to the issue.

The major debate has never been about extracting the oil; it has to do with the creation of the well in the first place—the drilling phase. And on this matter, many tempers have been volatile, with opponents over and again citing the Santa Barbara spill of 1969. Which, in fact, was a *drilling* disaster, not a production disaster.

On the heels of the *Deepwater Horizon* catastrophe of 2010, California governor Arnold Schwarzenegger, a Republican and a previous advocate of more offshore drilling in California, reconsidered his stance. "Why should we take on that risk?" he asked rhetorically. Then, referring to the potential royalties the state would be giving up, he stated that if he had a choice between making $100 million in royalties but also having Californians endure what was currently happening in the Gulf, or alternatively not having those royalties, then he'd rather find some other way to make up that $100 million.

With that, California's existing moratorium on *new* offshore drilling was extended.

As for Union Oil, the perpetrator of that 1969 disaster, it changed its name to Unocal in 1983; then in 2005 it was acquired by ChevronTexaco, which soon after dropped the "Texaco" part of the company name. Union Oil still, however, continues to conduct some production operations as Union Oil of California, a subsidiary of the Chevron Corporation.

◆　◆　◆

June 3, 1979.

It happened at about 3:00 a.m. Armando Rodriguez, a deckhand on a ship delivering drill pipe to the rig, saw it all. Illuminated by the derrick lights, a gusher from the exploratory well *Ixtoc I* exploded to a height of fifteen stories. Then a flash of sparks, followed by a near-deafening boom. A pillar of flame shot a thousand feet into the night sky. The drill tower collapsed into the platform, crushing it almost in half. Rodriguez saw men jumping into the sea to escape, silhouetted against the inferno.

Miraculously, sixty-three drillers were rescued. The semi-submersible rig *Sedco 135-F* crumpled in the flames, then sank. Oil gushed into the sea at a rate of at least 30,000 barrels per day.

5.1. The offshore drilling rig *Ixtoc I* exploded and sank in the Bay of Campeche on June 3, 1979, releasing up to 500,000 barrels of crude oil into the Gulf of Mexico. Until the *Deepwater Horizon* disaster, this event ranked as the biggest peacetime spill in history. Because none of the executives at BP had ever heard of it, they were doomed to repeat all of the same mistakes. *Courtesy of the US Environmental Protection Agency.*

The driller was Pemex, the Mexican government-owned oil company (yes, the same company founded by Edward L. Doheny of Teapot Dome Scandal fame). The site was in the Bay of Campeche in the southern Gulf of Mexico, sixty-two miles off the Mexican coast, where the water was about 160 feet deep (slightly less than that at the Santa Barbara disaster of a decade earlier).

The borehole had reached 11,800 feet when the problem began: drilling mud began to disappear. It was being pumped down all right, but less and less of it was circulating back up, which meant that the drill had struck some sort of void or a set of fractures. The engineers decided to yank out the drill pipe, remove the bit, then reinsert the tube and pump cement down the shaft to seal off the problem region. Once that cement had set, their plan was to drill back through their temporary plug. At this point, just as with the crew at Santa Barbara, the drillers had no inkling of how close they were to a major oil and gas reservoir.

The blowout came when they'd gotten the drill pipe only partially reinserted. The blowout preventer's shear ram didn't work, apparently because the shears happened to strike a reinforced coupling between a pair of sections of pipe. Mere moments later, the platform erupted in flames (fig. 5.1).

Pemex immediately began drilling two relief wells to stop the gusher. Because that is such a slow process, Pemex tried some other approaches as well. One contractor used a "junk shot" followed by cement to successfully seal the well, but that victory was only temporary; oil soon began gushing from around the casing. Another outfit built a collection dome dubbed a "sombrero," but that managed to collect only a small portion of the gusher. By August, sticky tar balls were washing up on South Padre Island, Texas. The disaster was now an international event.

In November, after five months of drilling and several misses, the relief wells finally struck home. Pemex employees began to pump in steel balls and cement to seal off the wild well. Unfortunately, the backpressure was too great for that tactic to work. It wasn't until March 25, 1980, that the gusher had lost enough of its gusto on its own to allow it to be successfully capped. That's right, nearly ten months after the blowout.

During that period, about 500,000 barrels of crude oil entered the Gulf of Mexico. Most of it remained in Mexican waters, but some drifted north and polluted more than a hundred miles of Texas beaches. Volunteers sprang into action to dig up thousands of sea-turtle nests and transport the eggs to unpolluted coastlines. Other groups in Texas sopped up oily muck day after day for months, only to watch more arrive on each incoming tide.

Mexico claimed sovereign immunity and never offered any retribution to Texas. President Jimmy Carter didn't push that matter, but he did make a national plea to try to wean the United States off its hydrocarbon addiction. Very few Americans listened.

The *Ixtoc I* spill wiped out fishing off the Mexican Gulf Coast for more than two years. As for the coasts themselves, most of the affected ones were sandy rather than rocky or swampy, which was fortunate since warm sand and surf accelerate the decomposition of oil. Moreover, *Ixtoc*'s oil was relatively "light"; that is, it contained a high percentage of the more volatile hydrocarbons, so a great deal of it evaporated before reaching shore. Some of the spill was also burned before it could disperse. It was, in other words, only because of a lucky confluence of factors that a spill of such enormous magnitude didn't cause far worse environmental damage.

Until BP's *Deepwater Horizon* disaster, Pemex's 1979 *Ixtoc I* spill held the record as the largest accidental spill in history. (Yes, there was one larger deliberate spill—actually a bunch of simultaneous deliberate spills, mostly on land—instigated by Iraq's retreating army at the tail end of the Gulf War of 1991.)

Some US jingoists have claimed that Mexican engineers just aren't as good as US engineers, and that explains why the *Ixtoc* blowout took so long to fix. That argument, however (its condescending tone aside), just doesn't stand up to scrutiny. Pemex indeed *did* bring in several US contractors. And even *they* still took ten months to plug the gusher.

Now you'd think that everyone in a high position in an oil corporation or in Louisiana government would know this history and keep it in mind as they approve offshore drilling projects. But did they? Nope. During one of the congressional hearings on the then-ongoing *Deepwater Horizon* disaster, a five-member panel of BP executives was caught flat-footed by a question about how their contingency planning had been affected by the *Ixtoc I* accident. None of them acted as if they'd even heard of *Ixtoc I*. As for Louisiana leaders, there seems to be no record of any journalist asking them that same question.

The point that completely slipped the grasp of the BP higher echelon is that in 1979, at a water depth of just 160 feet, Pemex unsuccessfully tried many of the same tactics that BP would attempt again unsuccessfully thirty years later at a much greater seafloor depth (more than thirty times as deep). Surely thirty years should have been ample time to develop a better engineering response. But no, BP hired engineers only to figure out ways to drill in deeper and deeper water, not to put systems in place to respond to the ever-increasing prospect of deepwater blowouts.

•   •   •

March 23, 1989.

Night was beginning to fall as the three-year-old supertanker *Exxon Valdez* left its loading berth and headed west through Valdez Narrows, then southwest through Valdez Arm, carrying a cargo of 1.3 million barrels of Alaskan North Slope crude. It was Good Friday and the second day of spring. The temperature hovered slightly above freezing and there was a bit of a drizzle, but the sea was calm and visibility was reasonably good: from the bridge, you could see about ten miles. Where Prince William Sound began to widen, the coastal pilot disembarked. The escorting tugs tooted and turned homeward, leaving the 987-foot supertanker to its own captain and his crew of twenty.

Ahead, the shipping lanes were confettied with ice floes and even a few small icebergs. Captain Joe Hazelwood decided to exercise caution. He steered his ship to portside and set a new course—one that headed the tanker straight toward Bligh Reef, which was well charted and identified by shore lights. He then handed the bridge over to his third mate, Gregory Cousins, with instructions to return the vessel to the shipping lane as soon as they passed the Busby Island light, about 2.5 miles prior to the reef. With that, Hazelwood went below to do some paperwork. And possibly to also have a few drinks.

What happened next made history. At 12:09 a.m. on March 24, 1989, the *Exxon Valdez* slammed straight into Bligh Reef. The impact peeled off several sections of the huge tanker's single bottom. Its oily cargo began spilling into the sea. Hazelwood reassumed command and spent the next hour trying to dislodge the vessel from the underwater rocks, sometimes running the 32,000-horsepower main engine at full throttle. He was unsuccessful, and in that respect he was fortunate. Marine engineers would later conclude that if he'd indeed gotten the *Exxon Valdez* off the reef in that damaged condition, it would have immediately sunk.

There remains a considerable disagreement about how much oil actually entered the environment from the tanker. The low-end estimate is about 257,000 barrels; the high-end is about 710,000. What is indisputable is that shorelines as far as 470 miles from Bligh Reef were fouled. Thousands of coastal fishers lost their livelihoods. A whole way of life disappeared for hundreds of families. As of this writing, twenty-four years later, you still can't lift a stone on some of those beaches and islands without finding black tar beneath it. Nor have all of the legal claims been fully resolved.

As with most man-made disasters, the *Exxon Valdez* spill was the culmination of a series of events and decisions that began many years earlier. And yes, the catastrophe could have been avoided if some voices of reason had prevailed. Instead, several of the individuals who did attempt to speak truth to power lost their jobs.

One could say it all began on March 13, 1968, when Atlantic Richfield and Humble Oil (now ExxonMobil) announced a huge oil strike near Prudhoe Bay on Alaska's north coast. This was several decades before the Arctic Ocean's ice cover began to melt appreciably, and it made little sense to build a tanker port at a place where it would be ice locked most of the year. Various alternatives were considered, including a resident fleet of icebreakers, a rail line with specially designed rolling stock, and even air transport (which was clearly a stupid idea from the get-go). The ultimate decision was to build a pipeline to transport the oil approximately eight hundred miles from the North Slope to a spot near the fishing community of Valdez (population four thousand), which happened to be accessible to deepwater ships via Prince William Sound. Even as environmentalists were shrieking in horror at this proposal, the three companies holding mineral leases on the North Slope banded together and, on August 14, 1970, created the Alyeska Pipeline Service Company. That outfit would not only build the pipeline, but also maintain it and be responsible for dealing with any spills.

The political battles continued for another three years. The majority of the fishermen on Prince William Sound were dead-set against the pipeline. The resident Native Americans were against it. Conservationists were against it. The oil industry, of course, was all for it. The citizens of the fishing village of Cordova and its surrounding region took their challenges to the courts. On appeal, those fishing interests lost to the oil companies.

In 1971, a group of Alaska's Cordova District residents flew to Washington, D.C., to testify before the House Committee on Fisheries and Wildlife Conservation in opposition to the proposed pipeline. In a chillingly prescient scenario, Alaska state representative Keith Specking described the prospect of a supertanker wandering off course in a storm, impaling itself on Bligh Reef, and spilling 250,000 barrels of crude oil into the sound. His testimony was duly recorded, then ignored.

Specking would ultimately be proven wrong about two details of his prediction: (1) the actual accident happened in calm rather than stormy seas and (2) the *Exxon Valdez* spilled a great deal more than 250,000 barrels.

The Trans-Alaska Pipeline Authorization Act passed easily in the House but became deadlocked by a tie vote in the Senate. Vice President Spiro Agnew stepped in and cast the deciding vote. On November 16, 1973, President Richard Nixon signed the legislation into law, and the pipeline project began.

It was, and indeed remains, a marvel of modern engineering. The oil needed to be heated and reheated along the way, so it wouldn't get too sluggish to flow in the arctic climate. Yet all that heat couldn't be allowed to melt the supporting permafrost, or else the pipeline would sink, kink, and rupture. This required the installation of heat exchangers on every support along the entire eight-hundred-mile route. Further, the flowing oil needed to be separated into batches by moving plugs, so if there happened to be a break, the volume of the spill would be limited. There were multiple pumping stations along the way, and they all had to be powered and maintained. And the pipeline could not be allowed to impede the annual migrations of herds of caribou and other wildlife.

The first section of pipe was laid on March 27, 1975, and the final weld was completed on May 31, 1977. After an additional three weeks of inspections, the oil began to flow. On August 1 of that year, the first tanker-load of North Slope crude left Prince William Sound for California.

For the next eleven years, the operation went pretty well. The pipeline delivered an average of about 650,000 barrels per day, which amounts to about 10 percent of today's total US production. Yes, there were a few negative incidents. One in 1978, ultimately attributed to sabotage, resulted in a spill of about 16,000 barrels onto the tundra. The others, however, were relatively minor. (There have since been a couple of other significant spills: for instance, one of 6,143 barrels in 2001 caused by a bullet hole and another of about 5,000 barrels in May of 2010 from an overflowed storage tank during a power outage.)

But between 1977 and 1989, Alyeska officials seem to have been lulled into a general sense of complacency that nothing serious would ever go wrong, let alone considering the prospect that they would ever need to contend with a major spill in the Prince William Sound. The budget for spill response gear was cut. Skimmers, booms, and other equipment were stored outside, where they were not maintained and got buried in snowdrifts. Spill response training was ignored. No plans were made to notify coastal communities in case of an emergency, let alone to involve the locals in any mobilized response. This, despite the fact that Alyeska was officially in charge of the whole show from the moment oil entered the north end of the pipeline until the departing tankers at the other end were safely out to sea.

Several Alyeska employees did express concerns over the years. One was Steve Eward, who worked at the Valdez loading terminal. From time to time, Eward noticed oil sheens on the water, small oil slicks, tar balls washing ashore here and there, and even oiled dead birds. His managers weren't interested in hearing about such things; they advised him that such pollution always eventually washes out with the tides, so there was no reason for concern. For Eward, however, this was not a good enough answer. Over a period of time he assembled a stack of notes documenting the sloppiness of the loading operations, then he hand-carried that pile of materials to the Coast Guard office in Valdez. The next day, his boss at Alyeska called him into his office. Resting on that manager's desk was Eward's report; the Coast Guard hadn't even bothered to file it, let alone read it. Eward was immediately demoted and shortly thereafter he left the company.

When the *Exxon Valdez* ran aground in 1989, Alyeska wasn't even remotely prepared to execute its responsibilities. The seas remained calm for the next few days, so initially the spill remained close to the crippled tanker. Yet the company did virtually nothing during those first critical days when it should have sprung into full action. Its excuse, remarkably, was that most of its response equipment still lay buried in the snow. Then, toward the end of the third day, a violent storm with 65-mile-per-hour winds blew in and scattered the congealing crude over thousands of square miles of Prince William Sound.

If Alyeska's corporate negligence was inexcusable, Exxon was even more culpable. The *Exxon Valdez* was a fairly new ship, having been launched just three years before the disaster and expected to have a life-time of twenty-five to thirty years. Yet by the time it was placed in service in 1986, every other major oil company in the world had long been con-structing its supertankers with double hulls: an outer one and an inner one. That way if a tanker did happen to suffer outer-hull damage, the inner hull would remain intact and no oil would escape. Exxon's bean counters, however, chose not to incur that extra expense. The *Exxon Valdez* had just one layer of steel sequestering its hydrocarbon cargo from the surround-ing sea.

Now if Exxon's managers were going to take a risk like that, one might think they'd at least want to be certain that a comprehensive spill plan and appropriate equipment were in place. As one of the owners of Alyeska, Exxon could easily have insisted on that. But did it? No.

After the big storm, the goo was so widely scattered that there was no longer any simple way to clean it all up. But that didn't stop Exxon from putting on a big show. One that left most of the affected Alaskans forever cynical of Big Oil.

Hundreds of "experts" were flown in from Texas and elsewhere— people who knew absolutely nothing about Alaska. The sky buzzed with helicopters and fixed-wing aircraft, all accomplishing essentially nothing other than to avoid colliding with one another. Boats were chartered and sent out without the necessary equipment. Local fishermen scooped up the spilled crude in five-gallon buckets, only to discover that Exxon offi-cials had not provided any means of disposing of it. One group of cleanup workers was assigned a quota of scouring a mile of coastline per day—when a realistic goal would have been more like a hundred yards per day. Local workers were admonished for moving rocks to get at the underlying oil; after all, the managers contended, the only thing that would show in the "after" photos would be the *tops* of the rocks, so that's all that actually needed to be scrubbed. The influx of outsiders vastly exceeded the few available public accommodations, and consultants and reporters alike found themselves sleeping in warehouses and garages. Sewerage systems couldn't handle the increased loads and they overflowed. The affected towns and villages all stank. Huge quantities of food had to be flown in—including canned meats, which had never been part of the local diets. And the entire region was soon littered with discarded Styrofoam.

Local officials found it difficult if not impossible to communicate with the oil company employees. A regional response group requisitioned eight hundred wooden baseball bats from Exxon—a perfectly reasonable request insofar as that's how local fishermen break ice from their boat railings and decks so their vessels won't get top-heavy in freezing weather. The request got mired because Exxon's accountants had no clue about conditions and practices in coastal Alaska.

Most seriously, however, were the sad facts that (1) there was never any comprehensive plan and (2) nobody had any personal accountability. After the big storm, Exxon took over the response from the demonstrably inept Alyeska, yet the parent company did little better. Managers arrived and left with revolving-door regularity, most staying only a week or two. Few seemed to have any clear set of objectives, and those who did seemed to have no concept of how to accomplish them. The entire operation was a mass of utter confusion.

On September 15, 1989, Exxon suspended its cleanup operation for the winter. It resumed limited cleanup efforts during the following two summers, then it declared its mission accomplished. As far as restoring the environment, that was that.

Captain Hazelwood was arrested and tried on four criminal charges. On March 22, 1990, a jury in Anchorage acquitted him of three of those offenses (including operating a watercraft while under the influence of alcohol) but found him guilty of the fourth: negligent discharge of oil, a misdemeanor. He was fined $50,000 and sentenced to perform one thousand hours of community service. After his appeals were exhausted in 1999, he served his sentence. In 2002, he paid off his fine to the state of Alaska.

Meanwhile, a class-action civil suit was filed against Exxon on behalf of about thirty-eight thousand plaintiffs, including commercial fishermen and others harmed by the spill. On September 16, 1994, an Anchorage jury awarded the group $287 million in compensatory damages (an average of less than $600 apiece after attorney's fees), plus $5 billion in punitive damages. Exxon appealed and the Ninth Circuit Court reduced the punitive part of the award to $2.5 billion. Exxon appealed this ruling as well, and on June 25, 2008, in a five-to-three decision, the US Supreme Court further reduced the punitive damages to $507.5 million. Exxon then returned to the lower court and argued that it should be liable for only 75 percent of that figure. In June of 2009, another federal court slapped Exxon with an additional $480 million in interest on the long-overdue punitive payment. As of this writing, twenty-four years after the disaster, the matter is still not completely resolved. In the meantime, more than eight thousand of the plaintiffs have died.

The costs, losses, fines, and jury awards had no long-term effects whatsoever on Exxon's bottom line. In 2009, Exxon reported profits of $40.6 billion, more than a ten-fold increase over its profit of $3.9 billion at the time of the disaster.

As for the crippled *Exxon Valdez*, the oil that hadn't escaped was offloaded, temporary repairs were made, and the vessel was moved to a shipyard in San Diego, where Exxon spent roughly $30 million to remove and replace about 1,600 tons of battered or missing steel. Before it was relaunched in 1990, the vessel was renamed the *Exxon Mediterranean*; a few years later, it became simply the *Mediterranean*. Because the Oil Pollution Act of 1990 (which Exxon unsuccessfully challenged in court) prohibited the supertanker from returning to Prince William Sound, it served on routes between Europe, the Middle East, and Asia under the Marshall Islands flag of convenience. (Yes, in other words, Exxon subsidiaries continued to transport oil in this dangerous, single-hulled tanker for about another eight years.) Then in 2008, the ship was sold to Hong Kong Bloom Shipping Ltd., which renamed it the *Dong Fang Ocean*, refitted it as an ore carrier, and registered it in Panama. As of this writing, it continues to ply the seas but is no longer capable of spilling a cargo of oil.

• • •

The US Congress reacted quickly to the *Exxon Valdez* fiasco. The House version of the Oil Pollution Act of 1990 had eighty cosponsors and passed by a vote of 375 to 5. The Senate version passed by a voice vote.

This law requires companies to have a plan for preventing oil spills, as well as a "detailed containment and cleanup plan" for instances when spills do occur. It imposes fines of up to $500,000 for failing to notify federal authorities of a spill. It bans ships that have been involved in spills from operating in Prince William Sound. It imposes penalties of $25,000 for each day of violation or $1,000 for each barrel of oil discharged. But it also caps offenders' liability at $350 million per spill for onshore facilities and deepwater ports, and just $75 million per spill for offshore facilities, plus various direct costs. Mere pittances for a major oil company.

This law clearly has a number of weaknesses. One is obviously the low dollar cap on liability. But perhaps the major one is this: although individual states are free to impose additional restrictions and fines, state jurisdiction does not apply beyond three miles offshore. Thus, in a case like the *Deepwater Horizon* disaster, the offending company's responsibility to the affected states always promises to result in a legal quagmire that will drag on for many years, if not decades.

•   •   •

It's human nature to ignore low-probability but high-impact risks in our everyday lives; after all, who worries about a tree limb falling on them while walking down their driveway, or getting food poisoning in a well-known restaurant? We know that such things indeed do happen; yet on an individual daily basis, they're not worth our getting concerned about.

Big oil spills—say a hundred thousand barrels or more—are also low-probability, high-impact events. But in these cases, the consequences are much broader than harming one individual. The health and economic welfare of large numbers of people can be adversely affected, and huge regions can be devastated environmentally. Yet the same human psychology that applies to falling trees often prevails here as well. And because oil companies are run by humans, it's not uncommon for entire organizations to adopt a lockstep "What, me worry?" culture. Then when something catastrophic does happen, everyone is stunned and nobody has the foggiest notion of what to do.

The simple fact is this: Given a long enough period of time, even a low-probability event is virtually certain to happen. It's a good bet that your hometown won't be hit by a meteorite next year, but don't let your grandchildren bet their inheritances that, over the next sixty years, a big earthquake won't strike San Francisco or a major hurricane won't wallop Miami or a freak blizzard won't bury Atlanta. We can't argue that such events are impossible, because they *have* happened in the past. And because they have happened, the law of large numbers tells us that they *will* happen again.

Is this also the case with man-made disasters? Yes, it seems to be, particularly when you factor in human groupthink mentality. Sooner or later, a disaster with the space shuttle was imminent. So was a deadly crash of the supersonic Concorde. As well as the collapse of major interstate highway bridges, such as the I-35W Mississippi River Bridge in Minneapolis and the I-10 bridge over Escambia Bay in Florida.

Likewise, a major supertanker accident like the *Exxon Valdez* was sure to happen someday, and some offshore wells such as the ones in the Santa Barbara Channel and the Bay of Campeche were guaranteed to go rogue. And, yes, eventually there was also bound to be a blowout on a big outer-continental-shelf drilling rig.

All of these exemplary disasters could have been mitigated to some extent through more cautious engineering at the front end of the projects. They could have been mitigated further through more comprehensive testing and inspection programs later on. And by doing so, some accidents here and there may have been avoided entirely. One hundred percent of the risk, however, would never have been eliminated. There will always be accidents in any man-made system, and every once in awhile, even if the probability is very low, some of those accidents will escalate into disasters.

Now every human group—be it a company or a community or a governmental entity—can adopt one of two general strategies for dealing with this reality. On the one hand, they can choose to be *reactive*; that is, they can simply conduct business as usual until there's a crisis, then everyone runs around frantically trying to figure out what to do about it. This, unfortunately, is a very common dynamic. It's how FEMA as well as the Louisiana government dealt with the flooding of New Orleans in 2005. It's also what Union Oil did at Santa Barbara in 1969, what Pemex did after the *Ixtoc I* blowout of 1979, what Exxon did after the *Exxon Valdez* grounding in 1989, and what BP did after the *Deepwater Horizon* disaster of 2010.

The alternative strategy is to be *proactive*. This means accepting the fact that crises will indeed occur and preparing for them well in advance. Brainstorm about everything that might possibly go wrong, and predict every need you can think of that can possibly arise. Set up an emergency management system whereby everyone understands the chains of command as well as the divisions of labor. Develop a means for quickly mobilizing all the personnel. Properly train everyone. Have systems in place to promptly deliver all the necessary physical resources to wherever they might be needed. Involve the locals (they're always a great deal more resourceful than typical outsiders assume). And so on.

In other words, don't wait until thousands of barrels of crude are spilling into the sea to begin thinking about what you're going to do about it. The tardier and more disorganized your response, the worse things are guaranteed to get before they start to get better.

Of course there are numerous impediments to engaging in such proactive contingency planning. In the private sector, where short-term profits pave the way to managerial career success and the costs of contingency preparation eat into those profits, managers may have a clear incentive to procrastinate or even ignore the issue. And in the public sector, competent disaster planning is seldom a visibly valuable public service until an actual catastrophe strikes. In other words, behaving proactively on this issue requires not only enlightened foresight, but often a great deal of personal courage as well.

So, does anyone actually do this? Plan for hypothetical disasters in advance? Yes. The US Coast Guard, for instance (despite the flack it sometimes takes for not doing more than it's empowered to do), is usually remarkably quick and effective at responding to many categories of disasters. In the civilian realm, the Red Cross does pretty well. And then there is Florida, where each of its sixty-seven counties got their acts together in the wake of the debacle of 1992's Hurricane Andrew. Today, that state's integrated emergency planning and management system is surely the best in the nation.

Florida's proactive approach to disaster planning, however, did happen to overlook oil spills. Over the course of its history, Florida has had plenty of hurricanes, notable hard freezes, several major droughts, occasional epidemics, a couple of major commercial plane crashes, and a number of shipwrecks—but never a big oil spill. After all, there are only a couple of offshore oil and gas wells in Florida, no major refineries, and only a handful of modest-sized petroleum tank farms (mainly to serve cruise ships and airports). And so, at the time of the *Deepwater Horizon* disaster, Florida was no better prepared to prevent BP's oil from fouling its pristine Gulf beaches than was BP itself.

Oops again.

• • •

United States senators have an average age of sixty; in the US House of Representatives, the average is about fifty-five. The average ages of Louisiana's state legislators are in the same ballpark. In other words, the widely publicized oil disasters of 1969, 1979, and 1989, as well as the Lake Peigneur disaster of 1980, occurred within most of these politicians' personal memory spans. As for that minority of current lawmakers who are too young to remember those significant events, the historical records are readily available. There is, in other words, no legitimate reason for legislative ignorance about such noteworthy historical screw-ups by the oil industry.

And yet, over and over, assurances by oil executives that nothing can go wrong are trusted as if they were factual. The truth is that drilling for oil and transporting it on the seas are risky operations. Things can go terribly wrong. They've gone wrong before, and yes, they *will* go wrong again.

Chapter 6

SOCIAL SCRUPLES BEDEVILED

The history of American industry is replete with marvelous stories of Yankee ingenuity juxtaposed with dismal accounts of environmental pillage and exploitations of the working class. The steel industry in western Pennsylvania, coal mining in Appalachia, gold and silver extraction in the West, and, yes, drilling for oil and gas—all began with a devil-may-care attitude toward the natural world and a lack of concern for the physical well-being of workers and locals. After all, given the vastness of Nature, what harm was a little pollution here and there? If some individuals didn't like this or that smidgen of environmental degradation, they were certainly free to move elsewhere, right?

By the late 1800s, however, an increasing number of naturalists began to raise concerns about the long-term consequences of unbridled industrial development. As realists, they did not expect to convince their government to impose standards of enlightened behavior on private companies; instead, they campaigned for the creation of public sanctuaries that industrialists and developers would never be allowed to despoil. As early as 1864, California designated Yosemite Valley as a state park (it would become a national park in 1901). In 1872, the US government created the country's first national park—Yellowstone—to prevent post–Civil War entrepreneurs from marring the beauty of that wonderland of geysers, hot springs, streams, lakes, and wildlife. Over the following decades, the list of protected lands expanded to include historic battlefields, archaeological sites, and dozens of additional national parks, including five small ones in Louisiana. Despite angry reactions from many of the captains of business and industry, it turned out that none of those preservation actions had any demonstrable detrimental effects on the nation's economy. Moreover, in virtually every instance, locals actually benefited economically from the creation of those parklands.

As this trend was just beginning, an organized labor movement emerged in the industrialized Northeast. Labor's objectives, of course, did not initially focus on environmental quality; they dealt instead with the more immediate and pressing issues of working conditions, fair wages, and industrial safety. As medical science progressed, however, it became increasingly clear that the matter of workplace environmental quality overlapped with the unions' concerns about safety. Specific issues included worker exposure to asbestos, coal dust, biohazards, radiation, and various noxious chemicals. And once again the industrialists screamed in protest. This time, many of them claimed that any governmental imposition of environmental standards in the workplace would drive them into bankruptcy.

But there was also a slightly different argument against the establishment of workplace standards, one that was somewhat more subtle and philosophical and which still resonates with many voters today. It went something like this: governments are run by politicians and bureaucrats, neither of which (as a group) has any particular expertise in industry. Regulating industry by governmental fiat is therefore certain to lead to stupid rules and inefficiencies. Better to let industry police itself, right? After all, who better knows what needs to be done in the workplace and how best to do it than the nation's businessmen?

By the mid-1900s, most states had at least some laws on the books establishing minimal air and water quality standards for the public. Those standards varied from place to place, and enforcement tended to be spotty at best. Then in 1948, the federal government created a minimum nationwide clean water standard. A corresponding national clean air standard followed in 1955. In the industrialized regions of western Pennsylvania, northeastern Ohio, and parts of Illinois, Indiana, and New York, compliances were often technologically challenging, expensive, and slow. Elsewhere in the country, however, those initial sets of environmental standards bordered on irrelevancy; most folks simply ignored them.

Then, in a one-two punch in 1970 and 1971, President Richard M. Nixon (yes, a Republican) signed into law the legislative acts creating the Environmental Protection Agency (EPA) and the Occupational Safety and Health Administration (OSHA). Whether in the workplace or at home and whether an individual was pro or con, it was no longer possible for anyone to escape thinking about the environment.

Not only did many company executives shriek (again), but so did many of the public, because as a part of the cascade of new regulations that followed, municipalities were no longer allowed to dump raw sewage into waterways or incinerate their garbage. And that meant increasing everyone's taxes and water bills to pay for environmentally friendly municipal sewage treatment and sanitary landfills.

Few at that time had any inkling of how well it would all turn out. Within two decades, the previously hopelessly polluted Ohio River was clean enough to swim in, and edible game fish were even returning to those waters. Recreational businesses and quaint restaurants sprouted on the once-grimy riverbanks of places like Pittsburgh, Wheeling, and Cincinnati. Today, people are boating and water skiing on streams that had been so chemically toxic and fouled by bio-waste that no sane person would even stick a toe in them.

Certainly the rapid pace of environmental improvements in parts of the Northeast was accelerated by the demise of the steelmaking industry. But no, environmental regulations didn't cause that particular industrial decline; big steel was doomed anyway because of broader economic forces, and the keener minds recognized that reality. Just as today's oil industry is also certain to crash sooner or later.

Could anyone possibly doubt today that the environmental regulatory changes were for the better? And, more to the point, would such remarkable improvements have come about if the Captains of Industry had been permitted to continue to police themselves? Yes, that's a rhetorical question. But it's worth keeping in mind when examining what continues to go on in Louisiana.

◆　◆　◆

During my (Ernest's) seven years in Louisiana, I never got used to hearing so many rigidly negative attitudes toward government regulation of any type. Because most of my academic interests related to natural disasters, construction practices in particular always piqued my curiosity. And much of what I saw here appalled me. One nearby subdivision under construction in Baton Rouge consisted of dozens of duplex townhomes with no partitioning firewalls in their attics (a flagrant violation of the fire codes in virtually every other city in the nation). There were few if any hurricane straps tying the roof rafters to the walls, nor were the sill plates properly anchored to the foundations—and this in a region subject to violent tropical storms and hurricanes capable of ripping off roofs or tumbling a home onto its side. The roof decking was chipboard instead of moisture-resistant plywood. The shortcomings went on. It was as if the contractors were begging for these new homes to collapse in a storm or burn to the ground in what would otherwise be a minor fire. And this was in 2004, centuries after folks knew better. Resource-poor Lisbon, Portugal, for instance, adopted fire (and earthquake) construction codes as early as 1756, including masonry firewalls extending above the roof lines between adjacent row houses.

One might expect that Louisiana's older homes would be the ones most prone to storm damage, but that is not the case. A process of natural selection has been going on for several centuries here—with the flimsiest old buildings succumbing long ago and the surviving antique dwellings having generally proven their durability. Ironically, it is many of Louisiana's newer homes that are most vulnerable, at least those built prior to 2006, when the state reluctantly enacted a baseline building code to qualify for federal assistance after the previous year's series of devastating hurricanes.

Beyond their disdain for construction codes, few Louisianans are enthusiastic about land-use restrictions. Chemical factories sprawl adjacent to low-income residential communities, oil refineries are situated next to college campuses, sewage plants border beautiful antebellum mansions and churches, and oil and gas wells sprout willy-nilly from agricultural fields and even some residential lawns. There is very little that the state inhibits its businesses and residents from doing. Only in 2008 was cockfighting banned (Louisiana was the last state to allow it). And you can still legally pop open a beer while on the road here, provided that there are at least one fewer open cans than the number of people in your vehicle.

Few Louisianans, however, believe that their quality of life could be better, for the simple reason that they seldom leave the state long enough to experience anything different. Even today, many of the older folks have never traveled beyond the next few parishes, let alone visiting New Orleans (which to some of them might as well be on the moon). Numerous middle-aged women (and even some men) in the western and central parishes have never seen the Mississippi River. Although studies of the mobility of US residents always result in somewhat fuzzy data, it's pretty clear that Louisianans rank lowest in their rate of emigration from their home state, with 90 to 95 percent of today's residents reporting having been born relatively near to their present abodes. (At the other extreme is Nevada, where only about 17 percent of today's residents were born in that state.) Ergo, is it any wonder that there has been no popular uprising against the power of Big Oil in Louisiana? After all, most Louisianans have never experienced anyplace that was *not* controlled by oil interests. Nor a place with strict building codes. Nor one with strong zoning and land-use laws. Nor, for that matter, one with stiff environmental regulations. Let alone a place with a culture of diligent enforcement of such regulatory standards.

How could any place on Earth be more egalitarian than that? Everyone does pretty much as they please, and that includes the rich and poor alike. Yes, and the oil companies.

◆ ◆ ◆

When the drillers first swarmed into the southern parishes in the 1920s, that region had almost no roads that led anywhere. Most communities were strung along cheniers or the narrow natural levees of the bayous, usually with a single street—typically not much more than a footpath— that began at a swamp at one end of town and terminated at another marsh at the other. Transportation was predominantly by boat, and most families owned several. Formal schooling was minimal. The daily language of the older folks was still French, and many of them could speak little or no English at all. There wasn't a whole lot of use for money, because most of the local economy ran on bartering. The wetlands, however, were bountiful, providing building materials (cypress, which is impervious to rot), furs, shrimp, oysters, fish, mudbugs (crawfish), ducks, and alligators. Mattresses were stuffed with fumigated Spanish moss; streets and sidewalks were paved with oyster shells. Plus, here and there rose patches of slightly higher ground that could be cultivated with rice or cotton or sugar cane or used to raise livestock. Even alcohol and firearms were available via fur and alligator-hide traders (and sometimes smugglers) who arrived by boat. This was the Cajun lifestyle for many generations, and yes, the locals were quite happy with it.

Even today, very few Louisiana residents live within view of the Gulf of Mexico—the two exceptions being near the small town of Cameron next to the Texas border and the sparsely populated Grand Isle, a narrow barrier island about forty miles west of the mouth of the Mississippi River. These are also the only two places where Louisiana has sandy beaches. The rest of the state's coastal region consists of marshlands, bogs, shallow lagoons, and thousands of low-lying islands, some of which come and go with the tides, others of which move and change shape with each tropical storm.

Lacking any notable beaches, Louisiana also lacks coastal resorts. Tourists outside of New Orleans consist mostly of fishers and hunters who don't spend a lot of money, nor could they find a way to do so if they wanted to.

Although the United States has twenty-three states with seacoasts, Louisiana's shoreline is unique in at least two respects: (1) only a tiny fraction of it is accessible by land, and (2) there is no way to measure the total length of that shore. The sometimes-quoted figure of 397 miles does not account for all of the numerous wiggles in the coast, the banks of the brackish bayous (whose currents reverse with the tides), nor the thousands of islands. If you start adding all that in, you can easily double the coastline length. Moreover, regardless of how accurate you try to be, you can also be assured that the resulting statistic will change within a month or so.

Even today, it's not easy to travel around in southern Louisiana. In fact, to drive most places in the southernmost parishes still requires a commitment to an adventure on narrow, poorly marked, and often unpaved roads that never take the shortest path between any two points. Regardless of where you start and where you're going, you can be guaranteed that your route will wiggle around a labyrinth of swamps, bayous, and lakes—provided, that is, that you don't get onto one of the many roads that ends abruptly at the edge of a swamp in the middle of nowhere. (Yes, today a GPS is helpful, but no, it's not a guarantee that you won't still experience a memorable, unplanned adventure.)

Even assuming that you don't get lost (and virtually every outsider does), your odometer will run up a mileage far out of proportion to the linear scale of the map you're following. The straight-line distance from Cameron to the city of Lake Charles, for instance, is 27 miles, yet the two land routes measure 57 and 50 miles, the latter involving a ferry. The lengthiest compulsory meanders are in the southeastern parishes. Grand Isle, for example, is only 23 miles from Port Sulphur as the crow flies, but by car it's a whopping 189 miles—all of which lie west of the Mississippi River.

Drilling, of course, requires a great deal of heavy equipment and supplies. There needs to be a way to get all of this paraphernalia to the well sites, which in this region are seldom in convenient locations. Yet you can't even lay down a functional *temporary* road on much of the soggy and semi-submerged land here.

The only practical way for the early drillers to transport equipment into the swamps was via barge. Yet, because most of these waters are too shallow for even the three-foot drafts of the shallowest of such vessels, that called for dredging. Before long, southern Louisiana was crisscrossed by a lacework of straight and narrow canals running in from the Gulf of

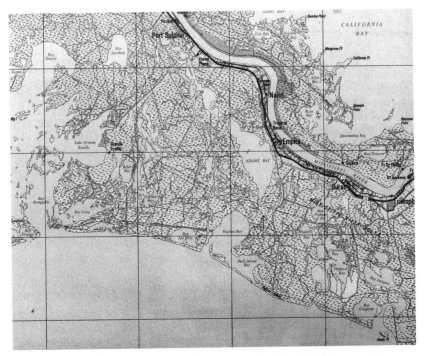

6.1. Louisiana's coastal regions are crisscrossed by thousands of canals once used to barge in drilling equipment or to pipe the extracted oil to collection stations. This example is in Plaquemines Parish. *Courtesy of the Louisiana Department of Transportation.*

Mexico to various drilling sites in the swamplands. Then, when many of those wells became productive (beginning in the mid to late 1920s), additional canals were dredged to lay pipelines farther to the north, where collection terminals could be sited on more stable ground. Today, more than 14,800 miles of pipelines slice through Louisiana's coastal wetlands, along with about 3,000 miles of navigable artificial channels.

Although most of the early wetlands wells have long been depleted, the abandoned equipment and a lacework of obsolete canals remain today (fig. 6.1). No, the state of Louisiana never did require the oil companies to remove their junk when they were done with it, let alone to fill in those canals that had outlived their usefulness.

Initially, such equipment canals were fairly narrow, just wide enough to minimally serve their function (a fifty-foot width was usually sufficient). The pipeline canals were even narrower, typically ten to fifteen feet. Over time, however, Mother Nature enlarged those dimensions. Although the tides here are not particularly strong (seldom varying diurnally by more than two feet), that is still enough to reverse the current in the artificial waterways twice per day. Over a period of decades, with about fifteen thousand flow reversals per decade, and with the canals running in fairly straight lines (as opposed to the naturally sinuous routes of the bayous), tidal erosion was inevitable, particularly during major storms.

The tidal currents scoured the canals ever wider, and the adjacent land grew soggy with saltwater, killing the vegetation that had helped hold the soil in place, until eventually it began to erode as well. Thousands of acres of formerly dry land began to disappear each year. Seawater intruded ever farther into the mainland. The steel pipelines and associated equipment began to deteriorate faster, accelerated by salt-induced corrosion. From time to time there were leaks and spills, which killed even more vegetation.

Today, about 80 percent of the entire nation's coastal-region land loss is in Louisiana. The state currently loses roughly twenty-five thousand acres per year to the tidal scouring of coastlines and canals—the equivalent of about four football fields per hour. Yes, a part of this land loss can be blamed on the artificial levees along the lower Mississippi River, which prevent annual flooding from depositing silt that in prior centuries replenished the land. Up to 59 percent of Louisiana's wetland loss, however, is not due to the river levees at all, but rather to the oil industry's marshland canals and pipelines.

Yes, if you're going to extract petroleum from the wetlands, then you clearly need to build canals. Nobody, however, can legitimately argue that those canals should be allowed to remain forever after the extraction is done and the wells are depleted. Yet the whole history of the oil industry— particularly in Louisiana—is a saga of conquering Nature, making money, then moving on and leaving the mess behind. Oh, and yes, fighting against pesky environmental regulations.

After all, even the natives here don't seem to want them.

◆   ◆   ◆

Louisiana does have a Department of Environmental Quality (DEQ). In its self-reported history, this agency traces its origins to an (undocumented) environmental movement in the early 1900s, a two-person Water Pollution Control Division in the late 1930s, a two-person Air Pollution Division established in the early 1950s, and a "small" radiation-control division in the early 1960s (which was primarily concerned with the X-ray machines in doctors' and dentists' offices).

Then in 1970, under President Richard Nixon and on the heels of the Santa Barbara oil spill of 1969, the federal government consolidated its own various environmental regulatory activities under one umbrella, naming the resulting federal bureaucracy the Environmental Protection Agency (EPA). This action was hardly applauded by the Louisiana legislature, which had always been xenophobic about Washington, D.C. In response, in 1972, Governor Edwin Edwards[1] created a Governor's Council on Environmental Quality, whose primary function seems to have been to keep an eye on the new federal EPA and to sound alarms if and when Louisiana was about to be stomped on by the Feds.

In 1983, the Louisiana legislature consolidated the state's own environmentally related operations and elevated the resulting organization to the status of a state agency, titling it the Department of Environmental Quality (DEQ). Its formal function was to enforce existing statutes (both state and federal) relating to water and air quality, radiation, soil contamination, hazardous waste, and wetlands protection, including activities related to drilling and minerals extraction. Meanwhile, drilling permits and related regulations fell under the jurisdiction of Louisiana's curiously named Office of Conservation (OOC), which in turn is part of its Department of Natural Resources.

Yes, that's right. In Louisiana, the Office of *Conservation* grants drilling permits and regulates most aspects of the oil, gas, and chemical industry.

Although such an ostensible separation of powers may appear on paper to be a good way to safeguard the environment, that's not quite how it works in practice. Residents who phone the DEQ with questions or to register complaints about pollution by oil companies are matter-of-factly referred to the pro-drilling OOC, which then usually ignores them. Citizens who show up in person at the DEQ headquarters to talk to regulatory staff members are informed that they can't do so unless oil company lawyers are also present at the same meeting. In the next chapter, we will give some examples of lawsuits filed by citizens' groups against Louisiana's DEQ for failing to enforce various *existing* state and federal environmental

---

1. Four-term governor Edwin Edwards was released from federal prison in January of 2011 after serving eight years of a ten-year sentence for fraud, racketeering, and extortion relating to legalizing gambling enterprises in Louisiana.

statutes. In most other states, such a flagrant pattern of disregard for its constituency by a state agency would lead to a major public backlash. In Louisiana, however, it is simply the customary state of affairs. Louisiana, after all, has a history of functioning a lot like a Third World petro-state, with a relatively immobile and largely uninformed population ruled by an oligarchy beholden to the oil industry's leaky buckets of cash.

If Louisiana's DEQ doesn't safeguard the environment, then certainly the state's unabashedly pro-drilling OOC can't be expected to do so. As a case in fact, a Louisiana friend of ours recently wrote to the OOC to get herself on the agenda of a public hearing about a drilling application filed by Devon Energy (based in Oklahoma but extracting much of its oil and gas in Louisiana). Devon's proposed gas well was to go in across the road from her front porch and was to run diagonally under her home. Numerous rusting, abandoned wells already dotted her eighteen acres, and she had concerns about the environmental and visual impacts of yet another well.

In response to that letter, our friend received a visit—not from anyone at the OOC, but from one of Devon's managers. Clearly, the whole process of holding a public hearing was a mere charade; Devon's drilling permit was a *fait accompli* before it was even applied for. No, Devon and the OOC didn't succeed in shutting her up, but her efforts were to no avail anyway. The new wellhead ended up 320 feet from her front porch, thus conforming to the statutory requirement that drilling not be done within 300 feet of an occupied dwelling.

Although the OOC is empowered to impose whatever additional site restrictions it judges to be appropriate on a case-by-case basis, its hearing panels seem to have never forced a driller to resite a proposed well *beyond* the statutory 300-foot *minimum* distance from a private dwelling. If a driller meets the minimum separation, then the application is approved automatically.

Of course our friend didn't receive a penny of compensation, nor did she expect to. After all, she owns only the surface land, not the mineral rights. She simply was asking the drillers to set up their derrick farther away from her, which they could easily have done since they were planning to drill diagonally anyway.

• • •

Today, if you relax on Holly Beach (just east of Cameron) and gaze out over the waters of the Gulf, your view is punctuated by hundreds of offshore oil platforms stretching as far and wide as you can see. A similar scene greets you at Grande Isle, 212 miles to the east. What you don't see unless you're on a boat is the thousands of offshore rigs between those two spots. As for the coastal swamps, marshes, and woodlands in between, nobody venturing into those regions can avoid running across hundreds of producing wells and hundreds of others long abandoned. And rusting pipelines. Furthermore, what nobody ever sees and few ever think about is the approximately twenty-seven-thousand offshore wells that have already played themselves out, and whose corroding wellheads still lurk on the seafloor, waiting for some future day when a combination of deteriorated metal and repressurization of the reservoir may combine to create future spills.

Why do Louisianans put up with this degree of environmental degradation and risk? Ask their political leaders, and they'll usually tell you it's about *jobs*. And here too the natives seem to be getting snookered.

• • •

Remarkably, the state government of Louisiana does not publish unambiguous statistics on the economic impacts of its oil and gas industries. Instead, it lists a pooled labor category called "mining and forestry," which includes gas and oil extraction. That *combined* sector currently is said to employ about 50,000 workers, or roughly 2.5 percent of the state's labor force of 2.096 million. Adding the spin-off employment (oil-related services, manufacturing, and transportation) is difficult to do, since no agency—state or federal—reports the statistics in that form. Researchers who have attempted to analyze this issue have come up with a range of figures; the highest (published by the *Christian Science Monitor*) reports that up to 17 percent of the state's jobs—or about 356,000—depend at least partially on oil and gas operations.

On the flip side, even this high-end figure implies that the oil and gas industries are essentially irrelevant economically to more than 83 percent of Louisiana's workers. Similar, for instance, to the current statistics in Hugo Chavez's petro-state of Venezuela.

Do such numbers, fuzzy as they are, reveal anything more? Maybe, maybe not. But when combined with some other figures and a calculator, they do raise some curious questions.

The oil and gas industries themselves claim that they collectively pump $65 billion annually into Louisiana's economy. Louisiana's gross domestic product is about $222 billion, so, if accurate, the industry's claim means that oil and gas activities drive about 30 percent of the state's economic activity. It also means that oil and gas cash flow alone dwarfs the state government's annual budget, which currently stands at about $26 billion.

One might think, then, that Louisiana, with a population of a modest 4.492 million people, ought to be a very prosperous place to live. But let's put some of the available numbers into a calculator and punch the division button. Here are a couple of the outcomes:

> Divide the $65 billion economic impact claimed by the oil and gas industry by the portion of the workforce whose jobs are claimed to be impacted (a maximum of 17 percent of the 2.096 million available workers), and we get a minimum average cash flow of a whopping $182,400 per worker per year. Yet, the actual average annual income of full-time workers in Louisiana's labor market is apparently only about $36,200. The discrepancy: more than five to one.

> Divide Louisiana's $222 billion GDP by its population of 4.492 million people, and we find that the state's GDP per capita is about $49,400. Yet Louisiana's actual median per capita income is just $15,508 per year, ranking it at or near the bottom of the fifty states. The discrepancy: at least 3.2 to 1.

Yes, we can quibble about the accuracy of some of the raw data in the above, or whether Louisiana really ranks fiftieth in personal income rather than simply being one of the bottom five, but that doesn't change the material conclusion: Only a small fraction of the money being spread around by Louisiana's oil and gas industries filters down to Louisiana's working class. So where is the rest of it going? Well, a small fraction of it does go into taxes and is ultimately spent on public services. That still, however, leaves a major chunk of the cash flow unaccounted for by the official statistics. Clearly, most of those other billions must be going to folks who *do not* draw a paycheck.

Welfare queens? No, that arithmetic just doesn't work. It would take more than 15 million of them to skew the statistics to that degree—roughly triple the entire current population of Louisiana. But if not to welfare chiselers, then where *is* this huge river of oil and gas money flowing?

If you average the incomes of fifty workers who each earn $36,000 per year, you obviously get an average of $36,000. But if you toss in a fifty-first person who makes $7 million, then the average jumps to $173,000. Fifty of those fifty-one workers earn well below that average, while just one earns a huge amount above that figure. In fact, this same kind of arithmetic also arises in many Third World countries. A relatively small number of people have huge incomes, the majority earn very little, but the average may not look all that bad.

What seems to be happening in Louisiana is this: Yes, the oil and gas industries pump huge amounts of money into the state's economy. Only a modest fraction of that cash flow, however, seems to find its way into local jobs and paychecks. Between 50 and 80 percent of it seems to be paid as royalties (unearned income) to holders of mineral rights and owners of dummy oil-development companies or else paid to various equipment-leasing vendors.

Moreover, the highest-paying nonexecutive jobs—those on the offshore rigs—are held by the most *mobile* sector of the workforce, many of whom don't even live or pay taxes in Louisiana. With their typical two-weeks-on, two-weeks-off schedules, some of them actually find it possible to maintain residencies as far away as California and New York. How many? Again, it's hard to tell. But in a study conducted back in 1983, approximately 10 percent of Louisiana's offshore workers at that time lived in other states. Since then, with the expansion of the offshore sector of the industry, that percentage has surely grown.

Moreover, if the number of oil-related jobs held by Louisiana citizens were impressively large, then why wouldn't the state or the industry tabulate and brag about the actual figures? And if all those jobs were high-paying ones, wouldn't that also be widely publicized? Instead, what we hear from Governor Bobby Jindal, Senator Mary Landrieu, and numerous other Louisiana politicians is the unsubstantiated assertion that more drilling creates more good jobs for Louisianans. The stark fact that most of the oil revenues never filter down to the working class is carefully avoided.

Workers who do snag offshore jobs generally earn in the neighborhood of $40,000 per year for an entry-level position, which is high for Louisiana but not exactly a prince's ransom. Experienced field engineers and project managers can earn triple that, but those openings are relatively few and are seldom handed to locals. If you're a Louisianan, the very best way to profit from offshore drilling is to own a business that leases equipment, sells supplies, provides transportation to and from the rigs, offers repair services, or something else along that line. The oil companies are happy to subcontract such activities to local businesses because that simplifies their own logistics while giving them flexibility in re-siting their operations and scheduling their own personnel. In other words, when a well plays itself out (and eventually all of them do), the companies can easily move on with minimal worries about what will happen to their local employees. They simply don't have very many of them.

When Barack Obama's administration announced a moratorium on OCS drilling on the heels of the *Deepwater Horizon* disaster, temporarily shutting down thirty-three deepwater drilling rigs, the group suing to reverse that action did not include the owners of those platforms or the oil companies or the oil workers. It was a consortium of Louisiana shore-based subcontractors who reeled at the thought of even a 1 or 2 percent reduction in their profits. To them, money was everything—even though the inadequacy of existing OCS safety measures and spill response technology had been clearly demonstrated by the accident.

The prevailing business and political philosophy in Louisiana seems to be this: the environment be damned and workers and jobs be damned. Let's just keep busy making money! Time's a-wasting!

• • •

One might think it would be a plus for Louisiana's economy if drillers were required to remove their abandoned equipment, fill in obsolete canals, and generally restore the environment to its prior condition when they leave a particular site. Certainly that would create local jobs, and it would also counteract at least some of the state's wetlands erosion problems.

Instead, for many decades now, the state's politicians and business leaders have actually exacerbated the destruction of Louisiana's wetlands. Probably the most egregious example was the construction of the Mississippi River Gulf Outlet (the MRGO, or colloquially "Mister Go"), a poorly conceived canal that, according to several scientists at the Louisiana State University (LSU) Hurricane Center (part of Louisiana's flagship university), played a major role in the 2005 flooding of New Orleans. This little-known waterway is actually longer than the Panama Canal: seventy-six versus fifty miles in length. Unlike the Panama Canal, however, which is used by about fourteen thousand vessels per year, the MRGO ultimately served about five hundred ships per year (less than an average of three vessels every two days). In fact, it was barely being used at all by the time of the Hurricane Katrina disaster. In April of 2009, it was formally decommissioned because of the high cost of redredging it and thereafter keeping it dredged, and as of this writing it is blocked off to navigation by a (leaky) riprap barricade.

The initial plan had been to provide a shipping shortcut between the Port of New Orleans and the Gulf of Mexico, bypassing about forty miles of the sinuous lower Mississippi River. A number of oil companies seem to have pushed for this project to go forward, including SoCal (now Chevron), Shell, and British Petroleum (now BP). Pressured by those companies as well as by other business interests (some of whom had been advocating the idea for the previous thirty years), the US Congress finally authorized the project in 1956. In 1958, with the engineering work completed and construction about to begin, the US Department of the Interior warned that the excavation of the MRGO "could result in major ecological change with widespread and severe ecological consequences."

That, in fact, is exactly what happened. When it opened in 1965, the canal was 650 feet wide at its surface and sloped down to a 500-foot width and a 36-foot depth at the bottom (sufficient for two ocean-going freighters to pass in opposite directions). Immediately, however, the tides and wave wash began to scour the muddy banks, and today much of the waterway is a half-mile or more in width, an average fourfold increase. Saltwater from the Gulf has gained an ever-expanding corridor into the wetlands of St. Bernard Parish. More than 25,000 acres (forty square miles) of adjacent land have disappeared since the waterway's opening. An additional 11,000 acres of cypress swamps have died, and 19,000 acres of previously brackish marsh have become saline marsh. An estimated 650,000 indigenous vertebrate animals died because of the environmental changes, and with them died the livelihoods of several hundred Isleno trappers, whose fur harvestings until that time had been sustainable.

Even as the MRGO grew in width over the decades, it was always a challenge to maintain its depth, and the Army Corps of Engineers found itself dredging the channel almost continuously. Keeping the canal navigable cost tens of millions of dollars more than the meager annual receipts from shipping tolls. Shippers used the canal less and less because of the continual inconvenience. Petrochemical companies never did use it much, and oil producers not at all, despite the fact that their ostensible needs had been a major impetus behind the project's approval. Although the alternative, the Mississippi River, involved numerous bends and a greater distance, it was also considerably deeper and wider and therefore not any more difficult to navigate, while only five or six hours slower.

In the 1980s, a number of scientists (including several at LSU) began sounding a different kind of alarm about the MRGO. The canal, they said, was an invitation to catastrophe because it could funnel a storm surge directly into New Orleans. Those scientists' concerns, however, went unheeded by the political establishment and the various state bureaucracies.

Then, in 2005, Hurricane Katrina came along. That category-3 tempest sideswiped eastern Louisiana and whipped up a storm surge of twenty-eight feet above normal high tide in the Mississippi Sound, which drove a monstrous mass of water into the mouth of the MRGO and directed it straight toward New Orleans. Just as scientists had predicted, the waterway overflowed its banks, levees and seawalls at its western end failed, virtually all of St. Bernard Parish was flooded, and several hundred of that parish's residents drowned. Because the MRGO intersected the New Orleans Industrial Canal, Katrina's storm surge also breached some of those walls, inundating portions of New Orleans and causing more deaths. (Additional deaths resulted from the failures of three poorly designed canals connected to Lake Pontchartrain, bringing the official total number of fatalities to 1,836.)

Prior to Hurricane Katrina, the population of St. Bernard Parish stood at 64,890. A month later, it was 13,924. Even three years after the disaster (July 2008), it had recovered to only 37,722, and as of this writing, it is in the neighborhood of 41,000. Clearly, there are thousands who haven't returned and probably never will. Many neighborhoods, including some upscale subdivisions, still stand totally vacant—their interiors rotting, polluted, and infested with vermin.

So why didn't the better thinkers prevail, the ones who had been sounding the warning for decades? Because they weren't the folks with the money. Numerous mid-sized companies are located along the New Orleans Industrial Canal, which connects via the Inner Harbor Navigational Canal lock (IHNC) to the Mississippi River in one direction and to the sea-level MRGO in the other. Three of those companies—although they weren't huge employers—had no choice but to use the MRGO from time to time, because some of their vessels wouldn't fit through the ancient (1923) IHNC. Those three companies were Bollinger Gulf Repairs, New Orleans Cold Storage (NOCS Ltd.), and Lockheed Martin's Michoud assembly plant, among whose products were the external fuel tanks for the space shuttle. If it weren't for those three, maybe it would have been possible to shut down the MRGO several decades earlier.

As it stands, with the space shuttle program ended, the remainder of the Michoud assembly plant's products will easily fit through the lock to the Mississippi River. Bollinger employs fewer than 250 workers at its New Orleans shipyard, and it has several dozen other facilities in southern Louisiana and Texas capable of handling its largest jobs. NOCS was located on the Industrial Canal only because its executives thought that some of its clients would arrive via the MRGO; the company has since relocated to a site along the river. In other words, the arguments that the MRGO needed to stay open because of *jobs* was spurious. The MRGO actually killed more people that it ever provided employment to. Not to mention the thousands of family homes it devastated through its flooding, most of those losses uninsured.

Although natural forces are indeed silting up the MRGO since dredging ended in 2005, they also are continuing to scour it wider. A monument to Katrina victims erected just a few years ago on the canal bank at Shell Beach, for instance, now juts from the water nearly 150 feet offshore. The boondoggle that cost $92 million to build and $906 million to maintain over fifty years will now cost many billions of tax dollars to fill in. And that future project will require considerably more dirt than was excavated in building the Panama Canal.

Once again, such is the price of believing the oil companies and the politicians they buy. They said they needed a MRGO to efficiently ship petroleum products. They didn't, and once it was built they rarely used it. They said it would be an economic bonanza for Louisiana. It actually brought in money only during construction (and those funds were from the federal government); toward the end of its lifetime, the public was actually losing as much as $20,000 for every ship that used the waterway. And then, of course, what was the value of all the lives lost and property destroyed when the MRGO channeled Katrina's storm surge into St. Bernard Parish and New Orleans?

Today the environmental status of Louisiana's southern parishes remains troubling. Environmentally abusive practices have wrought their devastation for almost a century now, creating an overwhelming amount of damage to correct. Meanwhile, big businesses, and Big Oil in particular, continue to lie to the electorate, claiming that they enhance Louisiana's quality of life and are continually creating jobs. The sad truth is that they don't and aren't.

Chapter 7

CHEMICAL VOODOO

In the United States as a whole, chemical pollution (including in inland waters) averages about 570 pounds per square mile per year. In Louisiana, the corresponding figure is roughly 1,800 pounds per square mile per year, more than three times as high. On a per capita basis, this amounts to about 7 pounds of pollution per person per year nationwide, but in Louisiana it is about 21 pounds per person—and in some poorer communities it averages more than a whopping 2,000 pounds per person per year. In fact, by virtually any measure, Louisiana is the most polluted state in the nation.

Meanwhile, the composition of Louisiana's pollution is different than in most other places. Elsewhere, the most common chemical pollutants tend to be inorganic acids leaching from old mines, airborne sulfur oxides from power plants, nitrogen oxides from engine exhausts, and heavy metals from various industrial processes. Yes, Louisiana also generates its share of these same inorganic toxic wastes. The lion's portion of the state's pollution, however, consists of hydrocarbon-based molecules, many of them synthetic (with names like hexachlorobenzene, tetrachloroetheylene, propylene oxide, formaldehyde, and so on).

Given the slow grind of natural selection, the human species has not had nearly enough time to adapt to many of the new organic chemicals mankind is now being exposed to. As a result, ingesting or breathing such synthetic hydrocarbon-based chemicals can often trigger cancers, neurological disorders, or genetic damage. And, of course, the people with the most continuous exposures are those most at risk. People, in other words, who live closest to the sources of such contamination. Including, yes, lots of poor folks in Louisiana.

• • •

When drillers strike oil, what they extract from the ground is a stew of hundreds of hydrocarbons whose actual mix can vary quite a bit from one oil field to another. Sometimes this mixture is thin and light colored; other times it can be thicker and almost tarry. Some deposits contain sulfur and other chemicals besides hydrocarbons. It is remarkable that chemical engineers have figured out how to transform such wide disparities of crude oil composition into a set of end products with such consistent properties. For example, gasoline produced at one refinery today is virtually indistinguishable from the same grade of gasoline produced anywhere else—even though the initial makeups of the crude oil may have differed significantly.

In the early years of the industry, crude oil was distilled in much the same manner as brandy or whisky: in a "batch" process. The goal at that time was to obtain kerosene, and the gasoline that was produced was simply discarded. After the kerosene was extracted, a thick, gooey mixture of heavy hydrocarbons and various contaminants remained behind. Depending on the initial properties of the crude oil, the distillers might sell this sticky residue for use in oiling roads, as a roofing material, or sometimes they would use it themselves to fuel their distillation boilers.

The transition from distilleries to refineries was evolutionary rather than revolutionary. It paralleled the development of markets for petroleum products other than kerosene and tar, particularly gasoline and diesel fuel. These new markets demanded more consistent chemistry than simple batch distillation could provide.

Today, thanks to some clever chemical engineering over the decades, each 42-gallon barrel of crude oil entering a modern refinery can produce between 19.5 and 21.5 gallons of gasoline, plus about 4 gallons of jet fuel, with the remainder going into other products. This is by any measure a monumental engineering achievement.

However, to accomplish this kind of chemical voodoo on a large scale, modern refineries are necessarily enormously complicated. Even more complicated are the petrochemical plants—those factories that combine refinery products with other chemicals to produce plastics, refrigerants, synthetic rubber, fibers, solvents, detergents, paints, pesticides, and a host of other commercially important products. And, yes, Murphy's Law does apply: Sooner or later, anything that *can* go wrong *will* go wrong.

• • •

Although storms have been directly responsible for only about 5 percent of the refinery accidents in Louisiana in recent decades, they are nevertheless a significant agent of environmental contamination. In terms of the quantity of pollution released, nature's tantrums have accounted for about 64 percent of the water pollution and 24 percent of the air pollution released by refineries (according to information provided by the refineries themselves and the Louisiana DEQ).

These figures, however, high as they may seem, only include pollution directly attributable to oil refineries; they don't include spills from ships, pipelines, and storage tanks where crude oil is stored en-route to other processing facilities, which are also susceptible to damage from storms.

St. Bernard Parish suffered such an en-route disaster during Hurricane Katrina in 2005. The Murphy Oil Company was temporarily storing crude oil in a collection of aboveground tanks surrounded by earthen berms designed to contain any oil that might escape in the event of a leak or spill. When the storm surge from Katrina rushed up the MRGO, its floodwaters swept over the berm of at least one 25,000-gallon tank and swirled through what was supposed to be its containment area. The tank began to float and, dislodged from its moorings, collided with some nearby equipment, which ruptured it. Before the floodwaters had receded, all of that oil had escaped into the surrounding neighborhoods—hopelessly contaminating thousands of homes and businesses. Although environmental regulations that might have prevented such an accident were certainly on the books at the time of that 2005 disaster, those regulations had not been enforced by Louisiana officials.

The Murphy spill resulted in twenty-seven consolidated class actions filed on behalf of several thousand homeowners and businesses. Murphy's defense lawyers were aggressive in pursuing procedural arguments to reduce the size of the class (ultimately to about eighteen thousand) and to seriously limit everybody's claims for remediation damages. To a considerable extent they succeeded.

In January 2007, a Louisiana court approved a settlement award, which was substantially less than the class had originally asked for. The total value of the award has been estimated at about $330 million (an amount that included at least $83 million Murphy already had paid through a voluntary settlement program.) Under this settlement, Murphy was required to spend $55 million to purchase properties in a "Buyout Zone," the area directly adjacent to Murphy's property that suffered the most extensive contamination. Murphy was also required to distribute $120 million to various other injured property owners, each specific allowance depending on the square footage of their property, the number of persons who lived there, and/or the estimated commercial loss. Lastly, Murphy was supposed to spend an estimated $72 million on remediation of the surrounding environment. Overall, the average compensation was less than $20,000 per property owner, even though some of the now-unlivable homes had been recently purchased for more than $300,000. Ultimately, many property owners simply walked away, leaving their mortgage banks—and eventually the federal government—to pick up the losses.

To actually receive a part of this settlement award, class members—the people whose homes and businesses were contaminated by the spill—were required to submit proof-of-claim documents and agree to release all future claims against Murphy. But, before they could do that, they obviously had to know that the lawsuit existed in the first place. Although notice was sent through the US mail, much of the affected area received little or no mail service for up to a year after the storm. Plus, due to the damage and contamination of their homes and businesses, almost all of the class members had been forced to relocate. To make up for the fact that the class members could now be living virtually anywhere, notice of the class action was printed in local newspapers and posted on a few websites. The court found that the settlement, as well as the efforts made to notify class members of their rights, was "fair, reasonable, and adequate." And Murphy was not required to accept any liability or otherwise make any admissions of wrongdoing for the spill.

◆　◆　◆

Storms aside, every now and then a refinery has a more serious accident—one that directly claims lives and compromises the health and safety of numerous others. Louisiana, to its good fortune, has never had a really big calamity along those lines. Maybe that helps explain why the state's leaders have been so lax about enforcing their existing regulations.

Still, Louisiana's leaders have certainly witnessed examples of such catastrophes. Just a short distance to the west, on March 23, 2005, a devastating explosion and fire at BP's Texas City Refinery killed 15 workers and injured more than 170 others. A report issued afterward attributed the accident to numerous failings in equipment, risk management, staff management, maintenance, inspection, and general health and safety assessments.

For these failings, BP was charged with criminal violations of federal environmental law. In February 2008, BP pleaded guilty to these charges and offered to pay a $50 million fine. The blast victims and their families objected, calling the proposed fine "trivial." The plaintiffs' appeal to the US Supreme Court, however, was unsuccessful, and in March of 2009 a federal judge approved BP's plea deal. Meanwhile, in addition to various violations of Texas environmental law, the Occupational Safety and Health Administration (OSHA) discovered over 300 federal safety violations and fined BP $21 million, the largest fine in OSHA history at the time. In October 2009, on the heels of a further investigation, OSHA imposed an additional $87 million fine—which broke the previous short-lived record as the largest in OSHA history—for the oil company's failure to correct 270 safety violations first identified in 2005 and for committing 429 addition violations in the meantime. BP agreed to pay $50.6 million of this fine, but at this writing its lawyers are still contesting the remainder.

•   •   •

Although Louisiana has not had any refinery disasters as violent as BP's 2005 Texas City explosion, there is still plenty of environmental contamination going on. Despite intricate and well-engineered systems and the employment of highly trained staff, accidents at refineries are actually fairly common. Although most of such mishaps are minor in the grand scheme of the entire energy economy, on average more than a dozen do happen every day in the United States. In Louisiana alone the average is 733 refinery accidents per year—or more than 2 per day.

In regions where industry is dense and environmental regulation is lax—as in Louisiana—risks to the local environment from workplace accidents greatly increase. If you include its offshore activities, Louisiana produces or transports 30 percent of the nation's domestic crude oil and 34 percent of our natural gas. Its seventeen giant petroleum refineries process 16 percent of our nation's petroleum. Louisiana is also home to more than 180 other petrochemical plants and hosts two of the nation's four Strategic Petroleum Reserve Storage facilities. The petrochemical industry accounts for nearly a quarter of its gross state revenue. And it has a notorious eighty-five-mile corridor along the Mississippi River, between Baton Rouge and New Orleans, where there are more plastic plants, oil refineries, and other chemical plants than anywhere else in the United States. Loose oversight has enabled these facilities to release large quantities of toxic chemicals into the local environment, with very little being done to clean up the mess. Greenpeace has labeled the state of Louisiana a "polluter's paradise" and has given that particular industrial corridor the designation of a Global Toxic Hotspot.

It was in 1987 that residents of St. Gabriel (population 6,677), which lies within this dense ribbon of industry and pollution, first realized that there were fifteen cases of cancer within just two blocks of each other. It turned out that there were seven more cancer victims living on a single block a half a mile away. As reports continued to crop up of numerous cases of cancer occurring in other small rural communities in this area, this particular industrial corridor began to earn its current nickname: Cancer Alley.

The residents of Cancer Alley are mostly African American, and many of their communities were originally founded by emancipated slaves. With the boom in the plastic and chemical industries after World War II and the help of Jim Crow laws, the petrochemical industry encountered little resistance to building its factories and refineries adjacent to these effectively disenfranchised black neighborhoods. Today, despite the large number of industrial facilities in the area, unemployment rates are still quite high in Cancer Alley. Most residents do not have a college education, and many lack even a high school diploma.

But just because many of the residents of Cancer Alley are low income and African American does that mean they should be exposed to more environmental contamination than other folks? Environmental justice is the concept that all people, regardless of race, color, national origin, or income, deserve fair treatment and meaningful involvement with respect to the enforcement of environmental laws. In other words, shouldn't *everyone* get to enjoy the same degree of protection from environmental and health hazards and *everyone* have the opportunity to object if they don't think this is the case? Based on Title VI of the Civil Rights Act, Congress passed the Environmental Justice Act, the Environmental Equal Rights Act, and the Environmental Health Equity Information Act in 1993. In 1994, President Bill Clinton echoed these sentiments by signing an executive order mandating this equal protection for minority and low-income populations.

Unfortunately, implementation of these laws and Clinton's environmental justice order has been rather weak in Louisiana. Many residents of Cancer Alley believe that they have been targeted to accommodate these industries and the resulting environmental contamination because of racism, and reports by a host of environmental justice groups support such claims. For one thing, according to the Centers for Disease Control

7.1. A portion of "Cancer Alley," the eighty-five-mile corridor of refineries and petrochemical plants between Baton Rouge and New Orleans. The state has seventeen mega-refineries and more than 180 petrochemical factories. ©2011 *Julie Dermansky.*

(CDC), the death rate from cancer in Louisiana is significantly higher than the national average. In 2007, there were 178.1 deaths from cancer per 100,000 people in the United States—but in Louisiana the number was 196.2. When only African American populations are considered, the national average death rate is higher at 216.3 per 100,000 people—but in Louisiana the number is higher still at 237.0.

Residents of Cancer Alley have attempted to sue the industries they believe are responsible for their poor health. Unfortunately, legal standards make it difficult to pinpoint which, if any, of the facilities is to blame for the excessive rates of cancer in the area. Residents have also organized to attempt to limit the siting of new noxious facilities in their neighborhoods. But, since the local governments in Louisiana traditionally support the needs of industry, so far the residents have had little hope of redress.

• • •

There has actually, however, been a bit of success in addressing issues of environmental justice in Mossville, Louisiana (population 375). Although not part of Cancer Alley, there are still fourteen chemical plants and refineries within or adjacent to this tiny and predominately African American community in southwestern Louisiana. According to federal and state records, these facilities release millions of pounds of toxic chemicals into the local air, land, and water every year. In 1998, the federal Agency for Toxic Substances and Disease Registry found that blood samples from twenty-eight Mossville residents contained high levels of dioxin, a cancer-causing chemical, that were three times the national average.

In 2005, a group of residents from Mossville traveled to Washington, D.C., to file a human rights complaint against their own government, alleging that the United States was not protecting their right to live in a healthy environment. There have been two positive outcomes of this petition. First, the EPA agreed in January 2010 to test whether Mossville qualifies as a federal Superfund site, a designation that would provide federal funding for cleanup and, potentially, relocation for residents who want to go. Secondly, the Inter-American Commission on Human Rights (IACHR) has also agreed to hear the petition.

IACHR is the international human-rights-monitoring body of the Organization of American States (OAS), of which the United States is a member. This commission has jurisdiction to investigate and report on human rights issues arising in any OAS country. The petition from Mossville residents is the first environmental human rights complaint from United States citizens ever to be heard by IACHR. If the board of commissioners determines that a human rights violation has occurred in Mossville, it will issue a report to recommend how the United States should address the violation and give a deadline to do so. As of this writing, the case remains unresolved.

However, even if the report finds that the United States has violated Mossville residents' right to freedom from racial discrimination or their right to protection against the destruction of the environment, the ruling would not be legally binding. IACHR gets its power from the American Convention on Human Rights, which the United States has signed but Congress has not yet ratified, so it is not binding law here. Even so, if the commission finds that the United States has violated the human rights of Mossville residents, it will shine an international spotlight on the issue, which could encourage the United States to address the problem even if it is not legally required to do so.

◆　◆　◆

Although environmental justice issues in Louisiana may be gaining some modest recognition on the international stage, Louisiana remains the worst state in the nation at enforcing federal clean air, clean water, and hazardous waste laws. While the EPA usually delegates the enforcement of these federal environmental laws to the states, a report released by that agency's inspector general in December 2011 concludes that the weak enforcement in Louisiana may be driven by a culture in which the state is expected to protect industry (a phenomenon we have already discussed in previous chapters). And it's true—businesses and politicians in Louisiana are still fighting bitterly to prevent any change to the state's lax regulatory regime. For Louisiana residents, like those in Mossville and Cancer Alley, fighting against this powerful culture can be extremely difficult.

The Tulane Environmental Law Clinic (TELC) has stepped forward to assist such residents by helping them sue companies and local governments for failing to enforce existing environmental protection laws. The mission of this clinic is to expand access to the legal system on environmental matters, especially for those who could not otherwise afford it, and to help community members participate effectively in decisions about environmental issues. In doing so, TELC also enables law students to gain practical experience in representing real clients.

Perhaps the most noteworthy TELC case occurred in the town of Convent (population 2,020), another predominately African American, low-income community in St. James Parish—right in the middle of Cancer Alley—that was already home to eleven chemical plants. In 1997, Louisiana's DEQ issued a permit to allow Shintech, the largest producer of polyvinyl chloride (PVC) in the United States, to build a plant that would be permitted to emit 611,700 pounds of contaminants into the air every year. TELC represented Convent residents in opposing this proposal. Ultimately, the federal EPA ruled that the permit granted by the Louisiana DEQ violated federal Clean Air Act regulations. As a result, Shintech abandoned its plans for this plant in 1998.

Although the outcome of this legal action was successful for the residents—who were not burdened with yet another polluting factory in Cancer Alley—the backlash from that success was loud and immediate. Then-governor Mike Foster, numerous state politicians, and many Louisiana business leaders screamed as if their knees had just been smashed by a crowbar. Foster himself called TELC "a bunch of vigilantes out there to make their own law," which of course was not the situation at all, insofar as the relevant laws were already on the books (not to mention that the federal EPA ended up agreeing with TELC's interpretation of the law). Foster and his secretary of the Department of Economic Development,

Kevin P. Reilly Sr., announced that they would use every legitimate method to defeat the clinic. As a tactic to pressure the president of the Tulane University to rein in the pesky student organization, Foster asked donors and supporters of the university to threaten to withhold financial support from the institution. Foster also threatened to revoke the tax-exempt status of Tulane, which at seven thousand employees has one of the largest workforces in the state.

Governor Foster had never demonstrated much empathy for poor people, and even less if they were both poor and black. He supported Grand Wizard Klansman David Duke's[1] run for the US Senate in 1996, and in Duke's prior campaign for office Foster contributed more than $150,000 to Duke's efforts—an ethical violation for which the governor eventually had to pay a small fine (with no apologies). And where did Foster get the money to bankroll his own political ambitions as well as those of David Duke? For one thing, Foster was earning roughly $200,000 in royalties each year from Exxon, which is undoubtedly part of what makes him unabashedly pro-oil and pro-industry.

Meanwhile, some of the state's worst polluters donate the most generously to selected Louisiana political candidates. Foster had no issue with the prospect of Shintech degrading the environment of a predominately black community, and he saw no problem with the Louisiana DEQ giving the go-ahead in direct violation of federal clean air standards. And, when asked if low-income residents seeking enforcement of environmental laws had a right to counsel, Foster shouted, "Let them use their own money, not Tulane's!"

When Tulane's administrators didn't capitulate to the governor's funding threats in 1997, Foster and some (white) members of the Louisiana legislature and business community sought revenge against TELC by lobbying the elected justices on the Louisiana Supreme Court—during a judicial campaign year—to change the student practice rule, which allows unlicensed law students to represent clients under faculty supervision as part of their legal education. Seemingly at the request of these critics, the Louisiana Supreme Court did actually amend the student practice rule so that it is now the most restrictive one in the nation. And there were no laws or court rules that required the court to open this process to public

---

1. And what happened to David Duke? He eventually served fifteen months in a federal prison after a plea bargain on charges of tax evasion and mail fraud. He was recently reported to be living and working in Australia.

hearing or public comment. There were no public proceedings or deliberations, and the court has not made public any of its reports or the results of its investigations.

Although today's TELC students can continue to represent clients in certain types of high-impact or controversial cases, there are now significant restrictions on who qualifies for representation. Before an individual can receive legal aid from a clinic, the student practice rule makes them subject to inflexible income guidelines that make the client subject to invasive tactics from opposing counsel concerning their personal finances. For community organizations, they must demonstrate their inability to retain private counsel and show that the incomes of at least 51 percent of their members meet the individual income guidelines. These amendments have severely limited access to the courts for grassroots organizations and low-income individuals. In her dissenting opinion, Justice Bernett Johnson stated that the Louisiana Supreme Court should not have curtailed a program that teaches students advocacy and gives previously unrepresented groups and individuals access to justice merely in order to satisfy some critics who were unhappy by the success of the clinic.

Despite the restrictions of the new student practice rule, TELC has continued to work toward establishing environmental justice in Louisiana and has had some modest victories. The following are a few representative examples:

- In 2004, a TELC action halted FTM Associates' practice of spraying sewerage sludge from Kenner on sugarcane fields near homes of residents of Covenant in St. James Parish.
- In 2005, TELC got a court to rule that Chalmette Refining of St. Bernard Parish had violated the Clean Air Act more than 2,600 times. The company was ordered to pay a small fine.
- In 2007, a TELC lawsuit led to a judgment that Louisiana's own DEQ had improperly waived the Clean Air Act requirements at a landfill. The DEQ was ordered to enforce the existing statutes at that particular site.
- In 2007, TELC successfully challenged the US Army Corps of Engineers' issuance of a permit to destroy a small section of wetlands bordering Timber Creek in St. Tammany Parish.
- In 2009, in an out-of-court settlement, EnerVest Operating agreed to clean up mercury leaked from meters used to monitor gas wells near the city of Monroe, where several streams were already under mercury advisories.

• In 2009, a permit was revoked that would have allowed the expansion of an industrial pipe landfill bordering the predominately African American community of Oakville in Plaquemines Parish.

In any other state, these rulings would constitute legal precedents—or formal examples—to be followed by future judges on future cases with similar fact patterns. But not so in Louisiana. While the other forty-nine states use a common law legal system based on the English tradition, Louisiana uses a civil law legal system inherited from the French and Spanish influences on its history. In common law states, judges are required to respect the precedents established in prior decisions. If the facts are similar enough, a common law judge must follow the example of previous cases—even if it is only a single ruling. In contrast, Louisiana civil law courts *may* consider a long series of similar previous decisions to be important and *possibly* determinative in subsequent cases, but they don't have to be—especially if it is only a single ruling. In Louisiana, judges rule based on their *own* interpretation of the laws on the books, not the interpretations of prior courts.

Yet despite the intricacies of the civil law system and the restrictions of the student practice rule, TELC has made noteworthy progress in promoting the enforcement of environmental laws and providing access to the courts for those seeking environmental justice in Louisiana. In so doing, TELC has also continued to provoke the ire of businesses and politicians who would rather continue to have things their way.

In early May 2010, just as the full gravity of the *Deepwater Horizon* disaster was becoming apparent, the Louisiana Chemical Association mailed a remarkable letter to its sixty-three corporate members. President Dan Borne's message: Chemical companies should stop donating to Tulane University and stop hiring Tulane's graduates. Borne also used his connections with Louisiana senator Robert Adley (who coincidentally is the majority owner of the Pelican Gas Management Company) to get a bill introduced to prohibit all state funding of legal clinics for low-income constituents. Why? Because TELC had initiated legal actions on behalf of various groups of citizens to compel the state's officials to enforce the environmental laws that were *already on the books.*

Borne argued that the mission of TELC was to attack business and industrial development in Louisiana. Senator Adley told the Senate Commerce Committee that Tulane accepts around $45 million in state money each year, yet it runs an environmental law clinic that chases jobs out of the state by suing industry and government agencies. But Tulane University president Scott Cowen pointed out that Tulane uses the state funding it receives to run its hospital, conduct cancer research, and draw in some of the state's brightest students with scholarships. Tulane Law School receives only around $30,000 from the state, and the interim dean, Stephen Griffin, reported that none of that money is used to fund TELC.

Borne's and Adley's timing, of course, couldn't have possibly been worse. Thousands of low- and middle-income citizens in the southern parishes were at that very moment in the throes of losing their livelihoods because of BP's huge oil spill. Yet Born and Adley were overtly attempting to undermine a nonprofit service that might help those very same victims get restitution from the parties responsible for the disaster.

Today, TELC tries to defuse and manage the controversy by stressing that it is the duty of all lawyers to expand access to the legal system. Former Tulane Law School dean Lawrence Ponoroff explained that the clinic is "neither anti-business nor pro-business." Instead, TELC represents clients with legitimate claims under *existing* laws who are otherwise unable to afford legal aid. Mercifully, the most recent attack on the clinic—Adley's bill—died in committee. But that does not guarantee that TELC's critics won't try again later.

Chapter 8

WHAT DO THE SIMPLE FOLK DO?

Around 1951, an honest, hard-working family man in one of the rural parishes of northern Louisiana had a disheartening experience, one that was all too common at this time. Yes, he was a real person, and we know this episode is true (at least in its essentials) because we've corroborated it with the handwritten mineral lease records in the nearby parish courthouse—entries that probably hadn't been examined by anyone else in more than sixty years. Because we promised the fellow's living descendants that we'd keep their surnames out of this account, we'll refer to that old-timer as "Tadpole."

In fact, most boys in those parts acquired irreverent monikers early-on that they continued to carry through life, long past the age when people from other regions might consider them to be undignified. Tadpole himself apparently never gave a second thought to his own nickname, even though he was now in his mid-fifties. Most of his buddies still went by tags like "Crow," "Slammer" (apparently derived from "salamander"), "Diller" (from "armadillo"), and "Turpin" (from "terrapin," a water turtle).

In the early 1950s, those men were all fully content with their day-to-day lives. They worked conscientiously Monday through mid-Friday, mostly farming and raising chickens and livestock or horses, but sometimes helping out at the local brick factory when a big order came in. Then, on Friday afternoons, they'd get together to fish or hunt, and when no game animals were in season, sometimes they'd all go out in the woods together and blast away at tin cans just for the hell of it. Yes, they did drink a bit of beer on Fridays and Saturdays, but not really all that much. After all, their wives were all southern Baptists, and they did respect their ladies. Those boys also gambled a bit on cards (usually bourré), but relatively little money ever changed hands. None of them ever *had* much in the way of money.

Sundays their wives ran the show and there was no buddying around with the guys. First, of course, came church services. Then, if the congregation wasn't having some sort of eating event, there would be dinner at home with Grampa and the extended family. In the afternoon, depending on the weather, there might be yard games with the grandkids and the dog pack. Once a month, there would be a somber Sunday afternoon trip to the churchyard to visit Gramama's grave (*gramama* being the grandmother on the maternal side). Sundays would end with listening to one of the Shreveport radio stations while gorging on leftovers and desserts and sweet tea. Then a glorious night of sleep before greeting the roosters on Monday morning to begin a new week.

So it went. Week after week, year after year. The air was clean, the nights were quiet, the grass was fresh smelling, the livestock were healthy, and the dogs were happy. Life was good.

Then Grampa died. The hundred-plus acres that Tadpole and his two brothers and their families had been living on and cultivating were still in the old man's name. The three siblings got together, discussed the matter, and designated Tadpole, the eldest, to hire an attorney to straighten things out legally.

A week or so later, attorney Jarvis (not his real name) offered to divide up the property, file all the necessary paperwork, and pay the appropriate taxes (actually, there was no inheritance tax on an estate that small; the only taxes were some modest property transfer assessments). Including Jarvis's own fees, the total was going to cost the brothers $500. Which, even collectively, the three of them didn't have to spare.

Whether Tadpole actually divulged to Jarvis that he and his brothers were cash-poor, or whether the attorney simply surmised it, is anybody's guess. In any case, Jarvis offered Tadpole an alternative: the three heirs to the property could transfer their *mineral rights* to Jarvis in lieu of the $500. After all, *they* were never going to drill for oil or gas, so why should they care about that? To sweeten the deal just a little, Jarvis promised that if natural gas were someday to be discovered beneath that property, then the brothers would be supplied enough of it to heat their homes free forever. (Not that free gas was all that big a deal, considering how short and mild the winters are in northern Louisiana.)

And so, in return for those legal services and a little bit of natural gas, Tadpole and his two siblings transferred to Jarvis their mineral rights, giving Jarvis or his designee the right to explore under the family property for whatever minerals might be found. And, with the exception of the small amount of fuel promised to the brothers, any minerals discovered and extracted would then belong to Jarvis, or whomever he might choose to lease or sell those resources to.

Barely a year later, a pair of surveyors showed up in the middle of Tadpole's pasture, explaining that they had been hired to stake out a gas well. Tadpole objected. Then he learned that as long as the well was more than three hundred feet from the nearest part of his house (and it was actually something like four hundred feet), he had no legal grounds for stalling the project. A few weeks later, a crew came in with a couple of truckloads of equipment, erected a derrick, strung in some electric lines, and began to drill.

For the next two months, the machinery droned day and night (under floodlights). It spooked the animals, and Tadpole had to move them to another part of the farm. When the well was finally completed and the derrick came down, Tadpole breathed a sigh of relief. That reaction turned out to be premature, however, because now the well's diesel-driven compressor ran through the night and ruined everyone's sleep. Tadpole planted a barrier of fast-growing shrubs as a sound barrier between the house and the invading monstrosity.

That, however, wasn't the last of it. Before the year was out, another well went in near one of his brothers' places. Then three more back in the woods, eventually mushrooming to seven. And yet another on the edge of the property. Traffic on what was once a lazy backcountry road began to whiz by at all hours. Several of Tadpole's hounds were killed by vehicles that never bothered to stop. He had to start confining his dogs—dogs that until now had always roamed free.

Tadpole died in 1971, and his portion of the property passed to his daughter, then eventually to her daughter, who still lives there today. The original well in the pasture near the house has long played itself out, yet capped pipes and rusted valves still jut from the ground today. The initial seven wells in the woods also stand abandoned and rusting, along with junk oil and gas tanks and various pieces of derelict rusting plumbing. But no, that doesn't mean it's over. For every well that was abandoned, a new one was drilled somewhere else in the vicinity. Plus, right adjacent to the property, there now stands a natural gas–processing plant, which feeds a pipeline that follows a wide, ugly swath that has been cleared straight through the woods.

Attorney Jarvis, of course, is also long gone. Normally, country lawyers eke out a modest living at best, but Jarvis managed to build himself an elegant home on several hundred acres which, notably, still doesn't have a single gas or oil well on it. That estate has been passed on to his descendants, several of whom continue to live there, breeding horses, driving expensive cars, and supporting political candidates who promise to be friendly to the oil and gas industries.

Jarvis wasn't the only attorney who figured out how to thrive financially from oil and gas in that rural region. The same general scheme was used by numerous other lawyers to acquire a considerable amount of personal wealth, way out of proportion to their own clients' meager financial resources. Today, if you visit the major gas-producing parishes in north-central and northwestern Louisiana and ask around regarding who owns the mineral rights, you'll discover that the overwhelming majority of that region's property owners don't actually own what lies under their land. Instead, the lion's share of those mineral rights are concentrated in the hands of a relatively few very wealthy families.

◆ ◆ ◆

So, is what happened to Tadpole and others like him legal? Did Jarvis *actually* have permission to do anything he wanted to the family land to get at the oil and gas beneath it? What does the law say about this topic?

In the United States, when land was originally deeded to individuals in the eighteenth and nineteenth centuries, the owner of the surface land also gained the right to mine whatever minerals might be found directly under his or her property, including oil and gas. The surface owner then had the freedom to keep, sell, lease, or give away those mineral rights at his own discretion. In most states, if the surface owner chooses not to keep his mineral rights, this creates a "mineral estate" that will be separate from the surface land from that point forward (the legal term for this is "severing"). After that, whoever owns the separate mineral rights is allowed to enter the property and drill or mine at his own whim. That person is free to use as much of the surface land as is *reasonably necessary* to explore, develop, and transport the underlying minerals.

But, as we have already seen, Louisiana is unique when it comes to dealing with issues related to oil and gas production. And, as we mentioned in the previous chapter, the state's civil law legal system is a bit different than the common law system used in other states. These differences mean that "mineral rights" in Louisiana aren't exactly the same as in the other forty-nine states. In the rest of the country, if you own a mineral estate, it means you already own whatever might be found under the property, even if you haven't actually found it yet. But in Louisiana, if you own mineral rights you don't actually "own" anything except the exclusive right to explore and develop whatever might be under the land. You do not own the minerals themselves until they are out of the ground and physically in your possession.

This may seem like a nit-picky distinction, but it makes a big difference in how oil and gas law is applied in Louisiana. Because the minerals themselves can't be owned until they are out of the ground, a separate mineral estate can never be created in Louisiana. Instead, the landowner can give, sell, or lease the *right* to extract minerals to someone else. This creates a mineral *servitude*, not a mineral estate.

Having mineral servitudes instead of mineral estates makes Louisiana unique among oil and gas producing states. And the reason the distinction matters is this: Article 789 of the Louisiana Civil Code of 1870 says "a right to servitude is extinguished by the non-usage of the same during ten years." In plain English, if you have bought or leased mineral rights in Louisiana but you do nothing for more than ten years, you lose those rights and they return to the owner of the surface land. That means that in order to keep your mineral rights alive in Louisiana, you *must* conduct good faith operations for the discovery and production of minerals—with a reasonable expectation of producing in paying quantities—within ten years. Once you have a producing well, the ten-year clock stops running. But, as soon as production stops, that ten-year clock starts ticking away all over again.

The ten-year clock was put in place specifically to promote more rapid development of mineral resources. And this pressure to produce (or forever lose your right to do so) certainly seems to affect how the owners of mineral rights treat the surface land in Louisiana. After all, why waste your time trying to make the surface owner happy when the surface owner is the one who gets your mineral rights if you don't develop a producing well in time?

•   •   •

So is the surface owner simply at the mercy of whoever owns the mineral rights? Not completely. The best way for the surface owner to maintain some control over what happens to his land is for him to anticipate what might go wrong and write a contract to preserve his or her wishes *before* transferring the mineral rights in the first place. Such a contract can protect the surface owner's property and way of life: it can specify that buildings, roads, livestock, crops, and other assets not be disturbed (or, if harmed, that they be restored). It can also reserve portions of the surface that will not be disturbed. Of course, this requires the surface owner to be very savvy about what the mineral extraction process might do to his or her land, and—like Tadpole—often the surface owner just doesn't know any better.

Without an advance contract, the owner of the mineral rights *can* pretty much extract the minerals at any time, using any methods, and without very much regard for the surface owner's wishes. Of course, even the unique system in Louisiana does not give anyone the right to *completely destroy* the surface land to get at the minerals beneath it. Louisiana courts have always held that the owner or lessee of mineral rights can use as much of the surface as is *reasonably necessary* for his or her operations and that these actions must be done with *reasonable regard* for the surface owner. But what counts as "reasonable"?

One of the earliest cases in Louisiana about damage to the surface land from mining operations took place in 1920. To make a little extra money, B.Y. Wemple (whose first name we don't know, since court records at that time tended to depersonify plaintiffs) sold his mineral rights to an oil company. That first company then sold them to a second company, which transferred the mineral rights to a third company, so by the time the operations were complete it was difficult to even be sure which company was responsible for B.Y.'s lost timber and destroyed fences. But it turned out it didn't much matter, because the court ruled that no matter which oil company owned the mineral rights, they were allowed to remove timber and disturb the surface land so long as it was "necessary" for extracting the oil and gas. The only way that B.Y. would be owed damages was if he could demonstrate that the operations had been unreasonable or excessive—which he couldn't—so, in the end, B.Y. didn't receive anything in return for the damage done to his property.

The first Louisiana case to result in an actual cash award for damage to the surface land took place in 1953. Mrs. Gladys B. Smith owned about 460 acres of land in northwestern Louisiana and had leased her mineral rights to a Mr. C. R. Schuster. After the drilling operations were completed, Mr. Schuster failed to fill and level a pit and remove debris, even though he had assured Gladys that he would do so. Gladys got frustrated, so she filled in the pit and removed the debris herself, then she sued for reimbursement. The court, without citing any particular law or authority, found that Mr. Schuster had a duty to restore the surface land and awarded Gladys $170 for her trouble. Although this wasn't a huge amount of money (an amount worth about $1,400 today), the court *did* recognize for the first time that the owner of mineral rights had at least *some* duty to restore the surface land.

Five years later, Murphy G. Rohner sued the Austral Oil Exploration Company after it completed its operations on his property in southeastern Louisiana. Murphy had a litany of complaints: the driller had assembled its derrick right in the middle of his cornfield, had driven its trucks *through* the cornfield (instead of using the constructed roadway), had also driven its trucks through Murphy's watermelon field, and his workers had eaten and hauled away some of his watermelon crop. In addition to the destroyed crops, Murphy said that several acres of his land had been rendered useless for future agricultural purposes because of the drilling operations—and this was a real problem since Murphy made his living by farming.

Luckily, Murphy had been smart enough to put a contract in place *before* conveying his mineral rights, and the contract contained a fairly typical provision for damage to timber and growing crops. So the good news for Murphy was that he did get compensated for the corn and watermelons that were destroyed (or eaten without permission). However, the court *denied* Murphy's claim for damage to the surface land where the drilling actually took place. If the land was now infertile because of the drilling operations, the court said, that was okay because it was due to the ordinary, customary, and necessary acts that must be done by drilling companies in order to put down a well. Since the driller had not been unreasonable or negligent (at least as far as the actual drilling was concerned), Murphy wasn't owed a penny for the damage to his now infertile surface land.

At the time these litigations took place, Louisiana courts had no specific mining laws to rely on to determine the outcomes of such disputes because the legislature hadn't made any yet—and, of course, decisions from other states weren't very useful because they didn't apply to the civil law system. So, with each of these early decisions, the courts played a role in shaping Louisiana mineral law. Unfortunately, the lack of specific laws to follow (particularly in a civil law system that relies on its rules being codified) led to various inconsistencies and unpredictability from the onset. And though a Mineral Code was proposed as early as 1938, an official codification of mining laws didn't actually take place in Louisiana until 1975. That's right, 1975!

But, even after oil and gas laws had finally been codified in Louisiana, the language of the Mineral Code did not and remarkably *still* does not expressly impose a duty to restore the surface of the land after mineral extraction. The text of the relevant law, Article 122, only requires the owner or lessee of mineral rights to operate in "good faith" as a "reasonably prudent operator," and it allows the parties to decide by contract what counts as reasonably prudent. The official comment to Article 122 notes that a prudent operator *does* have an *implied* obligation to restore the surface to "as near as practical to the original condition"; but, unfortunately, even an "official" comment only explains how the drafters think the law *ought* to be interpreted—the text doesn't create any specific law of its own.

Since the adoption of the Louisiana Mineral Code, only two cases seem to have awarded damages based on the implied duty to restore the surface land. In the first one, Dejean Broussard owned about twenty-one acres of land that he used primarily for grazing cattle. As was common for people of modest means, Dejean eventually sold his mineral rights. Sometime in the early 1960s, two producing oil wells were drilled on his property. When the production ended in 1977, Dejean sued for the restoration of his surface land. The court acknowledged the implied duty to restore the surface under Article 122, and Dejean was awarded $9,000.

In the second case, which took place in 1987, Charles Don Edwards also sued the mineral rights owner for damage to his surface property. The court likewise recognized that Article 122 created an implied duty to restore the surface. But, in this case, the court decided to look into whether the actions that caused the damage were "unreasonable." In the end, the court decided that most of the actions had been reasonably necessary for mining operations, so Charles was awarded the modest sum of $2,175 to fix his property.

In 2005, the Louisiana Supreme Court once again used "unreasonableness" as the measuring stick to determine whether or not damages were owed for surface restoration. The Terrebonne Parish School Board had sued Castex Energy Inc. for marshland loss that was caused by canals dredged in the course of mining operations. Although the school board had an advance contract in place, unfortunately that agreement didn't explicitly mention a duty to restore the surface or compensate for damages, so they had to argue that the duty was implied. In this case, the court concluded that when the advance contract is silent about the issue, Article 122 only imposes a duty to restore the surface to its original condition *if* there is evidence of *unreasonable* use. Since dredging the canals was not unreasonable—it was, in fact, *necessary* for the mining operation—the court found no duty at all to backfill the canals or to compensate the school board for the damage to its property.

As it turns out, these few court cases are actually quite unusual. In general, Louisiana property owners rarely challenge oil and gas companies for damaging their surface land. Maybe that's because most plaintiff's lawyers in the state know better than to tilt at windmills, for when they are stubborn enough to actually do so, they so rarely win. And even in those atypical cases where they do happen to win, they never seem to win enough to make the surface land completely "whole" again. Of course, because of Louisiana's civil law legal system, even successful litigations do not set binding legal precedents for future liability cases. As for unsuccessful lawsuits, however, they indeed do seem to establish a pattern of judgments that are sympathetic to the owners of mineral rights rather than the owners of the surface land.

So, are the surface owners totally out of luck? What about the state regulatory agencies—like the DEQ, or the Department of Natural Resources, or the Office of Conservation. Don't they care if oil and gas companies leave the land destroyed, contaminated, or littered with debris? The answer is sort of, but not really. The Office of Conservation is responsible for overseeing mineral operations and oil field cleanups, and it has a list of requirements for restoration, including plugging wells, closing pits, and limiting certain soil contaminants. The DEQ also has standards pertaining to the environmental quality. Both offices have direct enforcement authority, and surface owners can technically seek relief directly from these agencies. But, as we've seen in previous chapters, Louisiana state agencies have a poor track record of actually *enforcing* environmental laws, even the ones that are already on the books.

Unless the surface owner is smart enough to write an excruciatingly specific contract *before* selling or leasing his or her mineral rights, Louisiana is a safe haven for the oil and gas industry to do as it pleases. Whoever owns the mineral rights has the effective privilege to despoil the surface land, and whoever owns the surface (and all future owners of the surface while the mineral rights are active) will have to live with the consequences. In reality, the industry doesn't even need to *pretend* that it's trying to be a good neighbor to the owners of the surface land.

•   •   •

Yet another egregious case that, as of this writing, may still escalate further, involves the seventy-five or so heirs of Aristide Broussard, a French immigrant who bought three thousand acres of land in Vermillion Parish in the late 1800s. (Broussard is an extremely common Cajun name in southern Louisiana, and this particular branch of the Broussard family does not appear to be closely related to the Dejean Broussard we mentioned previously). Aristide's land was perfect for growing sugarcane, raising cattle, and trapping alligators, but that still wasn't quite enough to support his expanding family. So, like many other Louisiana families of modest means, Aristide sold the rights to the minerals under his property to Texaco.

Then, in 1942, Texaco also asked to lease an eighty-acre plot of surface land in one of Aristide's cow pastures. After the lean days of the Great Depression, it seemed to be a smart decision, as it would earn the Broussard family an additional $1,600 a year for the next seventy-five years (an amount that was later renegotiated to $100,000 a year). Texaco also threw in a Cadillac and a lifetime supply of free natural gas for Aristide to enjoy. It even promised jobs for his grandsons. So Aristide accepted, and Texaco built a large gas plant a few hundred yards from his home.

Over the years, Aristide's heirs continued to work on the family property, and some still do today. But while they were aware of some places in the pasture where grass simply didn't grow anymore, and some other locations where Texaco paid them extra not to graze cattle because there were too many pipelines, the Broussard family was never fully aware of exactly what Texaco was up to. It was not until a legal argument broke out between Texaco and another company working on the site that the Broussards learned that one of the wells had actually blown out in 1997. At that point the family hired environmental experts, who uncovered radioactive materials, aluminum pellets, and leaky saltwater pits contaminating their property.

Shortly thereafter, the Broussard family sued Texaco for the contamination of their land. This particular case, however, is a bit more complicated than the surface damage cases we discussed earlier in this chapter. Although Texaco does own the mineral rights to the land (which, as we have seen, gives them the right to use and sometimes damage the surface land), a lot of this particular dispute has to do with contamination associated with the activities of the gas plant, which was located on *surface land* leased to Texaco. With ordinary lease law also in play, the Broussards argued that the lease had been breached and that Texaco should be forced to vacate the property unless it was properly decontaminated.

The case was then complicated further when a company that initially seemed unrelated to the contamination suit got involved. Sabine, a subsidiary of Chevron, had been operating a pipeline across the street since 1964, and since 1990, the outfit had also been managing a crucial interchange of gas lines called the Henry Hub. Shortly after the Broussards sued Texaco, Sabine offered the family nearly $1 million to buy most of the contaminated land in question. This offer came with a letter informing the Broussards that if they did not accept, Sabine would be forced to expropriate the land through a perfectly legal court proceeding and pay the family a fair market value. And the reason Sabine was interested? Part of the Henry Hub, which plays an important role in setting the prices for natural gas futures, had somehow, inexplicably, migrated onto the family's own property. When the Broussards declined to sell, Sabine sued to take over the property, arguing that the company was acting in the national interest.

Although the outcomes of these complicated, interrelated cases have yet to be determined, already they have dragged on for so long that thirteen of Aristide's heirs have died. But, though these litigations cover a wider scope of law than the more straightforward mineral rights cases discussed earlier in this chapter, the Broussards' story further illustrates that oil companies aren't always the greatest neighbors.

•　•　•

If you were to take all of the producing oil and gas wells in Louisiana and spread them out evenly over the state, each of them would be just 1.04 miles from four others (north, south, east, and west). It would be impossible, in other words, to stand anywhere in the state without being within eyesight of a wellhead in every direction. Moreover, if you tossed into the mix all the state's defunct and abandoned wells, you wouldn't find any spot in Louisiana where you were more than about 1,200 feet from a well or associated equipment. And yes, the state motto is "Sportsman's Paradise."[1]

---

1. Dividing Louisiana's land area (43,200 square miles) by its 39,960 active inland oil and gas wells gives an average of 1.08 square miles per wellhead. If each active well were plopped in the center of a square that size, those wells would each be within 1.04 miles of another well in each direction (the square root of 1.08).

Courtesy of Lori Henry

Courtesy of Lori Henry

Courtesy of Lori Henry

8.1. Louisiana's woodlands, pastures, and swamps are peppered with more than sixty thousand abandoned wellheads and associated derelict oil equipment. Although the state technically requires oil and gas companies to remove such hardware after a well is exhausted, enforcement remains lax and can be avoided simply by claiming that a well has only been "temporarily" abandoned.

Two other states (Texas and California) each do have more currently active wells than Louisiana (although if you include offshore wells, Louisiana rises to second). But, geographically speaking, those are also much larger states. In terms of the *density* of drilling activity—wells per square mile—Louisiana is the undisputed champion.

Of course, the wells aren't actually spread out evenly; they are clustered where the oil and gas are. The sprawling, flat cotton fields of northeastern Louisiana, for instance, have only a sprinkling of them. The northwestern part of the state has lots of gas wells, but very little oil production. Most of the liquid petroleum is found farther south, around places like Lake Charles, Cameron, Lafayette, Baton Rouge, Plaquemines Parish, and, of course, offshore.

We've already seen how the owners of surface land in Louisiana are affected by all this extraction, but what about the general workforce? With 39,960 producing wells dotting the state's landscape, one might easily jump to the conclusion that a lot of Louisianans gain their livelihoods from participating in all that activity. As a matter of fact, however, the employment number is not all that large.

According to the Louisiana Workforce Commission, in 2010 there were only 8,500 people employed in the category of "Oil and Gas Extraction" in the state. This includes workers who were actively engaged in recovering hydrocarbons up to the point of shipment from the producing property. That same year, there were also 39,400 employed in the state under the heading "Support Activities for Mining." This includes individuals involved in office work, site preparation, monitoring equipment, maintenance, and transporting the products, although technically those products might also include minerals other than oil and gas. Finally, another 8,900 Louisianans were employed by the industry on a contract or fee basis for a variety of special tasks including moving earth, piloting helicopters, delivering supplies to offshore platforms, and so on.

So, if you include all the support activities and contract workers, the oil and gas industry employs a grand total of around 56,800 people in the state of Louisiana. This is out of a civilian labor force of 2,023,976, of whom 1,894,163 are actually employed. Divide out the numbers, and we find that only 3 percent of Louisiana's active workers gain their livelihoods directly from the oil and gas industry.

Why so few jobs for so many producing wells? As it turns out, getting oil and gas out of the ground just isn't all that labor-intensive. A small crew that knows what it's doing can sink a well to six thousand feet in just a few months. After that, the facility produces on its own with only occasional human intervention. And that job situation isn't likely to change anytime soon; total employment in the entire category of "mining" is projected to grow by only 7.5 percent by 2018 in Louisiana. In other words, an increase of about 4,000 jobs out of nearly 2 million over about six years.

Even if you are a Louisiana worker lucky enough to actually get one of these oil and gas–related jobs, the compensation you'll receive isn't particularly impressive. Most extraction occupations in Louisiana have an entry-level salary of around $25,000 a year. An experienced oil and gas derrick operator makes roughly $60,000, and a safety engineer might earn $75,000 a year (the salaries are, of course, higher if offshore).

Meanwhile, the CEOs and other oil and gas executives are funneling many millions every year into their personal bank accounts. CEOs of some of the better-known oil companies had official 2009 salaries of $1.5 million (ConocoPhillips), $1.8 million (Chevron), and $2.1 million (ExxonMobil). The CEO of BP, the company responsible for the *Deepwater Horizon* disaster, had a salary of $1.74 million in 2010—the same year the oil spill took place. And, as if those numbers aren't high enough already, it turns out that most CEOs actually make the vast majority of their money from bonuses that often dwarf their actual salaries. Consider, for instance, the same three CEOs we mentioned above. According to the *Wall Street Journal*, their total direct compensations (including bonuses) for 2009 were $14.2 million (ConocoPhillips), $14.7 million (Chevron), and $21.4 million (ExxonMobil).

• • •

In summary, we find that the majority of Louisiana's rural residents live within view of one or more unsightly oil or gas wells. Many of those folks also have to contend with the nuisance of constant noise from nearby gas compressors. Tens of thousands of the state's residents have wells on their property—paraphernalia that they themselves do not own and (in most instances) derive little or no financial benefit from. The state's courts are not sympathetic to attempts by property owners to force the oil companies to be good neighbors, and derelict equipment litters both woods and fields throughout most of the state. Further, the state laws actually encourage companies to preserve their future drilling rights by starting new wells soon after an earlier one plays itself out. Although all of this activity indeed creates jobs, it does so for only about 3 percent of the state's working population. The other 97 percent of working Louisianans derive minimal, if any, benefit. Meanwhile, most of the river of royalty cash flows into a very tiny number of already brimming bank accounts of the oil executives.

Why is this situation permitted to continue when it enhances the lives of so few and lowers the quality of life for so many? In the next chapter, we explore a large part of the answer.

Chapter 9

OF WISDOM AND FOLLY

American-style democracy was not designed to guarantee that only the best and the brightest would lead. Instead, the governing concept was more akin to a revolving door, where citizen-lawmakers would serve in office for relatively short periods (a handful of years), then return to private life before the trappings of power tempted them to pursue their personal interests at the expense of the public good. Those temporary office-holders might be great thinkers or mediocre thinkers or even sub-standard thinkers, but regardless, even their blunders would be corrected over time, provided that they didn't stay in office very long.

So went the thinking of the nation's founding fathers. Or at least the majority of them, which is all it took.

Prior to 2012, Louisiana voters got to elect seven members of the US House of Representatives (with two-year terms) and two members of the US Senate (with six-year terms). Beginning in 2012, due to a population decline caused by displacements following a series of devastating hurricanes in the years leading up to the 2010 census, Louisiana has lost one representative.

Over the past century, the overwhelming majority of Louisiana's lawmakers have had close ties to oil, gas, and petrochemical interests. It's worth taking a quick look at the nine politicians who represented Louisiana in Washington in 2012.

US Senator Mary Landrieu (D), b. 1955

By anyone's measure, Ms. Landrieu is one of the most conservative Democrats in the US Senate. In chapter 1, we described her sponsorship of the bill that opened up the outer continental shelf of the Gulf of Mexico to leasing and drilling, a poorly regulated initiative that set the stage for the *Deepwater Horizon* disaster shortly thereafter. She favored drilling in the Arctic National Wildlife Refuge, voted to ban the EPA from regulating greenhouse gases, supported continuing governmental subsidies to oil and gas companies, and voted yes on implementing the Bush-Cheney energy policy, whose only intellectual input had come from the energy industry itself (more about that in chapter 10). She also fought to reduce corporate liability for hazardous waste cleanup. The nonpartisan Campaign for America's Future gives her a 33 percent rating on issues relating to energy independence. The League of Conservation Voters gives her a 21 percent score on environmental issues.

In the 2010 election cycle, oil and gas interests donated at least $58,000 to Ms. Landrieu's campaign, in addition to thousands more she received from energy production and oilfield services operations. When a concurrent $17,000 contribution from BP came to light during the height of that summer's big oil spill, several watchdog organizations called on her to return that money. Landrieu's communications director Aaron Saunders responded, "Senator Landrieu has no plans to return donations from BP's PAC or BP employees. Campaign contributions from energy companies or from environmental groups have absolutely no impact on Sen. Landrieu's policy agenda or her response to this unprecedented disaster in the Gulf. The Senator is proud of the broad coalition she's built since her first day in the Senate to address the energy and environmental challenges in Louisiana and in the nation. This disaster only makes the effort to promote and save Louisiana's coast all that more important."

US Senator David Vitter (R), b. 1961

Mr. Vitter was initially elected to the US House of Representatives in a special election in 1999 after his predecessor resigned because of an adultery scandal. Vitter won his current US Senate seat in 2004. Although a devout Roman Catholic, in 2007 his phone number showed up on the client list of a Washington, D.C., prostitute. He apologized publicly but did not step down.

Vitter's stance on anthropogenic (human-caused) climate change has been inconsistent at best. In some instances, he has said he believes the scientific evidence; in other venues he has referred to climate change evidence as a "fraud." His votes have generally been pro–oil and gas, and he is opposed to governmental incentives for renewable energy. He voted against reducing oil imports 40 percent by 2025, and he voted against further increases in vehicle fuel efficiency standards. A few years ago, the League of Conservation Voters gave him a rating of 0 percent on environmental issues. That's right, zero.

Some sources put the oil and gas contributions to Vitter's 2010 campaign at about $250,000, while others claim they may have totaled as high as $523,800 (out of approximately $2.5 million in total donations). Regardless, it's clear that Vitter has been well supported by oil and gas interests. He won reelection in 2010 with 57 percent of the vote.

US Representative Steve Scalise (R, District 1), b. 1965

Mr. Scalise was elected to the US House of Representatives in 2008 in a special election to fill the seat vacated when Bobby Jindal became governor. His district includes most of the land bordering Lake Ponchartrain and some of the western suburbs of New Orleans. Since then, Scalise's voting record has been consistent with that of the rest of the Republican delegation from Louisiana: pro–oil and gas and anti-environment.

According to Open Secrets, a research group that promotes transparency in government, Scalise's main contributors in 2011 included $61,400 from oil and gas, $40,700 from sea transport (which includes companies that service the offshore rigs), and $40,106 from real estate interests. He is a member of the House Committee on Energy and Commerce.

US Representative Cedric Richmond (D, District 2), b. 1973

Mr. Richmond was first elected to his seat in 2010, garnering 65 percent of the vote in a district that encompasses most of New Orleans. The *Huffington Post* has described him as "one of the best-dressed people in American politics."

Although Richmond has not yet spent enough time in office to amass much of a voting record, he did vote *against* reopening the outer continental shelf to drilling and *against* banning the EPA from regulating greenhouse gases.

Remarkably, in his initial bid for office, Richmond managed to attract $1.1 million in campaign contributions with virtually none of it coming from the oil and gas industries. His major contributors were law firms, trade unions, and individuals. More recently, however, he seems to have teamed up with Representative Scalise to promote more domestic drilling.

US Representative John Fleming (R, District 4), b. 1951

Dr. Fleming, who first won his seat in 2008, is a navy veteran, a family practice physician, and a businessman who owns Fleming Expansions LLC plus at least thirty-three Subway sandwich shops. His district in northwestern Louisiana includes the city of Shreveport. In September of 2011, during an interview on national television, Fleming railed against the concept of increasing taxes on the rich, stating that although his businesses "made" more than $6.3 million per year, he and his family actually lived on only $400,000 per year, and that people like him cannot afford tax hikes and still be job creators. Pundits promptly pounced on various inconsistencies in Fleming's numbers, including the claim that he had created five hundred jobs. (If so, then the annual pay would have had to be considerably below the poverty level; is *that* what he was bragging about?)

Fleming, a member of the House Natural Resources Committee, supports drilling pretty much anywhere it can possibly be done. On energy and environmental legislation, he has consistently voted with the other Louisiana Republicans. On health care reform (despite being a physician himself), he is vehemently opposed to the affordable care concept.

Of the most recent $1.45 million raised for Fleming's campaigns, the health professions, which contributed $212,800, were the most supportive group. Second was oil and gas, at $122,450.

US Representative Rodney Alexander (R, District 5)

A Democrat while in the Louisiana state legislature and in his initial 2002 election to Congress, Mr. Alexander changed his party affiliation to Republican a bare fifteen minutes before the filing deadline for the 2004 election. His voting record in the House has been virtually 100 percent pro-oil and roughly 80 percent anti-environment, according to nonpartisan organizations such as the Campaign for America's Future and the League of Conservation Voters. He also has a relatively low rating of 39 percent from the National Association for the Advancement of Colored People (NAACP) for his blind eye toward minority issues, including environmental justice.

Alexander voted against tax incentives for renewable energy while voting for more drilling, he supported the implementation of the Bush-Cheney energy policy, and he voted against the regulation of greenhouse gas emissions. Environmentally, Alexander voted to de-authorize the "critical habitat" designation for endangered species, voted against increased AMTRACK funding (despite the fact that trains are considerably more fuel-efficient than cars), and voted to kill the "cash for clunkers" program, whose goal was to get old gas-guzzling and polluting vehicles off the highways.

Although Alexander has received campaign donations from various oil and gas interests, including the Pelican Gas Management Company, most of those contributions were modest. His major institutional supporters have been agriculturally related or connected to the health care industry.

In his 2010 reelection campaign, Alexander spent a total of $1,239,962.91 (and managed to raise slightly more), despite the fact that his district includes some of the poorest places in the nation, including the environs of the town of Lake Providence. There is relatively little oil or gas in that northeast corner of the state; the main product there is cotton.

US Representative Bill Cassidy (R, District 6), b. 1957

Dr. Cassidy is a physician specializing in diseases of the liver. He is also an associate professor of medicine at Louisiana State University. He initially won his congressional seat in 2006 in a district that includes the state capital of Baton Rouge and the bordering parishes.

Cassidy's voting record on energy, the environment, and deregulation mirrors those of his Louisiana colleagues: he is pro-oil and blind to most environmental issues. Despite the well-documented environmental tolls on the health of the average Louisianan, and despite his own professorial position in the School of Medicine, he remains opposed to virtually any public health care reform.

Special-interest group contributions to Cassidy's 2010 campaign chest included $176,000 from the health professions, $42,900 from sea transport, and $33,000 from oil and gas.

US Representative Charles Boustany (R, District 7), b. 1956

Yet another physician-politician, Dr. Boustany won his first race in 2004. His district encompasses the oil-rich southwestern portion of the state. He is on record as favoring the Keystone Pipeline and opposing any tax on carbon emissions and has enthusiastically invited investment in liquefied natural gas (LNG) in Louisiana.

Although Boustany did vote to extend the cash-for-clunkers program, beyond that he hasn't exhibited much independent thinking—instead consistently voting the line with the rest of the Louisiana delegation. The Campaign for America's Future gave him a rating of 0 percent on his stances relating to energy independence.

Boustany's seat was one of those affected by redistricting in 2012. In the previous election, he received donations of $129,750 from the health professions and $83,600 from oil and gas. His war chest for the 2012 election seems to have followed the same general pattern. In a bitterly fought contest against a fellow redistricted Republican in 2012, Boustany ultimately prevailed in a special run-off election.

• • •

In summary, eight elected individuals continue to represent the citizens of Louisiana in Washington: two in the Senate and six (down from seven) in the House. Of those eight, two are presently Democrats and six are Republicans. The past campaigns of five of those six Republicans and one of the two Democrats have been funded by significant amounts of oil and gas money.

Is it a mere coincidence that all but one of those eight have so consistently voted in favor of the oil and gas interests? Or that they clamor for fewer regulations of the industry? And that they turn such a blind eye toward environmental and quality-of-life issues?

• • •

At the state level, Louisiana has 39 senators and 105 representatives. No public interest group seems to have statistically analyzed all of these lawmakers' votes regarding the environment or energy independence (nor has anyone done so for most of the other forty-nine states). As for the prospect of listing those 144 Louisiana legislators and describing each of them here, we'll spare the reader. There is another way to qualitatively assess the influence of the oil and gas interests on the Louisiana state legislature, and that is to look at the statutory outcomes.

Let's begin in 1999, three decades after Louisiana's domestic production (onshore and in state offshore waters) had peaked. By then, Louisiana's total annual oil and gas production had dropped to just 19.4 percent of what it once had been but a generation earlier. So did this weaken the oil and gas interests' power over the state's lawmakers? Nope. Here are some examples of the deliberations of the 1999 state legislature and their outcomes:

Environmental Facilities. State Representative Arthur Morrell introduced a measure that would have imposed a five-year moratorium on the construction of new chemical plants in Louisiana, pending the Department of Environmental Quality's establishment of more scientifically based environmental standards. The resolution, however, died in the House Environment Committee.

Hazardous Materials. Concerned about the parking of rail cars containing hazardous materials in residential communities, Senator Cleo Fields introduced a bill that would have prohibited the storage of hazardous materials in rail freight cars, freight containers, cargo tank cars, or portable tank cars located within one thousand feet of any residence and would have imposed both civil and criminal penalties for violations. The bill was quickly killed by the Senate Environmental Quality Committee.

Used Oil. In an effort to address the fact that used oil facilities are unregulated by the DEQ, Senator Wilson Fields introduced a bill that would have required used oil collection centers, transfer facilities, and transporters to obtain hazardous waste licenses or permits authorizing such facilities to properly handle used oil. The bill was amended on the senate floor to eliminate the requirement that such facilities obtain a more stringent hazardous waste permit and instead merely required that such facilities obtain a permit authorizing their operation in accordance with rules and regulations promulgated by the DEQ. Despite this attempt to make the proposal more palatable to all parties, the bill was killed in the House Environment Committee.

Crimes/Enforcement. Senator Ron Landry introduced a bill to attempt to create the crime of environmental fraud by state employees. The crime was defined as any intentional action, inaction, omission, falsification, or concealment of environmental documents by state employees that caused or might have caused damage to the life or health of a person. The bill would have also obligated any state employee with knowledge of the commission of environmental fraud to report the offense to the local district attorney, and it would have authorized a citizen suit in the event the district attorney did not prosecute. However, the bill died in the House Administration of Criminal Justice Committee. In other words, environmental fraud in Louisiana is still *not* a crime.

Fees. Act 839, introduced by Senator Noble Ellington and Representative Dan Morrish, was signed into law on August 15, 1999. Although there is a chemical accident prevention program in Louisiana, this new act prohibited the DEQ from imposing fees under the program against the propane gas industry, so long as their facilities are permitted or inspected by the Louisiana Liquefied Petroleum Gas Commission or their use of liquefied petroleum gas is for fuel in an agricultural process.

And yes, this pattern repeats through the following decade. By 2011, the Louisiana Mid-continent Oil and Gas Association (LMOGA) had grown considerably more brazen, actually bragging on its website about its lobbying victories with the Louisiana state legislature. Here are a few examples, in the LMOGA's actual words (italics added for emphasis):

- HB 258 by Rep. Richie Burford, R-Stonewall, would have changed from three to ten years the prescriptive period for an action to recover underpayments or overpayments of mineral royalties. *LMOGA opposed this bill.* The legislation was eventually voluntarily withdrawn *after heavy lobbying by LMOGA* and other industry groups.
- HB 389 by Rep. Pat Connick, R-Marrero, would have provided that certain releases of future medical claims relating to the BP oil spill are null and void and therefore unenforceable, allowing an injured party the opportunity to file suit at anytime in the future. *LMOGA opposed this bill.* The legislation was ultimately defeated on the House floor.
- HB 422 (constitutional amendment) and HB 436 (statutory companion) by Rep. Reed Henderson, D-Chalmette, would have levied a tax of 50 cents per 1,000 cubic feet on the use of pipeline more than one mile in length for the transportation of natural gas through Louisiana. *LMOGA opposed this bill.* Rep. Henderson's bills gained no support in their committee of origin and were defeated.

- HB 547 by Rep. Richie Burford, R-Stonewall, would have defined "timely payout" relative to the payment of royalties within 180 days of production for proceeds totaling $100 or more annually. It also called for a company to mail a notice to the mineral lessor explaining the reason behind the delay in payment. *LMOGA opposed this bill.* The bill was voluntarily withdrawn.
- SB 77 by Sen. Buddy Shaw, R-Shreveport, would have provided for the recoupment of unit well costs and risk charges. *LMOGA opposed this bill.* The legislation was voluntarily deferred following testimony in the Senate Natural Resources Committee.
- SB 97 by Sen. A. G. Crowe, R-Slidell, would have eliminated the use of most dispersants and the issuing of permits allowing them in the event of an oil spill. *LMOGA opposed this bill.* The bill was reported favorably out of the Senate Environment Committee but was defeated on the Senate floor.
- SB 145 by Sen. Dan Claitor, R-Baton Rouge, provides that the historic gulfward boundary of the state of Louisiana extends a distance into the Gulf of Mexico three marine leagues from the coastline or nine geographical miles. *LMOGA worked to include an amendment to address some tax issues.* The amended bill was passed out of both houses and sent to the governor, where it was signed and enacted into law. (Act 336)

It is commendable that the LMOGA so readily discloses the details of its influence on Louisiana lawmakers. If there is a bill introduced in Louisiana that affects the oil industry or the environment, you can be sure that the LMOGA will be on top of the issue immediately, and it will brag that it has done so. If the LMOGA opposes a bill, it is unlikely to even come up for a vote. And if the LMOGA favors a bill, it will almost always pass in a flash.

This isn't just a screwy short-term anomaly. It's the way things have been in the past in Louisiana, and it's the way it continues to be. Today, the documentation is just a bit better.

•   •   •

State legislators are not full-time employees. In Louisiana, the legislative session alternates year by year between sixty days and eighty-five days, minus Fridays, Saturdays, Sundays, and legal holidays. For this, the lawmakers are paid $16,800 per year plus a per diem that typically totals

$9,540 to $13,515 per year. They also receive up to $3,000 per month for a legislative aide, plus a vouchered expense allowance capped at $50,340 or $54,315 (depending on whether it is an odd or even year).

In accordance with the philosophy of the founding fathers, this degree of economic incentive is unlikely to attract many full-time career politicians—or at least many committed ones. After all, how many qualified people, for a mere $16,800 per year plus expenses, would take the time to properly prepare themselves before attending all the necessary meetings, let alone to conduct all the background research to cast knowledgeable and responsible votes?

Lobbyist organizations such as the LMOGA can always out-muscle legislators in terms of time, money, staff, and printed words. If you're interested in becoming a Louisiana legislator and you're overtly pro-environment, your *opponent* is likely to be the guy who attracts the financial assistance to run a successful campaign.

•   •   •

Today, Louisiana produces about 49 million barrels of crude oil per year (inland and from state-owned offshore waters), down from a peak of 476 million barrels in 1970. Taken alone, these numbers might suggest that oil is a dwindling economic activity in the state, and that therefore the continued influence-peddling by the oil/gas industry should not be a major concern to today's Louisianans.

Actually, however, there are a series of reasons why the oil industry continues to spend huge sums of money to control the Louisiana government. Even though a diminishing amount of petroleum is being extracted within the state, *more* of it is being processed there. A whole lot more.

In 2010, for instance, 588 million barrels of oil were extracted from all federal outer continental shelf (OCS) waters. Of this quantity, 519 million barrels, or 88.3 percent, was pumped ashore in Louisiana. Although a portion of this petroleum continued on through pipelines to a final destination in some other state (principally Texas), a lion's share of it went to Louisiana's seventeen mega-refineries, where it was processed into gasoline, jet fuel, and other products, including various products that supply Louisiana's petrochemical industry. This state of affairs gives the oil and gas interests a considerable incentive to assure that, in the future, they will *continue* to operate in a setting of lax state regulations and preferential tax treatments.

Meanwhile, in 1981, the state had another significant oil-related development: the opening of the Louisiana Offshore Oil Port (LOOP), whose construction irrevocably destroyed several hundred acres of marshland. This huge facility, standing in 110 feet of water eighteen miles out in the Gulf from Port Fourchon, can simultaneously and efficiently unload up to three of the largest of the world's supertankers. The petroleum from their holds is pumped to on-land storage facilities (one of them a salt dome with a capacity of 50 million barrels), or else it is transferred directly to various refineries. The LOOP facility is owned by three companies: Marathon Oil, Murphy Oil, and Shell Oil, so of course they are the ones that reap the profits from this huge operation.

Yes, the facility supports jobs: at present, it employs about 160 full-time workers. And if we include the multiplier factor for spin-off jobs, a total of about 323 Louisianans owe their livelihoods to the LOOP. Despite these unimpressive employment numbers, however, the LOOP does handle a great deal of oil: about 17 percent of the entire nation's oil imports, or about 570 million barrels per year.

So, why does the oil/gas industry feel it must continue to buy off the Louisiana government? Not so much because of the 49 million barrels being extracted within the state annually, but more so because of the additional 1,089 million barrels that enter and exit the state each year from OCS production and the foreign oil handled through the LOOP.

• ◆ •

In chapter 8, we pointed out that Louisiana's landscape is peppered by tens of thousands of derelict oil and gas wells, and that the state Office of Conservation has done relatively little to force the oil companies to clean up those messes. In the present context of how laws are made in Louisiana, we need to say a bit more about that part of the story. The relevant state agencies, it turns out, actually have no real fangs to force oil companies to clean up after themselves.

Yes, the Louisiana statutes do require that the surface land must be restored to its previous condition when production ceases. Often, however, multiple wells are drilled under a single mineral lease, and in such instances the Louisiana courts usually rule that if one well is still producing while a nearby one is not, then neither well site needs to be restored until *both* wells are unproductive. Compounding the matter further is the wimpy legal definition of well abandonment. Wells that are played out and capped *do* sometimes recover slightly over a period of years, to the point where some additional petroleum may become extractable. An oil company therefore can simply claim that a well has been "temporarily" abandoned with the intention of returning to it at some unspecified future date, and that simple piece of paperwork generally gets the company off the hook for a number of years or decades. Or even forever.

By the 1980s, with inland oil production dwindling and offshore production booming, the larger oil companies focused most of their attention offshore. Because their inland leases still had some resale value, they began selling them to smaller (and therefore less-capitalized) companies. Over the years, many of those smaller producers also left behind various pieces of worn-out or otherwise unsalvageable equipment for the next operator to worry about. Mostly, of course, this was on privately owned land.

Although the state motto "Sportsman's Paradise" was coined in 1958, ecotourism was not aggressively promoted until a few decades later, just as Louisiana's oil sector was in transition from inland to offshore. Sportsmen nationwide who were accustomed to the scenic beauty of other parts of the country flocked in to explore this new and mysterious place. Many, if not most, were appalled. Yes, the Louisiana wetlands and forests *would* be extraordinarily beautiful if only the oil industry hadn't turned so many of those scenic regions into junkyards.

The oil industry quickly recognized that a public relations problem was brewing. Not so much with the disappointed fishers and hunters from other states; those guys were going to buy petroleum products regardless. Oil's concern was that it might lose some of its sway with Louisiana's own lawmakers. And if that happened, the golden goose could get cooked.

Nobody has ever admitted who actually wrote the 1993 legislation that resulted, but, suspiciously, it was fully supported by the oil lobby (most vociferously by the Louisiana Oil and Gas Association, LOGA). In the resulting act, the state of Louisiana instituted an Oilfield Site Restoration (OSR) program under the duties of the Office of Conservation (OOC). But no, this program did not exactly deal with the plethora of abandoned wells, which, after all, might only be "temporarily" abandoned. Instead, it only addressed "orphaned" wells, which are wells for which the OOC records can no longer identify the party actually responsible for restoring a particular site.

The part that Louisiana politicians loved most: those site restorations wouldn't cost the state's taxpayers a penny. Instead, they would cost the oil companies a penny—literally. Yes, the statute assessed producers *one cent per barrel* on all oil extracted within the state's boundaries. It did not, of course, apply to OCS oil or to imported foreign oil.

At that time, crude oil was selling for $16.75 per barrel. The one-cent levy on each barrel therefore amounted to a tax rate of 0.06 of 1 percent (0.0006). As time went on, the original one-penny tax was increased to 1.5 cents, with a corresponding equivalent for natural gas. As of this writing, however, oil prices hover around $120 per barrel, so the assessment is now barely one one-hundredth of 1 percent. Yes, it was quite ingenious of LOGA to push for the passage of such a bill. The amount it currently generates for the restoration program statewide is in the neighborhood of $4 million annually.

So how does this level of cash flow stack up against the size of the task? The Louisiana OOC and its OSR program do not report a figure for the total number of well sites in need of restoration; all they tell us is that there are presently about 2,800 orphaned sites on the waiting list. But if we start with the total number of wells successfully drilled over the years and subtract the number still operating or having been removed, we get a total of about 60,000 unrestored, inactive inland wells in the state. This figure does not seem to be inflated; the *Daily Comet* of Lafourche Parish computed the total number of restoration sites statewide as 220,000 (some of which are not wells, but related defunct operations). The *Daily Comet*, September 12, 2010, goes on:

> The state has entirely lost track of some wells. For instance, there are 74 wells in Lafourche and 23 in Terrebonne designated code "28," which means "Unable to locate well, not plugged and abandoned." Another 50 in Lafourche and 15 in Terrebonne are listed as "Temporarily abandoned," even though they were permitted as long ago as 1959.
>
> [A spokesperson for the OOC] said the orphan-well program is tasked only with handling sites that have no designated responsible party. . . . "In America, we don't go and take somebody's contract away from them, and tell them how to handle their lease or produce mineral resources," he said. . . . "Any citizen is welcome to bring complaints about a well they believe needs more attention from its regular inspection program. The regulator can't bring people into compliance with an issue if no laws are being broken."

Between 1993 and 2010, Louisiana's Oilfield Site Restoration Program spent $65.1 million to plug 2,453 orphaned wells, restore 596 production pits, and remove 295 other derelict production facilities. At this current rate of progress, it will take until the year 2025 to restore all of the sites on the program's currently approved waiting list. It will take until the year 2310 to restore all 60,000 sites that are currently in need of restoration. And if the 220,000-site estimate of the *Daily Comet* is correct, the task will take more than a millennium at the current rate of restoration. In one of the greatest understatements in Louisiana history, a Lafourche Parish official stated that the OSR is "grossly underestimating the problem."

So, with so much to do and so few financial resources available to do it, how are the restoration projects prioritized? By a commission, of course, ten members. The chair and vice-chair are career bureaucrats from the state Department of Natural Resources and the Office of Conservation. Four members are appointed by the oil and gas industry. One represents the Louisiana Land Association. Two are from environmental groups. And the final member is appointed "at large" by the governor.

If you are a Louisiana property owner and you want to have an old well removed from your property, your first challenge is to establish that the well is actually orphaned and not simply "temporarily" abandoned. Once you have done that, you can submit your application to the Oilfield Site Restoration program. The commission decides who is served first, giving priority to those situations that jeopardize health or safety. For instance, if you own coastal land that has subsided to the point where a previously dry-land well is now underwater and poses a hazard to boaters, you may float closer to the top of the OSR list.

As for getting to the tippy top of the list? Who knows? After all, the commission is stacked at least six to four in favor of the oil/gas industry.

◆ ◆ ◆

Louisiana's orphan well program, not unremarkably, left many of the state's rural landowners dissatisfied. Neighboring Texas, for instance, spends as much *each year* to clean up abandoned well sites as Louisiana has spent in the past seventeen years. Moreover, if you happen to *know* who is responsible for restoring your property, then Louisiana's orphan well program doesn't apply to you at all.

Then came a court case that caught the oil industry completely off guard. The plaintiff, William G. Corbello, owned 320 acres of land in Calcasieu Parish where Shell Oil and a series of other operators had been extracting petroleum since 1929. In 1961 the surface lease was extended, but only for 120 acres of the property and only for thirty years. In 1991,

Mr. Corbello reminded Shell of the upcoming termination date and his expectation that Shell and Iowa Production would honor their prior contractual agreement to restore the property. Instead, Shell built an oil terminal on a five-acre parcel within the leased acreage, which it operated for the next two years. By then, Corbello and his family had gotten irate enough to file a lawsuit for trespassing, breach of contract, pollution, and various other injuries. He also hired a scientific consultant who discovered that the property was seriously polluted by salt (at about eight times the legal limit) and hydrocarbons (at thirty-five times the legal limit). Further, this pollution was found to extend down into the soil as deep as twenty-five feet.

Efforts to reach a mutually acceptable out-of-court settlement were to no avail, and the plaintiffs (there were five of them now) decided to exercise their right to a jury trial. At this point, one has to wonder what was going on in the heads of the defendants' attorneys. Instead of simply advising their clients to go out and clean up the mess as they were contractually and legally obligated to do, they embarked on a series of delaying tactics. It wasn't until May of 2000 that the trial was finally held. In the courtroom, the corporate attorneys arrogantly argued that since the property at issue had a market value of only $108,000, that figure should be the limit of the defendants' financial responsibility. In other words, once they reached that threshold, they claimed, they were legally free to pollute to their hearts' content.

Members of the jury not only didn't buy it, they were appalled by the defendants' environmental insensitivity. They deliberated only a short time before finding in favor of Corbello and his four co-plaintiffs. The award was $927,000 for Shell's failure to vacate the leased premises after the surface lease expired; $33 million to restore the leased premises to their 1961 condition; and $16,679,100 for Shell's illegal disposal of saltwater on the leased premises. The plaintiffs were also awarded $689,510 in attorney fees and $65,000 to pay their expert scientific witness.

But no, that didn't end it. The oil companies appealed both the verdict and the award. They succeeded in getting the $927,000 reduced to $32,500, and the appeals court made a few other minor adjustments. Most of the outcome, however, remained intact, including the $33 million cost of site restoration, which the justices ruled was necessary to protect the Chicot Aquifer, which supplies drinking water to the city of Lake Charles (population 72,000) and numerous smaller towns. In that region, there are spots where the aquifer is only fifty to seventy-five feet below the surface.

In February of 2003, nearly eleven years after Corbello filed his initial complaint, the case landed before the Louisiana Supreme Court. In a tortured and convoluted forty-five-page opinion, those justices once again tinkered with some of the language but left the $33 million part of the award intact. Amazingly, an ordinary Louisianan had actually beaten the oil companies!

End of story? Nope. Corbello and his four co-plaintiffs apparently decided to simply abandon the property and pocket all of that money, which the Supreme Court ruling actually permitted them to do. As of this writing, it still remains unclear to what extent that particular piece of land will ever be restored. Or, for that matter, what will happen if the Chicot Aquifer does get contaminated from the oil companies' pollution on the Corbello property.

As can be expected, the oil interests shrieked in horror at this outcome. Accusations of judicial incompetence were bandied about, along with speculations of judicial impropriety. Was it possible, with $33 million already laying on the table, that some of the justices had been bribed? Who knows? After all, this is Louisiana, and a lot of curious things *do* happen here.

In the wake of the *Corbello v. Iowa Production* case, the oil and gas lobby quickly swarmed the state legislators. The result was Act 312, passed in 2006, which provides that any monetary awards for onsite remediation are actually used for that purpose. Such funds are now placed under the jurisdiction of the court and are drawn upon only by the Office of Conservation after that office conducts separate hearings to determine the best strategy for site restoration. Plaintiffs' attorneys immediately objected that this law's provisions impair the plaintiffs' rights to unfettered access to the court system as mandated by the Louisiana Constitution. They specifically argued that a hearing officiated by a bunch of bureaucrats was not the same as a jury trial. In 2008, however, the Louisiana Supreme Court affirmed the constitutionality of Act 312.

In summary, and regardless of all the hoopla about the orphaned well program and Act 312, not much has happened to actually restore Louisiana's landscape. The oil companies still demonstrate little interest in doing so on their own volition, and in fact they tend to do everything within their power to avoid cleaning up their messes. The state Office of Conservation is essentially toothless regarding enforcement of the existing statutes and regulations. The only way a property owner may have a chance of getting an oil company to remove its abandoned equipment is to go to court and file what industry lawyers refer to as a "nuisance lawsuit." Not only does that involve a considerable out-of-pocket expense for the plaintiff, but it's quite possible for such an action to drag on for as long as ten years to get a single site remediated.

Is it any wonder that so many Louisianans simply take a deep breath and learn to live with all the junk heaps in their backyards?

Chapter 10

DRILL, BABY, DRILL

Picture this: One day you hear on the news that there has been a drastic decrease in the global supply of oil. Soon you notice that one gas station after another is closing due to lack of supply. You need to put fuel in your car to get to work, but some retailers enforce a ten-gallon limit per customer and others are open for business only on alternate days. These closures and restrictions lead to bumper-to-bumper lines that stretch on for blocks. Tempers flare and fights break out. Politicians start calling for gasoline rationing programs, and several states enforce odd-even rationing, where cars with odd numbers as the last digit on their license plates can purchase gas only on odd numbered days, and vice versa.

Is this a future scenario concocted by some alarmist? Nope. It already happened, almost forty years ago.

In October of 1973, oil prices doubled in response to an Arab oil embargo. The situation arose when Syria and Egypt launched a surprise attack on Israel, known as the Yom Kippur War, and President Richard Nixon decided to deliver weapons and supplies to the Israeli military. In response to this US involvement, members of the Organization of Arab Petroleum Exporting Countries—consisting of Iraq, Kuwait, Libya, Qatar, Saudi Arabia, the United Arab Emirates, Egypt, Syria, and Tunisia—decided to use oil as a weapon to undermine US support of Israel. The posted price of petroleum was suddenly increased by 70 percent (to $5.11 a barrel) and the oil ministers agreed to continue to cut production over time in 5 percent increments until their economic and political objectives were met.

The effects of this "oil price shock" were immediate. The retail price of a gallon of gasoline jumped from a national average of 38.5 cents in May 1973 to 55.1 cents in June 1974. As the price of oil skyrocketed, economies around the world experienced recessions and high inflation. In an attempt to promote domestic oil exploration to replace the reduction in foreign supply, the US government issued price controls to limit the price of "old oil," allowing newly discovered oil to be sold at a higher price. While this tactic indeed encouraged many US companies to search for ways to develop new sources of oil—even in hostile Arctic environments—it also resulted in the withdrawal of old oil from the market. This created an artificial scarcity and only made the problem worse.

Eventually, Secretary of State Henry Kissinger convinced Israel to withdraw from the fighting. This was enough to convince the Arab oil producers to lift the embargo in March 1974. The damage, however, had already been done, and the crisis was regarded as the first episode since the Great Depression to have a sustained negative economic effect on the world economy.

In response to these events, the Nixon administration announced "Project Independence," a goal to achieve energy self-sufficiency in the United States by 1980. The plan stressed a national commitment to energy conservation and the development of alternative sources of energy. Initiatives included the conversion of oil power plants to coal (a resource that is domestically available), the completion of the Trans-Alaska Pipeline System (to promote domestic oil production), the diversion of federal funds from highway construction and into mass transit (to reduce dependence on oil), and the lowering of highway speeds to 55 miles per hour (to increase fuel economy). Although quite a few of these initiatives were successfully completed, the goal to achieve energy self-sufficiency by 1980 was not met. Not even close.

In April 1977, motivated by the lessons of the big oil embargo of four years earlier, President Jimmy Carter addressed the nation about the importance of altering our energy policy, calling it the greatest challenge our country will face during our lifetimes. He stressed the importance of balancing our growing demand for energy with our rapidly shrinking resources. "We must be fair," President Carter told the nation. "Our solutions must ask equal sacrifices from every region, every class of people, and every interest group. Industry will have to do its part to conserve just as consumers will. The energy producers deserve fair treatment, but we will not let the oil companies profiteer."

But Carter's attempt to forge national energy awareness was also ultimately unsuccessful. Rather than reducing our dependence on oil, the United States instead suffered from another energy crisis when oil prices nearly doubled again in 1979. This time the price increase occurred in the wake of the Iranian Revolution, when Iran dethroned its shah. Protests severely disrupted the Iranian oil sector, and production was greatly curtailed and exports were suspended. Even when oil exports were resumed under the new regime, they were at a much lower volume and often erratic. Oil prices rose once again.

With the impact of the 1973 embargo still fresh in the nation's mind, the result was widespread panic. Oil prices jumped from $15.85 per barrel to $29.50 per barrel in twelve months. The long lines at gas stations reappeared. Unfortunately, because the average vehicle at the time consumed between 0.5 to 0.8 gallons of gasoline per hour while simply idling, it is estimated that Americans wasted up to 150,000 barrels of oil *per day* while idling their engines in lines at gas stations to buy fuel.

In an attempt to reduce US vulnerability to future temporary supply disruptions, the Strategic Petroleum Reserve (SPR) was created in 1975. Maintained by the US Department of Energy, the reserve is located at four sites near the Gulf of Mexico: two in Texas (Freeport and Winnie) and two in Louisiana (Lake Charles and Baton Rouge). At these four locations the SPR can currently store up to 727 million barrels of oil. As of January 31, 2012, there were 659.9 million barrels being held in reserve in this manner. The Energy Policy Act of 2005, however, directs the secretary of energy to fill the SPR to 1 billion barrels, which will require a physical expansion of the facilities.

The 1975 Energy Policy and Conservation Act controls access to the SPR. If there is an event that causes a severe oil supply interruption, like the 1973 embargo, the president can order oil from the reserve to be released to the market and, within thirteen days, that oil can be distributed by competitive sale to help keep oil prices from spiking too severely. This technique was used to lessen the effects of oil price increases in 1991 during Operation Desert Storm and also in 2005 after Hurricanes Katrina and Rita.

If the events of 1973 didn't teach the nation a lesson, it seems that the repeat performance in 1979 should have finally awakened us to the reality of our dependence on oil—and all the associated negative consequences. Instead, the SPR enables the United States to somewhat avoid the negative economic impacts of temporary reductions in oil supply, maintaining our dependence on oil even in the face of events that ought to be teaching the opposite lesson. So, what has the nation really learned from all this?

• • •

We have already mentioned that Louisiana's inland and near-offshore oil production is dwindling. Figure 10.1 shows how dramatically the state's

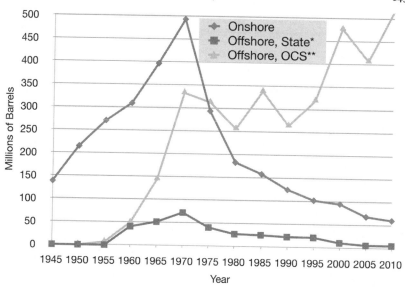

10.1. Louisiana's oil production peaked in 1970, both onshore and in offshore state waters. Oil production in federal OCS waters near Louisiana continues to show a potential to increase, although not all of the resulting crude is destined for the US market. *Data from the Louisiana Office of Conservation.*

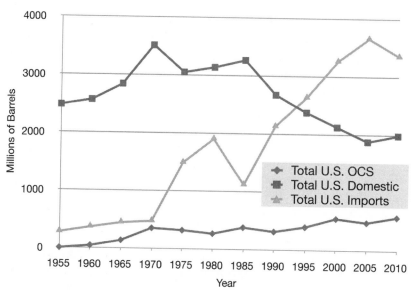

10.2. US domestic oil production has been in a general decline since about 1985. Imported oil first exceeded domestic production in 1991. *Data from the US Department of Energy.*

production has actually declined since its peak in 1970. Similarly, as we see in figure 10.2, the sum of all oil production nationwide is probably forever past its peak.[1]

Because oil takes millions of years to form, the amount of oil that can be extracted from the planet on a human timescale is finite. Eventually, we will reach (or may have already reached) a point in time where global oil extraction is at its maximum point. After that, the rate of oil production will enter a terminal decline, when supplies of oil will only continue to shrink. This concept is known as "peak oil."

There is plenty of debate about when the global peak in oil will occur—or whether it has already occurred. Some experts claim we already passed peak oil back in 2008, whereas some more optimistic US government analysts think global oil production won't peak until 2037. Despite such debate, even the most hopeful forecasters agree that in our lifetimes, or the lifetimes of our children, oil production will reach its peak and then begin to decline.

Passing global peak oil does not mean that oil will stop being produced overnight, but it does mean that oil companies will find it to be increasingly difficult, and eventually impossible, to continue raising their yearly levels of production. According to the US Energy Information Administration, all or nearly all of the largest oil deposits in the world have already been discovered, and most are already being tapped. In fact, oil *discovery* already peaked way back in 1964, and since that time the volume of newly discovered oil has, on average, steadily fallen every year. It may be possible to make up for some of the reduction in oil supply with emerging technologies, which could make the production of unconventional sources of oil, such as tar sands and oil shale, more economically feasible. But, as global populations and demand for energy continue to grow while oil supplies dwindle, cheap and plentiful oil will eventually become a thing of the past.

As we already saw in 1973 and 1979, rising oil prices will have a huge effect on the world economy. And, while the price shocks in the 1970s were only temporary, the rising prices that follow peak oil will be permanent. With so many countries dependent on oil, the economic effects

---

1. Yes, some analysts believe that the exploitation of US oil shale deposits can turn the United States into a net exporter of oil in about another decade or so. If so, however, this would have huge negative environmental consequences and would only be a temporary situation in any case. Whatever the source or the timeline, oil is certain to eventually become depleted.

could also lead to social and political unrest. This is particularly true in countries like the United States, where the demand for oil far exceeds the domestic supply, compelling imports from politically volatile parts of the world. This lack of energy security could leave the United States vulnerable to future embargoes and, as in 1973, endanger our freedom as a sovereign nation to act altruistically in our foreign affairs. Yes, the crisis may be delayed through the controversial use of hydraulic fracturing (fracking) and related technologies, but, no, it cannot be averted indefinitely.

In addition to economic concerns and issues of energy security, we also have to think about the specter of global climate change. Oil, natural gas, and coal are all carbon-based fuels that emit enormous quantities of carbon dioxide into the atmosphere during combustion. According to the Intergovernmental Panel on Climate Change (IPCC), a group of 2,500 scientists from all over the world tasked with evaluating the most current scientific data on climate change, carbon dioxide is the most significant anthropogenic (human-caused) contribution to climate change. Global atmospheric concentrations of carbon dioxide have increased from a natural pre-industrial level of approximately 280 parts per million to 392 parts per million in 2011—a level that already far exceeds the natural range over the last 650,000 years as determined by glacial ice core samples. In February 2007, the IPCC asserted with more than 90 percent confidence that these anthropogenic emissions have led to "unequivocal" warming of the climate system. Historically, the United States has been the number one emitter of carbon dioxide. Though China overtook the United States in total emissions in 2006, the United States still has the highest level of per capita emissions in the world.

Unfortunately, rising levels of carbon dioxide in the atmosphere are doing more than raising average land temperatures around the globe. Global ocean temperatures are also increasing, causing coral bleaching and contributing to sea-level rise through thermal expansion. Glaciers and snow pack are melting away in both hemispheres, which further exacerbates sea-level rise and may contribute to water shortages (snow that melts earlier in the spring is no longer available to feed streams later in the summer). Sea-level rise also means the potential submersion of low-lying land and even the salinization of some freshwater resources. Changing patterns of precipitation already seem to be leading to drought in some areas and recurring floods in others. There is also observational evidence to support the claim that since 1970 the frequency and intensity of North Atlantic hurricanes has been increasing.

The international community has already attempted to address the dangers posed by climate change through the negotiation of the Kyoto Protocol. This international agreement took force in February 2005 after Russia signed on, and it committed ratifying countries to cut their greenhouse gas emissions 6 to 8 percent below their 1990 levels by 2012. The United States was supposed to cut its emissions to 7 percent below 1990 levels, but it never actually ratified the Kyoto Protocol and thus was not legally compelled to do so. Unfortunately, many of the quantitative targets agreed to by ratifying nations were also unmet by the time the Kyoto Protocol expired in 2012, and so it is still unclear exactly what impact these international efforts have had on the issue of anthropogenic climate change. Additionally, despite the efforts of multiple international conferences, the international community has, as of this writing, been unable to agree on a treaty to replace the Kyoto Protocol.

Despite the difficulties associated with international cooperation, it seems clear that the residents of Planet Earth will somehow need to reduce their reliance on hydrocarbons in order to halt the negative effects of global climate change. It also seems obvious that Americans ought to reduce their dependence on oil to protect our economy and national security. And just think of how much better off the United States would be today if it had heeded President Jimmy Carter's sage advice and worked over the last forty years to promote conservation and the development of alternative energy technologies.

◆　◆　◆

Unfortunately, just as efforts to protect the environment in Louisiana are often stymied by backlash from the oil industry, attempts to alter national energy policy have met with similar opposition. Consider the example of the Global Climate Coalition (GCC). Though the group's name may lead one to suspect it's an environmental organization, the GCC was actually a group representing industries whose profits were tied to fossil fuel consumption. Created in 1989 in response to the first Intergovernmental Panel on Climate Change (IPCC) report on the science of climate change, early members included Amoco, the American Petroleum Institute, Chevron, Chrysler, Exxon, Ford, General Motors, Shell Oil, Texaco, and the partisan-supported US Chamber of Commerce.

For more than a decade, the GCC led an aggressive (and well-funded) lobbying and public relations campaign to convince the public and politicians alike that there was no need to act to combat climate change. In addition to challenging the scientific integrity of the IPCC process, the GCC questioned the fundamental science behind the specter of climate change. The organization distributed a video to hundreds of journalists maintaining that increased levels of carbon dioxide would increase crop production and help feed the hungry people of the world. Scientifically speaking, increasing concentrations of carbon dioxide *could* increase plant growth in some parts of the world, within limits—but this narrow viewpoint completely ignores the myriad other negative consequences that would result.

Even as the GCC publicly denounced the science behind climate change, a document filed in a federal lawsuit revealed that their own scientific and technical experts had already stated in internal reports that the science could not actually be refuted. But, as it turns out, the GCC didn't really have to prove the science of climate change to be wrong. All they had to do was spread enough doubt and confusion to reduce public concern and delay government action—and at this goal they largely succeeded. Some environmentalists have compared their tactics to those once used by the tobacco industry, which for decades insisted that the science linking cigarette smoking to lung cancer was uncertain.

In the lead up to the first big international conference to tackle the issue of climate change, Earth Summit in Rio de Janeiro in 1992, the GCC and other industry interests successfully lobbied the US government to avoid any mandatory controls on carbon dioxide and other greenhouse gas emissions. Then, throughout the 1990s, the GCC conducted a multi-million-dollar advertising campaign in the United States challenging the merits of reducing carbon emissions and the Kyoto Protocol itself. That campaign claimed that emission regulations would only result in unemployment, reduced economic growth, and extremely high energy prices for consumers.

The GCC website, which has since been deactivated, was decorated with numerous photos of happy children playing in idyllic farms, but it did not provide any information about the organization's budget or the sources of its funding. And, since the GCC was not registered as a non-profit organization, it was not required to make public disclosures of its Internal Revenue Service (IRS) tax filings. From the information that is publicly available, however, it is clear that the Global Climate Coalition spent tens of millions of dollars opposing action on climate change. According to the *Los Angeles Times*, it spent at least $13 million in 1997 just on its anti-Kyoto ad campaign—an amount roughly equivalent to Green-peace's entire annual budget. Additionally, Common Cause, a group that investigates the effects of money in politics, has documented more than $63 million in contributions from members of the GCC to pro-oil politicians between 1989 and 1999.

However, as it became clearer that the science behind climate change was irrefutable and the need to react to climate change was real, a number of GCC members reconsidered the negative public-relations implications of their involvement in the group. DuPont and British Petroleum (now BP) left the GCC in 1997; Shell Oil withdrew in 1998; Ford departed in 1999; and DaimlerChrysler, General Motors, and Texaco opted out in 2000. Then, in 2002, the GCC decided, in its own words, to "deactivate." Before its website was also deactivated, it claimed "the industry voice on climate change has served its purpose by contributing to a new national approach to global warming." And what was that national approach? No action at all. In fact, some former GCC members, including the National Association of Manufacturers and the American Petroleum Institute, even today continue to lobby against any law or treaty that would sharply curb emissions of carbon dioxide.

•   •   •

While the GCC and other industry interests undoubtedly played a role in discouraging US action on climate change in the international arena, what about our energy policy here at home? Unfortunately, the hydrocarbon industry has left a big blot there too.

When President George W. Bush took office in 2001, one of his very first actions was to create the National Energy Policy Development Group, nicknamed the "Energy Task Force." Vice President Dick Cheney (a former CEO at Halliburton, one of the world's largest providers of oil-field products and services) was appointed as the chairman. The group was supposed to develop a national energy policy that would help the private sector and state and local governments "promote dependable, affordable, and environmentally sound production and distribution of energy for the future."

Besides Mr. Cheney, the Energy Task Force was comprised of the secretaries of the State, Treasury, Interior, Agriculture, Commerce, Transportation, and Energy Departments, as well as other cabinet and senior administration-level officials. The members held meetings over the course of three and a half months to develop their policy recommendations. During these meetings, the Task Force solicited input from other experts regarding US energy policy.

But from whom, exactly, did they get this input? None of the meetings were open to the public and the White House refused to release a list of participants. However, evidence indicates that the policy recommendations came primarily from petroleum, coal, nuclear, natural gas, and electricity industry representatives and lobbyists. The *Washington Post* obtained documents showing that executives from major oil corporations—Exxon-Mobil, Conoco, and Shell—met frequently with Task Force participants while they were developing the policy. Cheney was also reported to have met personally with the chief executive officer of BP. It seems at least forty meetings took place between the Energy Task Force and representatives of the energy industry and its interest groups. But, when asked, most of these executives said they had not participated or did not know about it (though they were not under oath when answering).

If the Energy Task Force was accepting input from the oil industry, surely it also accepted input from the environmental perspective as well, right? Well, sort of. On April 4, 2001, representatives of thirteen environmental groups were able to meet with the Task Force, though Mr. Cheney himself did not attend that meeting. Those who attended report that half the meeting was spent on various members introducing themselves, and no further meetings with environmental groups ever took place. These environmental groups speculate that the single meeting in which they were allowed to participate was only an attempt to appease them, since a draft of the final report had apparently already been written *before* the meeting took place.

The extreme secrecy surrounding how the Energy Task Force made its decisions prompted Judicial Watch, an organization that attempts to promote transparency and accountability in government, to file requests for disclosure of Task Force materials under the Freedom of Information Act, a law that grants public access to government-held data. When the Bush administration denied the requests to make the information public, Judicial Watch and the Sierra Club sued. They argued that the refusal was a violation of the Federal Advisory Committee Act of 1972, which requires committees set up by the president to provide advice and conduct their business in public. But, Mr. Cheney pointed out, there is an exception to this law. If the committee is comprised entirely of federal employees and officials, then they can conduct their meetings in secret. But while the official membership of the Energy Task Force fit these parameters, Judicial Watch and the Sierra Club argued that so many energy industry lobbyists were so deeply involved in the process that they were effectively members of the committee, and thus the law should require what went on at these meetings to be made public.

In July 2002, a district court judge ruled that Judicial Watch and the Sierra Club deserved to know the degree to which private citizens and corporations had taken part in the work of the Energy Task Force. Cheney, however, did not accept this ruling and appealed to the US Court of Appeals, arguing that complying with the ruling would force him to reveal information that by law he was not obligated to reveal. The US Court of Appeals agreed with the first judge and ruled that Cheney had to disclose at least some of its records to show how the Task Force had developed its recommendations. Cheney appealed again, this time to the US Supreme Court.

The Supreme Court's ruling was sympathetic to the White House's need to insulate itself from lawsuits, but it did not actually rule on whether the transparency law ought to be applied. Instead, it sent the case back to the lower courts. Despite avoiding the actual issue at hand, the ruling still provoked a significant amount of press attention because Justice Antonin Scalia—who supported Cheney's side of the argument—refused to recuse himself from the case even though he had gone duck hunting with Cheney while the case was still pending (coincidentally, in Louisiana). A Supreme Court Justice's decision on recusal (whether or not to abstain from participation in a case where there might be a conflict of interest) is final and cannot be challenged. In the end, in May 2005, the US Court of Appeals finally ruled that the Energy Task Force did not have to disclose information about its deliberations.

Today, we still don't know exactly how Cheney's Task Force made its decisions. What we do know is that although the final report mentions the importance of energy efficiency and conservation, as a whole their recommendations have a decidedly pro-energy slant. We know that much of the wording contributed by Chevron's CEO concerning how the government could "eliminate federal barriers to increase energy supply" were incorporated directly into the final report. These recommendations included easing permitting rules, scaling back regulations and oversight of offshore drilling, and a request to lift the drilling moratorium on portions of the outer continental shelf—which President Bush in fact did in

2008. The American Petroleum Institute also offered a long list of suggestions for US energy policy, including a draft of a proposed executive order requiring all federal agencies to issue detailed statements on regulatory actions that might "adversely affect energy supply, distribution, or use." The draft was nearly identical to an order President Bush issued just two months later. The Task Force's final report also presented an extremely rosy picture of the offshore drilling industry, stating that newer drilling methods "practically eliminate spills from offshore platforms" and "enhance worker safety, lower the risk of blowouts, and provide better protection of groundwater resources."

The full extent to which the Energy Task Force recommendations may have guided decisions at federal agencies is still unclear, particularly when it comes to the notoriously lax Minerals Management Service (MMS), which was in charge of overseeing drilling on the outer continental shelf. For example, did their pro-energy recommendations play a role in a 2003 MMS decision not to require offshore rigs to install acoustic shut-off switches? These remote-controlled switches, required in other countries like Norway and Brazil, are put in place to seal off an underwater well even if the rig above is destroyed. When the MMS considered requiring installation of this particular failsafe, oil companies complained about the $500,000 price tag (which was exaggerated) and argued that the switches were ineffective. Ultimately, the MMS made the switches optional. The Macondo well was not outfitted with such a device—but if it had been, the *Deepwater Horizon* disaster would most likely have been prevented. The MMS also failed to implement new cementing policies or act on known concerns about other key components on drilling rigs.

Many of the recommendations made by the Energy Task Force were eventually adopted into the 2005 Energy Policy Act. That legislation provided $6 billion in subsidies for oil and gas development and waived royalty payments in several regions in the United States. Some companies were allowed by law to pay their royalties with oil, rather than money, which is a considerably less transparent system that is more vulnerable to abuse. The 2005 Energy Policy Act also provided $1.5 billion in direct payments to companies to incentivize drilling deepwater wells, while at the same time curtailing the authority of states to oversee oil and gas exploration off their coasts under the Coastal Zone Management Act. The law also weakened environmental protections for offshore drilling, making it easier to exclude a broad range of exploration and drilling activities from

10.3. The Natural Arches region in Utah is one of the scenic sites the US Congress has been under pressure to open up to drilling. *Photo by the authors.*

analysis under the National Environmental Policy Act—a fact that has been cited as a reason that the *Deepwater Horizon* site was not subjected to a more thorough environmental scrutiny prior to drilling.

As the Bush administration's second term drew to a close, it made one final decision that conservationists called "a fire sale" and the administration's "last great gift to the oil and gas industry." On December 19, 2008, the US Bureau of Land Management (BLM) announced an auction of more than fifty thousand acres of oil and gas parcels alongside, and sometimes within view, of three national parks in Utah: Arches, Canyonlands, and Dinosaur. One potential drilling parcel was located just 1.3 miles from Delicate Arch, a natural bridge so iconic that it's on Utah's license plates. If drilling were allowed to occur on that parcel, visitors to Arches National Park would be able to see drilling machinery while looking through the arch.

This issue prompted an act of civil disobedience from environmental activist Tim DeChristopher, a twenty-seven-year-old economics major at the University of Utah. DeChristopher decided to participate in the auction, and actually managed to win $1.7 million in leases—even though he had no intention of paying or means to pay. While many environmentalists view him as a hero for attempting to protect the land in question, he was convicted in 2011 of interfering with and making false representations at a government auction. He was sentenced to two years in prison, fined $10,000, and ordered to serve three years probation.

In the meantime, an alliance of environmental groups filed a lawsuit to try to halt any further leasing in these regions, arguing in part that drilling would pollute the air in the legally protected national parks. In January 2009, a judge granted a temporary restraining order to prevent the BLM from moving forward with the leases. Then, in its first action to overturn Bush administration energy policies, the Obama administration announced in February 2009 that it would cancel the drilling leases on more than 130,000 of the acres in question. Interior Secretary Ken Salazar announced, "We need to responsibly develop our oil and gas supplies to help reduce our dependence on foreign oil, but we must do so in a thoughtful and balanced way that allows us to protect our signature landscapes and cultural resources."

In response, energy producers sued, challenging the Obama administration's cancellations of the leases. A US district judge ruled in September 2010 that the lawsuit came too late, because the oil companies had failed to file within the statutory ninety days of the February 2009 announcement. Although this decision was appealed, as of this writing it appears that the position of the Obama administration has prevailed.

Overall, then, it seems that many of the policy and regulatory failures that laid the groundwork for the *Deepwater Horizon* disaster and our continued dependence on nonrenewable oil can be traced back to the Bush-Cheney era. And, although we can't be sure exactly what went on with the Energy Task Force, it seems clear that oil companies and energy industry lobbyists indeed dominated the development of US energy policy. This has resulted in a regulatory system that is full of loopholes favorable to the industry and agencies that are supposed to be overseeing the industry that instead are being essentially run by oil lobbyists.

◆ ◆ ◆

Even after the devastating results of the *Deepwater Horizon* disaster, oil and gas interests along the Gulf Coast have largely succeeded in continuing to block reform. After that devastating spill, President Barack Obama announced a six-month freeze on new deepwater drilling, a temporary moratorium that affected about thirty-three future projects. Although not a single oil-producing well in the Gulf was actually shut down, Louisiana governor Bobby Jindal declared that Obama's temporary moratorium was a "second disaster," on par with the devastation of the oil spill itself.

But the opposition didn't stop there. A federal district judge in New Orleans (who himself had significant personal energy investments) ruled against the moratorium, claiming outlandishly that it could eliminate up to 150,000 jobs and cause "irreparable harm" to the Gulf economy. In fact, the actual potential job loss was closer to a few hundred jobs, and BP had already agreed to compensate those particular workers. Nevertheless, Louisiana senator Mary Landrieu held up President Obama's nominee for the Office of Management and Budget, a totally unrelated issue, due to her belief that the temporary pause in deepwater drilling was having "detrimental impacts" on her state.

None of this reduction in production ever materialized, however. Despite the oil spill, the offshore tracts produced more oil by a big margin in 2010 than in 2009. The Louisiana Workforce Commission also declared in a December 2010 press release that Louisiana employment was "at its highest level since April 2009."

But the powerful network supporting the anti-moratorium offensive had the desired result. By April 2010, the Obama administration had already approved nine permits for new deepwater projects in the Gulf, even though the moratorium wasn't supposed to be lifted until November and Congress had not yet passed any new legislation to address the key regulatory failures that had led to the *Deepwater Horizon* disaster in the first place.

And so, forty years after we were first alerted to the dangers of our national dependence on oil, the oil industry is still loudly singing the same tune: *drill, baby, drill.*

Chapter 11

THE OIL INDUSTRY'S GIFTS KEEP GIVING

In 2011, the five largest oil companies—ExxonMobil, BP, Shell, Chevron, and ConocoPhillips—reported a combined total of $140 billion *in profits*. ExxonMobil has been growing in leaps and bounds over the past few years. In 2005, it surpassed Walmart as the world's largest publicly held corporation (when measured by revenue; but Walmart still has the largest number of employees). In 2008, ExxonMobil was the world's most profitable company. In 2010, it occupied eight out of ten slots on the list of the "Largest Corporate Quarterly Earnings of All Time," and five out of ten on the "Largest Corporate Annual Earnings" list. In the first quarter of 2011, it reported profits of $10.7 billion. It then reported a virtually identical $10.7 billion in profits during the second quarter of 2011—a 41 percent increase over the same period in 2010 and a 161 percent increase over 2009. In fact, due partially to rising gas prices, Exxon had 35 percent more profits in 2011 than in 2010.

The other big oil companies have been doing quite well, too. Shell pocketed $6.9 billion in profits in the first quarter of 2011, followed by $8.7 billion in the second quarter. For Chevron it was $6.2 billion, and then another $7.7 billion. ConocoPhillips managed $3 billion, then $3.4 billion.

Given these huge profits, are the big oil companies using the money to invest in research that could create jobs, improve consumer offerings, and accelerate alternative energy production? Not really. In fact, three of the big five oil companies spent large fractions of their profits to buy back shares of their own stock. In the second quarter of 2011, ExxonMobil spent $5.5 billion, more than half of its total earnings, on stock buybacks. Chevron spent $1 billion this way, and ConocoPhillips spent $3.1 billion, or *91 percent of its profits* that quarter. These numbers were similar to what was done in the first quarter as well. Such buybacks are almost guaranteed to send stock prices up by boosting earnings on each outstanding share and thereby attracting more investors. They are also particularly self-serving, because who benefits the most from the increased stock prices? The company's top executives who hold stock options along with their multimillion-dollar salaries.

Meanwhile, the Gulf of Mexico and the coastal states still struggled to recover from the *Deepwater Horizon* disaster. Fishermen reported the worst season they could remember, with catches down 80 percent or more. Shrimp boats came home nearly empty or else hauled in discolored shrimp with no eyes or other deformities. Tar balls and dead dolphins continued to wash up on central Gulf beaches. Many locals reported strange rashes, coughing, breathing difficulty, eye irritation, and a host of other sudden health problems. Yet BP, the oil company responsible for the spill, still reported *profits* of $7.1 billion for the first quarter of 2011, followed by $5.6 billion for the second. The company plans to continue to expand its drilling operations in the Gulf.

The oil companies generate these huge profits mainly because of the rising price of oil. But has the success of these oil giants had a positive impact on the struggling US economy? Not really. Higher prices at the pump have taken big bites out of household budgets and other businesses, particularly the transportation industry. Overall consumer spending has accordingly been reduced. In April of 2011, the US government reported that the growth of the gross domestic product, the broadest measure of economic activity, had slowed from 3.1 percent in the fourth quarter of 2010 to 1.8 percent. Combined with soaring unemployment rates, high gasoline prices have taken a serious toll on average Americans and put a damper on US economic growth.

In the face of a struggling economy, what is it, exactly, that allows the oil industry to continue being so profitable? Here's the hard truth: in our present economic system, there is virtually no way for anyone to do without petroleum products. If you use mass transportation instead of your own vehicle to commute, you're still contributing to the consumption of oil, and the price of your bus or train ticket reflects that reality. Bicycling might be a bit more benign, except that your bike tires are still made from petroleum and so is your rain poncho. Even getting around on horseback won't necessarily break you free, because your horse feed was probably grown on farms fertilized by petroleum products and tilled and harvested by motor-driven equipment.

Unfortunately, the pricing of oil products is simply not subject to classical supply-and-demand economics as, for instance, are consumer electronics or hammocks. With such conventional products, the higher the price, the lower the demand. But with petroleum, higher prices have relatively little impact on demand, because consumers have no other options. Nor do other industries (e.g., the airlines or trucking) have much choice other than to pay the asking price. That asking price is set unilaterally, and not by those who own the natural resources in the first place—the citizens of the nation and their government. It is actually set by those who stand to profit from it.

• • •

So what is the federal government's legitimate role in assuring that consumers are not exploited too severely by the oil companies? One might argue that the price of petroleum products should be regulated in the same manner that public utility prices are regulated. After all, that would be in the public interest, right? But, of course, nothing like that has ever been considered by Congress, and it's unlikely it ever will. Instead, our politicians uncritically spout the theory that everyone benefits collectively from the oil industry because of the jobs it creates and the taxes it pays.

And how much *do* the oil companies pay in taxes? The American Petroleum Institute claims that the oil industry pays a tax rate of more than 40 percent. This number, however, is misleading because it lumps together US and foreign taxes, including taxes that are deferred but not yet paid. Although all US companies must pay taxes on profits earned abroad, they can defer that bite until they actually bring the money home. Instead of doing that, the big five oil companies use a tactic of hoarding cash overseas in tax havens, which cuts their actual tax rates drastically. For example, ExxonMobil uses at least twenty tax shelters—wholly owned subsidiaries domiciled in the Bahamas, Bermuda, and the Cayman Islands—that shelter the cash flow from their foreign operations in places like Angola, Azerbaijan, and Abu Dhabi. Overall, ExxonMobil has tens of billions in earnings it keeps permanently reinvested overseas.

Additionally, US companies are given a foreign tax credit for any taxes that they pay to other countries. Foreign governments can collect money from oil companies at least two ways: (1) through royalties—fees for depleting their national resources—or (2) through corporate income taxes. An oil company is allowed to deduct a royalty from its US tax liability as a cost of doing business, which may shave as much as 30 percent off the outfit's tax bill. Foreign income tax, on the other hand, is 100 percent deductible. And, with this loophole in place in the US tax code, many foreign governments call all their taxes "income taxes" in order to attract businesses from abroad. Altering this tax credit, which is essentially a subsidy, would save the US government billions of dollars each year.

Meanwhile, there are multiple other tax breaks in the statutes that allow oil companies to reduce their tax liability. For example, the domestic manufacturing tax deduction was designed to keep factories and jobs in the United States. Companies that manufacture in the United States can therefore deduct 9 percent of their income from operations that are attributed to domestic production. But is this really an appropriate tax break for oil companies drilling domestically? It's not as if they can pick up an oilfield and move it overseas. This is also one of the larger tax breaks that oil companies receive, and if eliminated, it would save the US government over $1.7 billion a year.

Then there's the percentage depletion allowance. For any industry, the value of capital equipment can be partially deducted. The oil companies use this tax break to treat oil in the ground as their own capital equipment, allowing them to deduct about 15 percent of the money generated from every single well from their taxes. But who is it that actually owns the oil when it's still in the ground? Is it actually capital equipment already belonging to the oil companies? Or is it a natural resource, belonging to the people of the United States, that the oil companies are simply extracting? Eliminating this tax break for oil companies would save the US government at least $1 billion every year.

Meanwhile, of course, like every other industry, oil producers are also allowed to write off normal business costs like wages, fuel, repairs, and hauling expenses.

So what is the result of all these tax breaks? In reality, despite billions of dollars in profits, oil companies routinely pay significantly less than the 35 percent top corporate tax rate. In 2011, Chevron paid just 19 percent in taxes. But perhaps the worst offender of the big five oil companies is ExxonMobil, which paid *absolutely nothing* in federal corporate income taxes in 2009, even though it made $45 billion in profits that year. For 2010, Citizens for Tax Justice reported that ExxonMobil paid only 17.6 percent in taxes, which is a lower tax rate than the average American. For 2011, Reuters reported that ExxonMobil's rate was closer to 13 percent.

Even though the oil companies don't contribute much to the federal government in the way of taxes, they do spend millions upon millions of dollars every year trying to influence and control it. The Center for

Responsive Politics reports that ExxonMobil spent $27,430,000 on lobbying in 2009 alone. OpenSecrets.org reports that the big five oil companies collectively spent $75 million on lobbying in just the first half of 2011. This helps explain why Democrats (some of whom have been trying to eliminate tax breaks for oil companies for many years) have made such little headway on this issue.

The oil industry argues that these tax breaks encourage domestic oil production and provide jobs for millions of Americans. Critics say that such subsidies are unwarranted, especially given the fiscal challenges the United States is currently facing—not to mention the huge profits the oil companies are bringing in. Nancy Pelosi, minority leader of the US House of Representatives, has stated, "There is no reason American taxpayers should subsidize Big Oil's profits." Representative Ed Markey, a Democrat from Massachusetts, agrees: "Instead of asking seniors for a cut in Medicare or Social Security, it's time for the oil companies to do their part and contribute to solving our debt crisis."

President Barack Obama has consistently called on Congress to end the over-generous federal subsidies to the oil industry, arguing that the money should instead be spent on alternative energy sources and conservation. But, on March 29, 2012, the most recent attempt to end these oil subsidies was rejected by the US Senate. Although fifty-one senators were in favor of ending the subsidies and only forty-seven were opposed, the vote fell short of the sixty votes needed to overcome the threatened Republican filibuster.

Is there an explanation for why so many Republican senators would want to keep providing billions of dollars in tax breaks to what is already the most profitable industry in the history of humankind? Such subsidies are not widely recognized as good economic policy; even some economists on the right have argued that they should be eliminated. They are also not popular; an NBC News poll found that 74 percent of Americans would like to do away with most tax breaks for oil companies. Republican senators who would like to get rid of such overly favorable tax treatment include Mark Kirk from Illinois, Susan Collins from Maine, Dan Coats from Indiana, and John Thune from South Dakota. Perhaps most shockingly, former President George W. Bush, the quintessential Republican oilman, is on record as saying that we simply don't need oil subsidies when the price of oil is above $55 per barrel. Today, oil costs more than twice that amount.

So why haven't such excessive tax breaks been repealed? The answer is actually pretty clear. The fifty-one senators who did support repealing such subsidies collectively received $5,873,600 in campaign contributions from Big Oil, or about $115,170 per senator. And what about the forty-seven senators who voted to protect Big Oil's tax breaks? Collectively, they received $23,582,500 in campaign contributions from the petroleum industry, or about $501,755 per senator—more than four times as much.

• • •

As we discussed in chapter 10, even the most optimistic forecasters agree that global oil production will soon pass its peak and begin to decline. Some scientists argue that we have already reached the peak. So, when conventional techniques have extracted the most easily available oil, will the political power and influence of the oil industry also decline?

Not automatically. Aside from campaign contributions to friendly politicians, the oil industry also spends a great deal of money researching and advancing techniques for extreme methods of oil and gas extraction. Perhaps the most controversial of these techniques today is induced hydraulic fracturing, or "fracking" for short.

Fracking is a technique developed by oil and gas companies to release deeply trapped petroleum and natural gas. Here's basically how it works: A well bore is drilled into a reservoir rock formation, generally five thousand to twenty thousand feet down, then the bit is twisted so the borehole continues horizontally for up to another mile or so. At that point, a highly pressurized fracking liquid is injected into the well. The pressure of this liquid creates new cracks and channels in the rock, which can allow for recovery of hydrocarbons that would formerly have been inaccessible. According to the Interstate Oil and Gas Compact Commission, almost 90 percent of oil and gas wells in the United States today undergo some degree of fracking to stimulate production.

There are, however, some major environmental concerns associated with the fracking process. For starters, only 30 to 50 percent of the fracking fluid is ever recovered; the rest is left permanently underground. And although an average well can use up to 5 million gallons of water over its lifetime for fracking, it's not just water that is being pumped underground. Fracking fluid is typically a slurry of water, proppants, and chemical additives. Proppants are particles, such as resin-coated sand or high-strength ceramic materials, which are designed to hold fractures open once they have been created. Chemical additives usually make up less than 2 percent by weight of the total fluid, but they can vary widely in toxicity. Some additives are safe enough to be used in food products and others are used in household products (like soaps, furniture polishes, and paints); but others are known toxins, carcinogens (cancer-causing chemicals), or neurotoxins (chemicals that damage the nervous system and can cause brain disorders). The latter sometimes include lead, uranium, mercury, ethylene glycol, radium, methanol, hydrochloric acid, and/or formaldehyde.

A 2011 study identified 632 chemicals used in natural gas fracking operations, 279 of which have not been well described in scientific literature, which means that they have still not been sufficiently studied to determine all of their possibly detrimental health effects. Of the 353 that had been studied, more than 75 percent could affect skin, eyes, respiratory, and gastrointestinal systems; about 50 percent could affect brain, nervous, immune, and cardiovascular systems; 37 percent could affect the endocrine system; and 25 percent were known carcinogens and mutagens. The study also indicated that these chemicals posed possible long-term health effects that might not appear immediately. A US House of Representatives Investigative Report from the same year stated that of the 750 compounds often used in fracking, more than 650 contained chemicals that are known or possible human carcinogens.

Luckily, many of these chemicals are regulated under the Safe Drinking Water Act (SDWA). So that should keep our groundwater from getting dangerously contaminated, right?

Wrong. Despite the widespread use of fracking and the risks it poses to human health and safe drinking water, the EPA currently *does not* regulate the injection of fracking fluids under the SDWA. Why not? Because the 2005 Energy Policy Act officially exempts fracking fluids from drinking water regulation. This exception has become known as the "Halliburton Loophole," partly because it was recommended by former vice president Cheney's Energy Task Force (which we discussed in chapter 10). Before taking office, Cheney was the CEO of Halliburton, the company that patented fracking in the 1940s and remains one of the three largest manufacturers of fracking fluids today. Additionally, Halliburton staff members were actively involved in a 2004 EPA study that claimed fracking "poses little or no threat" to drinking water and concluded that no further study of fracking was necessary.

Although the Occupational Safety and Health Administration (OSHA) requires companies to submit a "Material Safety Data Sheet," or a list of chemical components in the products they use, so safety can be determined (and this even applies to college chemistry labs), a company is allowed to withhold information if it is designated as "proprietary" (information considered to be a trade secret). Part of the argument supporting the Halliburton Loophole is that the chemicals used in fracking are trade secrets. The US House of Representatives Investigative Report from 2011 indicated that between 2005 and 2009, there were 279 chemical products used in fracking that had at least one component listed as a trade secret.

Without knowing what chemicals are being included in fracking fluid, regulators cannot easily test for their presence in nearby groundwater. This prevents regulators from documenting changes over time and thus makes it difficult to prove that fracking is (or is not) contaminating the environment with toxic substances. According to the Oil and Gas Accountability Project, "the oil and gas industry is the only industry in America that is allowed by the EPA to inject known hazardous materials—unchecked—directly into or adjacent to underground drinking water supplies."

Although the oil and gas industry argues that fracking is perfectly safe and that further regulation would only deter domestic oil and gas production, there have been over one thousand documented cases of water contamination near fracking sites, as well as cases of sensory, respiratory, and neurological damage due to ingested, contaminated water. Common complaints include murky or cloudy water, black or gray sediments, iron precipitates, soaps, black jelly-like grease, floating particles, increased methane, gassy tastes, and rashes from showering.

In 2009, thirteen water wells located near fracking sites in Dimock, Pennsylvania, were contaminated with methane; one of those water wells even exploded. Drinking water was also contaminated with arsenic, manganese, aluminum, iron, and lead, all at several times the federally mandated maximum contaminant level for safe drinking water. Even today, confusion still remains regarding whether the water in Dimock is safe to drink. In December 2011, the EPA sent an email to several residents indicating that the water was fine. A month later, in January 2012, the EPA reversed its position and asked its hazardous site cleanup division to take immediate action to protect public health. In the meantime, Cabot Oil and Gas, the company conducting the nearby fracking, has financially compensated residents and even constructed a pipeline to bring in clean water. But the company still denies that "any of the issues in Dimock have anything to do with hydraulic fracturing."

In the town of Pavillion, Wyoming, complaints from residents about the quality of their drinking water prompted the EPA to conduct a groundwater investigation. The EPA discovered methane and other chemicals, such as phthalates, in private well water. Samples from the local aquifer also contained gasoline, diesel fuel, benzene, toluene, xylene, methane, and other synthetic chemicals used in fracking fluid. The benzene concentrations found in these samples were well above SDWA standards. In December 2010, the EPA issued a report stating that fracking was the most likely source of this groundwater contamination. The US Department of Health and Human Services' Agency for Toxic Substances and Disease Registry has recommended that owners of tainted wells use alternative sources of water for drinking and cooking, as well as being sure to have proper ventilation when showering. Encana, one of North America's largest natural gas producers, is funding the alternate water supplies—though not admitting any responsibility for the contamination, of course.

Despite these instances of contaminated drinking water, Ohio governor John Kasich has decided to encourage oil and gas companies to partner with the state of Ohio to make fracking a major component of his economic plan. (Perhaps not coincidentally, Kasich also received about $214,000 in campaign contributions from the oil and gas industry.) Before 2011, there were only a few hydraulically fractured wells operating in Ohio, but by February 2012 there were forty—and the governor's spokesperson estimates there could be five times as many by next year. But while some folks in the state of Ohio may benefit economically from increased fracking within its borders, it seems clear that nobody is properly respecting the rights of the *majority* of the affected Ohio landowners.

In October 2011, More Welch, an Ohio resident, attended an open house hosted by Cunningham Energy to inquire about what it would mean to sell the rights to the oil and gas under his land. Representatives from Cunningham Energy, a West Virginia–based oil and gas company, were outright deceptive in answering his questions, misleading Welch about the terms of the lease and quoting him a vastly under-market price. When Welch asked if the company used chemicals in fracking, a Cunningham representative first told him, "We don't put any chemicals down in the ground. We just use regular, fresh water." Later another representative backtracked and said they use "sand and water with household chemicals" like "dishwashing detergent."

In response to incidents like this, Democrats in the Ohio state legislature have introduced bills that would require the disclosure of chemicals used in fracking. Another bill proposes a moratorium on fracking in Ohio until the EPA concludes a study of its effects on drinking water. A recent poll found that 72 percent of Ohioans would support this move. But industry resistance and lobbying has been fierce, and Republicans have stonewalled such bills at the committee level.

So can anything be done about the negative health and environmental impacts of fracking? In his 2012 State of the Union Address, President Obama stated his intention to force fracking companies to disclose the chemicals they use. Then in April 2012, Obama signed an executive order establishing a new high-level task force on natural gas development, to ensure that advanced drilling techniques, including fracking, are "safe and responsible." Natural gas industry groups have criticized the order, arguing that state-level oversight is already good enough. Meanwhile, environmental groups point to contaminated drinking water in Dimock and Pavillion and hope that federal oversight of fracking can be improved by the task force.

There has also been an attempt by the US Congress, in both the House and the Senate, to pass a bill that would amend the SDWA to repeal the Halliburton Loophole exemption. The proposed Fracking Responsibility and Awareness of Chemicals Act (FRAC Act) would require oil and gas companies to disclose the types, amounts, and combinations of chemicals used in the fracking process. By requiring full public disclosure, the FRAC Act would give regulatory agencies and the public—including the people directly impacted—the information they need to conduct comprehensive water testing and trace potential contamination. Oil and gas companies would also be required to apply for a permit from the EPA before they injected any chemicals near drinking water supplies. Although the FRAC Act was introduced on June 9, 2009, the 111th US Congress adjourned without taking any action. And though the bill has been reintroduced in both houses, as of this writing, Congress still has not passed the FRAC Act.

A few oil- and gas-producing states have taken matters into their own hands and developed their own regulations governing fracking. In New York, the town board of Dryden (adjacent to Ithaca and the Cornell University campus) passed a zoning law that prohibited gas drilling within town limits. In February 2012, a New York state court ruled for the first time that towns have the right to ban drilling if they want to, despite a state law on the books promoting the development of oil and gas. The court agreed with the town's argument that New York state laws shouldn't override the authority of local governments to protect their constituents. This is a decision that could potentially set a national precedent for how local governments can regulate gas drilling and fracking.

However, other attempts to deal with drilling and fracking at the local level have met with considerably less success. Although a 2009 decision by the Pennsylvania Supreme Court upheld municipal rights to develop zoning laws that excluded oil and gas drilling, the oil and gas industry fiercely lobbied the Pennsylvania legislature to rewrite the state's oil and gas laws to overcome this barrier. The result was Act 13, which took effect in April 2012 and gives gas companies in Pennsylvania the right to drill anywhere, overturn local zoning laws, and seize private property. It even deters physicians from disclosing specific health impacts from fracking fluids. The law also empowers the state's Public Utilities Commission—a body of appointed, not elected, officials—to withhold revenues from towns that refuse to delete anti-drilling provisions from local zoning codes. The bill was passed over objections from local officials, environmentalists, and a handful of legislators who argued that it goes against three hundred years of local zoning and elevates the rights of gas companies above the civil rights of people and communities. Although Act 13 raises many constitutional issues that could become avenues for future legal challenges, for the time being the oil and gas industry has gotten everything they wanted in Pennsylvania—and more.

•   •   •

In addition to controversial techniques like fracking, the oil and gas industry has been actively fighting for increased access to deepwater drilling—before the full impact of the *Deepwater Horizon* disaster has even been resolved. Drillers are already probing dozens of new oilfields across the Gulf of Mexico, and there are more rigs designed to drill in deepwater—defined as two thousand feet or deeper—than there were before the catastrophic spill. By 2020, deepwater oil will likely account for around 9 percent of global oil production.

The Gulf of Mexico is a particularly attractive location for deepwater drilling. It's centrally located to the world's biggest consumer of oil—the United States—where drillers can easily tap into a vast network of pipelines and refineries. It's in a politically stable part of the world, and, despite industry complaints, royalties, taxes, and regulation in the United States are among the lowest in the world. Also, its untapped oilfields are enormous. Currently, the Gulf produces an average of 1.5 million barrels of oil per day, which amounts to 27 percent of US oil output, but satisfies only 8 percent of US oil demand. (The remainder of US demand is satisfied with other sources of domestic oil and foreign imports.)

But while politicians in Louisiana have continued to push for increases in deepwater drilling, the politics of drilling in a neighboring Gulf Coast state have turned decidedly sour since the *Deepwater Horizon* disaster. Former Republican Florida governor Charlie Crist withdrew his support for offshore drilling as the impact of the 2010 oil spill spread. Crist argued that the BP calamity was proof that it simply wasn't possible to have drilling that is safe enough or clean enough, and that it would be devastating if a spill like BP's were to occur near Florida's beaches, since the state of Florida depends so heavily on tourism. A Quinnipiac University Poll in June 2010 found that 51 percent of Floridians agreed with Crist and opposed more offshore drilling. Although this may not seem like much of a majority, it was a massive swing from two months earlier, when only 27 percent of Floridians opposed increased drilling. With the public behind him, Crist called a special session of the Florida legislature to advance a constitutional amendment that would prevent oil drilling off Florida's immediate coastline. That session, however, adjourned quickly, with a party-line vote of sixty-seven to forty-four. The Republicans were in favor of adjourning the session and ignoring the proposed constitutional amendment.

The Gulf of Mexico is not the only place where increased deepwater drilling is being considered. In October 2011, the Obama administration announced that it was moving forward with oil-drilling leases off the coast of Alaska—leases originally issued by the Bush administration in 2008—despite environmental groups and Alaskan native organizations claiming that US regulators don't know enough about the Arctic's marine life and ecosystems to properly supervise drilling in the region. In March 2012, the US Department of the Interior approved Shell's proposed oil spill response plan for drilling in the Arctic Ocean north of Alaska. This effectively grants permission for Shell to begin exploratory drilling. The proposed drilling season would end in October, when it gets too dark and icy to drill in Arctic waters.

In the wake of the *Deepwater Horizon* disaster, the Department of the Interior required Shell's oil spill response plan to prepare for a blowout three times larger. Shell's plans include the use of a cap, similar to the one that failed to seal the gushing BP well, as well as numerous sensors and automatic shut-off systems that are more advanced than what the BP rig had. If oil did enter the water, Shell and the Department of the Interior agreed that containing it with booms would be ineffective, as floating sea ice would obstruct their use. Backup plans include dispersants, burning the oil, and skimming it off the surface.

Environmental groups, meanwhile, have been quick to point out that these backup plans have the potential to be ineffective in Arctic oceans. Dispersants can leave marine life more exposed to oil's harmful effects, and it's not clear they would even work at such northern latitudes—for even in mid-summer the low-angle sunlight and extremely cold water might fail to activate the chemicals. Flammable materials added to burn floating oil slicks are also likely to be less efficient in the Arctic. And although Shell plans to have icebreaker ships available to create sea paths for skimmers, the broken ice itself may make it more difficult to recover spilled oil. Not to mention that if oil gets under the ice, it could stay there almost indefinitely since it won't be degraded by sunlight or bacteria.

The last resort in the event of a spill would be to drill a relief well, which Shell is required to be able to do. However, drilling such a well could take anywhere from three to six months—time that wouldn't necessarily exist if a spill were to happen toward the end of summer, with its increasing darkness, cold, and encroaching ice. There's also the risk of early winter storms, like the one that happened in 2010, just over a week after Shell's proposed drilling season would end. That brutal storm covered an area twice the size of Texas and produced blizzard conditions, coastal flooding, and hurricane-force winds, prompting Alaska's governor to declare a state of emergency. Had a spill happened in close proximity to such a storm, no cleanup response would have been possible. To avoid such dangers, ideally, two wells should be drilled in parallel, in order to have a relief well ready at all times, even though this would add hugely to Shell's drilling costs. Thus far, the Department of the Interior has not required Shell to take this precaution.

Despite successfully having its oil spill plans for the Arctic approved, Shell is continuing to fight against the opponents of offshore drilling. In a unique legal approach, Shell filed suit in February 2012 against more than a dozen environmental organizations it thinks are likely to challenge its plans for drilling exploratory wells in the Arctic Ocean. Since the Arctic drilling season is so short, Shell wanted to make sure that environmental groups would not wait to file suit until the eve of drilling, which could delay operations for another full year.

•   •   •

Although oil and gas companies often work in concert to influence the way they are regulated, lately some members of the club have been fighting amongst themselves. In September of 2011, a federal report on the *Deepwater Horizon* disaster concluded that BP and its contractors—Halliburton and Transocean in particular—all share responsibility for the deadly explosion and the ensuing oil spill by violating a number of federal offshore safety regulations. The report stated that a key cause of the explosion was a faulty cement drilling barrier at the well site. But the report also concluded that BP was "ultimately responsible" for making sure operations were conducted at the site "in a way that ensured the safety and protection of personnel, equipment, natural resources, and the environment."

BP, however, was not accepting all this responsibility without a fight. In December 2011, it sued Halliburton over the quality of the cement slurry used to seal the well casing, and whose failure had apparently triggered the gusher. BP specifically claimed that Halliburton employees had intentionally destroyed the records of early test results performed on the same batch of cement slurry, as well as physical cement samples used in the testing, so as to "eliminate any risk that this evidence would be used against it at trial." BP also sued Transocean, which owned the rig, and Cameron International Corp, which had manufactured the failed blowout preventer. Various aspects of those civil lawsuits and countersuits promise to drag on for years to come.

On November 15, 2012, the US Justice Department and a federal grand jury indicted BP and three of its employees on *criminal* charges, including eleven counts of felony manslaughter and obstruction of Congress. In a news conference, Assistant Attorney General Lanny A. Breuer commented, "The explosion of the rig was a disaster that resulted from BP's culture of privileging profit over prudence." The company pleaded guilty and was immediately fined $4 billion—the highest fine in US history. The three indicted employees are still facing trial. This still leaves BP open to numerous civil cases, with potential liabilities beyond the many billions it has already spent in cleanup and as initial monetary restitution to the thousands of victims.

Amazingly, it was only one day after those criminal indictments—November 16, 2012—that another rig exploded in the Gulf of Mexico and killed three workers. This one, owned by Black Elk Energy Offshore Operations, was operating about thirty-five miles southeast of Grand Isle, Louisiana; and, fortunately, it didn't cause a spill. The Bureau of Safety and Environmental Enforcement (BSEE), however, immediately revealed that the company had been cited for forty-five "incidents of noncompliance" over the previous two years, in addition to an October accident that had resulted in the hospitalization of six workers. Oh, and most of the company's workers—including the three fatalities—had been hired in the Philippines. Once again, none of Black Elk's operations had anything to do with Louisiana jobs, nor were they even related to any more than a handful of *American* jobs for that matter.

So, given such an arrogant and irresponsible record of past performance, is there any reason to trust the oil and gas industry in the future?

Chapter 12

CAN AMERICA LEARN?

For more than a century now, the people of Louisiana have been cocooned in an experimental laboratory where the oil and petrochemical industries have been granted everything they've asked for. Numerous rounds of empirical results are now in, and as we've seen in previous chapters, the results aren't pretty. Still, the industry continues to try to dupe residents of other states into believing that the oil and petrochemical interests can be trusted to pursue the public good. Trusted to be environmentally responsible. Trusted to ensure worker safety. Trusted to create lots of well-paying jobs. Trusted to shower financial rewards on local and state economies. And trusted to make the nation and the world a better place for future generations.

Ah, if only those poor companies weren't subjected to so many pesky regulations (which, in fact, are rarely enforced). And not expected to pay so much in taxes (which, in fact, they don't). And not hounded by "liberal" reporters every time something goes wrong. And not have their lies and payoffs exposed from time to time by the minority of "maverick" politicians who decline to be bought off and must be silenced via negative campaign ads.

In fact, from the time of the very first oil well that polluted Jules Clement's rice farm in 1901, Louisiana has become the poster child for how things turn out when the oil industry is allowed to get its way over and over again. The industry promises to be environmentally responsible, yet it never has actually behaved that way. It vows that it can regulate itself, but it has never reliably done so. And while it claims to create jobs, the Louisiana Workforce Commission itself reports that only 3 percent of working Louisianans owe their livelihoods directly to the oil and gas industry. As for the promised prosperity, after more than a century of false industry claims and promises, Louisiana still ranks near the bottom of the fifty states in per-capita income, educational attainment, health, and virtually every other measure related to quality of life.

In addition to experiencing some of the worst effects of the *Deepwater Horizon* disaster, Louisiana has had quite a few of its own oil-related catastrophes. In 1980 an exploratory well at Lake Peigneur punctured the roof of a salt mine, turning an 11-foot-deep lake into a 1,300-foot-deep cauldron and destroying the personal property of numerous local residents. In 2005, the Mississippi River Gulf Outlet (MRGO), which oil companies had fiercely advocated, contributed immensely to the devastation caused by Hurricane Katrina by channeling the storm surge directly into St. Bernard Parish and parts of New Orleans. That flooding also triggered the release of 25,000 barrels of oil that irrevocably contaminated several thousand homes (many of them brand new) and businesses in St. Bernard Parish. Murphy Oil, the company responsible for that particular spill, ended up paying about $330 million to victims in a settlement—but never accepted any liability or admitted any wrongdoing.

The state of Louisiana is littered with abandoned drilling debris; there are presently 60,000 to 220,000 sites (estimates vary) requiring restoration. Most of these old well sites are on private property, but when surface owners attempt to sue for restoration, the judgments of the Louisiana courts are almost always more sympathetic to oil companies than to property owners. And, in addition to rusting, derelict drilling equipment, over 14,800 miles of pipelines and 3,000 miles of artificial channels slice through Louisiana's coastal wetlands, contributing to the erosion of more than 25,000 acres of land per year. Many of these pipelines are also corroded enough from saltwater that they are starting to leak or are in imminent danger of doing so, further contaminating Louisiana's environment.

Even though a diminishing amount of oil is being extracted through drilling in Louisiana, the oil industry continues to spend huge sums of money to control the state's government because so much petroleum is processed and refined there. While just 49 million barrels annually are presently extracted statewide, at least 1,089 million barrels enter Louisiana from a combination of outer continental shelf (OCS) production and foreign oil offloaded at the Louisiana Offshore Oil Port (LOOP).

Much of this petroleum is processed and refined in an eighty-five-mile corridor between Baton Rouge and New Orleans, where there is a denser conglomeration of oil refineries, plastic plants, and related chemical facilities than anywhere else in the United States. Unfortunately, since Louisiana is the worst state in the nation at enforcing clean air, clean water, and hazardous waste laws (both federal and its own), this dense corridor of industry has generated massive amounts of environmental

contamination and has earned itself the rude nickname "Cancer Alley."
Nearby residents have little hope of redress—either in stopping the siting of new petrochemical facilities or in getting compensation for their
illnesses—because local governments in Louisiana continue to support
the interests of industry over the needs of the commoners. In fact, when
the Tulane Environmental Law Clinic (TELC) stepped forward to provide
legal assistance to various injured low-income residents, then Governor
Mike Foster encouraged donors to withhold support from the university
and lobbied elected judges to change the student practice rule. The Louisiana Supreme Court dutifully complied.

Louisiana politicians also fiercely opposed President Barack Obama's
temporary moratorium on new deepwater drilling after the *Deepwater Horizon* disaster—despite their home state experiencing the worst
impacts of the spill. Even though the moratorium affected only about
thirty-three future projects, Governor Bobby Jindal declared that it was
a "second disaster," on a par with the devastation of the oil spill itself, and
Senator Mary Landrieu held up a nomination on a totally unrelated issue
due to her stance that the temporary pause in deepwater drilling was having "detrimental impacts" on Louisiana. Though none of this ostensible
harm ever materialized, the Obama administration ended up approving
new permits for deepwater projects before the moratorium was scheduled
to be lifted—and before the key regulatory failures that led to the *Deepwater Horizon* had been addressed.

In fact, most of the lawmakers in Louisiana behave as if they've forgotten the not-so-distant past, and they certainly seem oblivious to the lessons of history regarding regulation of the oil and gas industry. Of course,
the continuous gusher of campaign contributions from the oil and gas
industry isn't helping jog their memories of past failed promises. Of the
nine politicians who represented Louisiana in Washington in 2012, seven
of them received a combined total of about a million dollars from the oil
and gas industry (the exceptions are Representative Rodney Alexander,
who received only modest donations from oil and gas interests, and Representative Cedric Richmond, who received virtually none). Can it be a
mere coincidence that such politicians vote in favor of oil and gas interests
so consistently?

◆　◆　◆

More so than any of the world's other sovereign nations, the United States
is hugely dependent on oil. Our transportation sector is almost totally

reliant on it. The US military (the largest in the world by a factor of ten) gulps up huge quantities of the stuff, even in peacetime. Petroleum sustains much of our industrial sector, not just as a fuel, but also as a raw material for manufacturing a wide variety of products. Overall, oil has a huge impact on our nation's economy—some even argue that it is an economic necessity. And, as demand for petroleum continues to grow, the oil industry lobbyists insist that increased drilling, including deepwater drilling, is *essential.* But don't worry, they tell us, it's totally safe and won't hurt the environment. In fact, they contend that drilling is actually being *over-regulated* in America.

But does the oil industry's record actually support the claim that drilling is safe and environmentally friendly? History seems to tell a different story. A bit more than four decades ago, in 1969, several hundred thousand barrels of crude oil contaminated 35 miles of pristine coastline in Santa Barbara, California. Then, in 1979, around 500,000 barrels gushed into the Gulf of Mexico over a ten-month period from the *Ixtoc I* exploratory well. That oil spill wiped out fishing off the Mexican coast for more than two years. In 1989, between 257,000 and 710,000 barrels of oil (estimates vary) fouled shorelines in Alaska as far as 470 miles from the spot where the *Exxon Valdez* tanker crashed into a reef. Thousands of local fishermen lost their livelihoods and oil still remains on some of those shores today. Although that particular disaster was not directly a drilling accident, it was certainly attributable to our dependence on oil as well as the irresponsibility of the Exxon corporation in failing to prepare itself to contain and clean up such a spill.

Most readers surely remember the devastating impacts of the *Deepwater Horizon* disaster in 2010. The image of the burning rig, with flames surging fifty stories into the sky. The mourning families of the eleven workers who lost their lives. The frustrating months of failed attempts to contain the spill. And the horrifying sight of a blooming oil slick in the Gulf of Mexico, where at least 4.9 million barrels of crude oil polluted more than 500 miles of US coastline as well as the water column that supports a wide variety of sea life.

These tragedies, plus various other well blowouts and major discharges around the globe in recent decades, demonstrate in clear and painful terms just how devastating our reliance on oil has become. Unfortunately, however, we don't seem to be learning our lesson; although President Obama announced a temporary freeze on new deepwater drilling after the most recent spill, that moratorium was soon lifted and new deepwater drilling projects have been approved in the Gulf of Mexico and in the harsh Arctic environment off the coasts of Alaska. All without any significant changes or updates in drilling regulations or safety protocols. Which, once again, is exactly what the oil industry wanted.

• • •

Unfortunately, Louisiana politicians aren't the only ones being bought off by generous campaign contributions. To a remarkably large extent, oil and gas interests have succeeded in their crusade of devious persuasion aimed at lawmakers and voters across the country. After all, what could be more patriotic than assuring that US citizens (and their military) always have enough oil? Despite the stark example set by Louisiana, the promises from the oil and gas industry keep flowing—and politicians (as well as many of their constituents) keep swallowing them. Yet, rather than taking into consideration the effects their actions are having on human health, the economy, the environment, and the nation's future, the big oil companies only seem to be considering the effect their actions have on their own profit margins.

Clearly, mainstream America needs to ignore the industry's cries about being over-regulated and determine whether the oil and gas industry should actually be regulated *more*. For example, we may need to reconsider the protections provided by the 1990 Oil Pollution Act, under which prospective drillers are required to "prove" their ability to handle a "worst-case spill." BP's application to the former Mineral Management Service (MMS) under this law claimed they could handle a worst-case spill of 160,000 barrels per day. However, the company did not mention exactly how the oil would be captured or at what rate; it neglected to analyze how nearby wetlands would be affected or accessed; and it also didn't specify how cleanup personnel would be hired, trained, or mobilized. The MMS also waived the requirement for a focused environmental impact study, so the application was never sent to the EPA for review prior to drilling authorization. Then, when the *Deepwater Horizon* exploded, BP turned out to be incapable of containing even a tiny fraction of the amount of oil it claimed it could easily handle (exactly as did Exxon a few decades earlier). This curious Oil Pollution Act also places a liability cap of just $75 million per spill for offshore events, plus various direct costs—even though the price tag of the BP spill will ultimately total multiple billions. It's clear that this law is deeply flawed. It urgently needs to be revised in a manner that prioritizes the nation's environment ahead of the interests of the oil companies.

Although big oil spills are admittedly low-probability events, we do know that many such episodes have happened in the past. Does it make any sense to assume they won't occur again in the future? The impacts of each of the historical examples could have been mitigated to some extent through more cautious engineering, more comprehensive testing and inspection, more thorough environmental impact assessments, and more proactive crisis planning. With these precautions, maybe some of these accidents could have even been avoided entirely. But, unfortunately, additional precautions cost money—money that oil companies will never be willing to spend unless required to do so by stiff and well-enforced regulation.

In addition to the impacts of disastrous oil spills, history also teaches us about the negative impacts that disruptions in oil supplies can have on our highly oil-dependent economy. The 1973 Arab oil embargo and the 1979 Iranian revolution seriously shocked our economy—and those incidents were only *temporary*. Although the oil companies are reluctant to admit it, the reality is that oil and gas are non-renewable resources. No matter how you frame it, supplies of hydrocarbons are *finite*. Someday, we will pass global peak oil (we may have already done so) and cheap and plentiful oil will become a thing of the past. There is no escaping this conclusion, and no prospect of wishing away this fundamental fact. No amount of political rhetoric will reverse it. No quantity of political donations will deter it. Mankind *will* run out of oil, and sooner rather than later. Youngsters already alive today will live to see it happen. And that's that. Anyone who argues differently is either a fool or a liar.

Our excessive dependence on oil presents many threats to US interests—economically, militarily, politically, and environmentally. Reduced supplies will lead to ever-increasing oil prices, which will harm the livelihoods of everyday Americans. Already, billions of US dollars flow annually to hostile nations to pay for foreign oil—money that could be used to grow the domestic economy and create jobs at home. Our dependence on oil also keeps our military involved in politically volatile parts of the world and often ties our hands in the foreign policy arena by forcing us to depend on countries that do not share our other values. Meanwhile, the dangers of climate change have been proven to be quite real (evidenced by melting glaciers and polar ice, rising sea levels, and altered weather patterns, for instance). Shouldn't we stop listening to the oil lobbyists and shift our dependence from hydrocarbons to renewable sources of energy in order to protect our economy, sovereignty, and environment?

Such a much-needed shift will become increasingly difficult to make as both population and energy demand continue to grow. There's no doubt about it: we *need* energy. We need it for transportation. We need it to light and heat our homes and businesses. We need it to run our refrigerators, TVs, computers, and smart phones. Our dependence on energy and the use of electronic technology continue to grow every day (some of you may even be reading this book in digital form). But while we certainly do need energy, we *don't* need so much of it to come from hydrocarbons. It won't, however, be an easy task to convince the oil companies, who have billions of dollars sunk into the current energy system and are deriving huge profits from the production of oil, to stop lobbying against renewable energy and instead start investing in it.

◆ ◆ ◆

OK, the need for renewable energy has already been promoted before by numerous scientists and political analysts with little power to do anything about the situation. Realistically, then, is there anything that can be done to impede the hydrocarbon hucksters and their Pied Piper parade toward economic and environmental doom?

As a matter of fact, yes. It won't be simple, and some of the rich and powerful will certainly fight such a program tooth and nail. Nor will the ultimate goal of energy independence be accomplished quickly. The benefits, however, will slowly begin to accrue right from the beginning. Properly documented and reported, such interim gains will potentially be a powerful influence in keeping the nation on track over the decades to come.

The key needs to be a new national energy policy that would include all aspects of energy development, production, distribution, consumption, and taxation. Unlike the 2005 Energy Policy Act, which included the recommendations of Vice President Dick Cheney's secretive and hydrocarbon-industry-dominated Energy Task Force, the nation needs an energy policy that honestly takes into consideration the long-term impacts that our various energy sources and uses have on our economy and environment. The result should be an enforceable strategy to provide affordable, sufficient, and environmentally friendly energy to US residents. And not only for the present, but also for the future and for generations yet unborn.

Rather than remain vague about this, let's list a few specific possibilities. Some of the following strategies will admittedly be too controversial to adopt immediately or in the exact form presented here. However, given that there are always alternative ways to pluck a goose, the following ideas give a flavor of the kinds of proactive things that might be done:

- *Public Utility Designation.* The United States will never consider nationalizing its domestic oil companies, even though this step has been taken in numerous other nations, including Canada, Mexico, Russia, Ecuador, Iran, Iraq, Libya, Nigeria, Saudi Arabia, Venezuela, and Argentina. Short of such drastic government takeovers, however, domestic oil producers could be designated as *public utilities*, similar to our current electric companies and water companies. They would remain privately owned by their stockholders, but those companies' profits and product prices would be strictly regulated, with increases approved only after formal justifications and appropriate public hearings. Yes, there would be numerous legal and regulatory issues to work out here, but given that such standards have already been successfully developed for domestic electric and water companies and natural gas utilities, there is no reason a similar system cannot be created for oil producers and refiners. After all, whose oil is it? If the petroleum in the ground is indeed publicly owned, then shouldn't the public also have some control over how much it pays an oil company after those hydrocarbons are extracted, processed, and distributed?
- *Speculative Profiteering.* According to the Department of Energy, the average price per barrel of crude increased from $31.61 in July 2004 to $137.11 in July 2008. During this same period, oil production kept pace with demand while the costs of refining and distribution rose only modestly. Most of this huge price increase, it turns out, was due to a small army of futures speculators who drove up the tab, much as home prices grew so outlandishly during the last housing bubble.

  To the consumer, however, buying petroleum products is different than buying a home. You can bargain on the price of a home, and you can walk away and buy a cheaper one or not buy one at all. Not so with gasoline; prices at the pump seldom vary by more than a few cents per gallon, and if your car is out of gas, you probably have little choice but to buy some. In doing so, you are not just purchasing fuel, you are also pumping money into the bank accounts of the futures speculators. In April of 2012, the *New York Times* reported that approximately one dollar of the then-current price of gasoline was due to the financial shenanigans of futures speculators who never physically took possession of so much as a drop of the oil they were speculating on.

For such an economically essential commodity as oil, futures speculations should be banned and even criminalized in the interest of the public welfare and national security. After all, such speculation adds nothing of any value to the economy as a whole, but merely extorts money from the public and pumps it into a small number of already overflowing individual bank accounts.

• *Environmental Restoration.* Yes, drillers are already required by law to restore each site of their operations after they abandon it, which, unfortunately, usually means thirty years or more down the road. We now have clear evidence of the folly of this idea; oil companies have a virtually null track record of compliance. Not only is much of today's rural Louisiana a trash dump of derelict wells and equipment, but the same problem is also apparent in parts of other states, including Pennsylvania, Wyoming, Texas, and West Virginia. The federal EPA estimates that there are about 1.2 million abandoned wells nationwide and that 200,000 of them may not be properly plugged. Clearly, we cannot depend on the industry's mere promises to clean up their messes *after* their facilities are no longer productive; we need to insist that they demonstrate their good-faith intentions by cleaning up the environment *before* they begin to drill.

How would this work? Before a leaseholder would be allowed to bore a new well, that outfit would first need to restore several (say, two or three) previously abandoned sites. Those restoration sites wouldn't necessarily need to be the company's own; they could include wells originally drilled by companies that no longer exist (of which there are many). Either way, the prospective driller would earn vouchers allowing, say, one new well permit for every two sites restored to their pre-drilling condition. These vouchers could also be bought, sold, or traded. And they could be earned by restoring not only wellhead sites, but also the sites of defunct storage facilities and abandoned pipelines and canals (equating, for instance, a quarter-mile of canal to one wellhead). But wouldn't this add a lot to the price of gasoline? Not if the procedure is properly designed and integrated with a comprehensive national energy policy. After all, the oil companies are *already* supposed to be spending money on site restoration. Restrict their profits (possibly via public utility designation), eliminate third-party futures speculations, and make some adjustments to the tax codes, and there will be plenty of money to spend on restoring the messes the oil industry has left behind over the past century. And yes, such restoration will create numerous domestic jobs—*meaningful* jobs.

- *Revise the Corporate Tax Codes.* In 2009, ExxonMobil earned a profit of about $35 billion. Its federal income tax bite that year was $0. To accomplish this remarkable feat, the company maintained a full-time tax workforce of almost one thousand lawyers, accountants, analysts, and various support personnel. Together, those folks created and filed a tax return that ran to a whopping 24,000 pages—much too voluminous, in other words, for any individual IRS examiner to actually read, let alone critically analyze it.

  None of this tax-avoidance activity had any redeeming social value, nor did it create any more energy, since it was achieved largely by legally funneling otherwise-taxable profits into some twenty wholly owned ExxonMobil subsidiaries in other countries. In other words, this huge profit, which was extracted from the American consumer (who technically owned much of the oil in the first place), wasn't even plowed back into the US economy.

  Yes, the major portion of ExxonMobil's tax-avoidance success is due to offshore money-transfer schemes that are also available to other large corporations as well as to some wealthy individual Americans. Those beneficiaries all argue (usually with convoluted logic) that these tax-dodge loopholes should be retained and even expanded, even though in any given year as many as one-fourth of US corporations already pay no federal income taxes at all. The oil companies, however, get additional breaks not available to other sectors of the economy, in the form of a depletion allowance and an accelerated depreciation on equipment. Although *all* of these kinds of unpatriotic tax-dodge loopholes should clearly be repealed, the ones that preferentially favor the already-privileged oil companies should definitely be retracted. There are much better national-interest uses for such tax give-aways.

- *Replace Oil with Electricity and/or Hydrogen.* This aspect of a national energy policy will be helpful only if the electricity and/or hydrogen are generated from renewable sources (see below). Even then, it's not a complete savior because current technology doesn't allow some applications to run on electricity (aircraft and military tanks, for instance) and petroleum will still be needed as a raw material for making plastics and other materials. The idea, however, would be to channel the available petroleum only to those places where electrical energy is not currently a realistic alternative. This would eventually reduce the demand for petroleum by an estimated 50 to 80 percent.

Except in some of the northernmost states, for instance, few homes *need* to be heated by natural gas or fuel oil. Electric heat pumps usually work just fine, they are reliable, and their efficiencies can be enhanced in colder climates by burying their external heat exchangers below the frost line (suitably designed versions, of course). Hydrogen fuel, if the proper infrastructure is developed, can be a realistic home-heating alternative for even North Dakota and Alaska. And burning hydrogen produces no carbon dioxide (or worse, carbon monoxide) because its only combustion product is water vapor. As for cars, there are now electric versions that operate pretty well on rechargeable batteries or hydrogen fuel cells.

And where would the necessary hydrogen come from? No, you can't mine it, and any that happens to enter the atmosphere is so light that it quickly rises and floats off into space. It's easy to make, however, if you have ample electricity and some water. Every high school chemistry student learns how to do this, and, yes, you can actually do it in your own basement using tap water (but no, that wouldn't come close to being economically feasible).

The attainable goal, however, would be this: through tax codes, direct incentives, and (maybe) appeals to patriotism, transfer as much of the nation's energy needs as possible from petroleum to electricity and hydrogen.

• *Renewable Electricity.* No, this is not a pie-in-the-sky idea; wind-turbine technology is well proven and is currently being used commercially around the world. Even in the United States, several dozen large wind farms sprawl over deserts and farms in California, Texas, and Kansas. Although their capital costs remain slightly higher than other methods of electrical power production, the operating costs of wind turbines are quite low (since they use no fossil fuels at all except for lubrication). Of the top ten manufacturers of these devices, however, four are Chinese, two are German, one is Danish, one is in Spain, one in India, and only one (General Electric) is based in the United States.

The United States offers numerous geographical sites windy enough to generate significant amounts of electricity. Although a number of wind farms are operating profitably in the Great Plains, however, remaining undeveloped is the US continental shelf, where the cost of erecting pylons and the risk of tropical storms presently render the economics somewhat less attractive. On the other hand, wouldn't this be a great adaptive use for defunct oil platforms?

The other well-proven way to generate renewable electricity, of course, is through photovoltaic panels. Again, however, most of these devices are presently manufactured and used in countries other than the United States, including some nations that are not particularly sunny (Germany, for instance).

Clearly, a national energy policy should immediately encourage the greatly expanded use of existing wind and solar technologies for the generation of electricity and hydrogen.

• *Increase Research Funding for Other Renewable Energy Technologies.* Three technologies in particular offer tremendous promise if the practical challenges can be overcome. One is thermonuclear fusion, using heavy hydrogen extracted from seawater. A second is to exploit the natural thermal gradient in the oceans, which are considerably warmer near the surface than at depths of a few thousand feet. (The feasibility of this approach was demonstrated in a pilot project off the coast of Hawaii in the late 1970s, after which funding for further research was withdrawn by the Reagan administration.) A third possibility is to extract power from the Gulf Stream, which averages sixty miles in width, three thousand feet in depth, and flows at a speed of about five miles per hour.

• *High-Speed Rail.* In Florida, Governor Rick Scott killed a high-speed rail project approved by the previous administration despite the fact that the engineering work had been completed, most of the right-of-ways had been acquired, and two independent analytical studies had projected that the system would be profitable within a mere two to three years. It's not clear what the man was thinking. Because trains can be electrically powered, they offer a tremendous opportunity to reduce the nation's dependence on petroleum. For medium distances (say up to five hundred miles or so), high-speed rail transportation can be essentially as fast as air travel, while the operating costs per passenger-mile are only a fraction of that of aircraft or highway vehicles. Clearly, this idea, which has been proven practical in much of Europe and parts of Asia, needs to be embraced in the United States as well.

• *Synthetic Fuels.* Although ideally the nation should quit burning any fuel that contains carbon, the reality is that there are some important applications (aircraft engines, for example) where no practical alternatives lie on the horizon. Although natural petroleum took millions of years to form, we do know that the fundamental processes involved microbes acting on biomasses under extreme pressure. Theoretically, such processes can be sped up considerably under suitably engineered conditions. Synthetic ethanol, for instance, is already being used as a gasoline additive. Other approaches along this line have been proposed to create other biofuels, and further research in this direction indeed merits funding.

• *Expand Recycling.* The energy cost of manufacturing virtually anything is lower when using recycled materials. In fact, in the United States, most steel products are presently made from recycled scrap; and for aluminum items, roughly half are. Although recycling is now a routine operation in most of the larger cities in the country, this is not, however, the case in many of the smaller communities. A national energy policy needs to address the issue of how to expand recycling to places that do not now do it.

• *Pay as You Go.* Perhaps the most controversial aspect of any national energy policy will relate to how it affects the price of gasoline. In most of the world, consumers now pay the equivalent of two to three dollars *more* per gallon than the average price at the pump in the United States. Some of this difference is due to disparate distribution costs, but most of it results from higher gasoline taxes. That excess tax revenue, in turn, is usually used to subsidize mass transportation and to maintain a nation's physical infrastructure. An important side effect, of course, is that higher gasoline prices also reduce energy consumption. If the United States increased its federal tax on fuels, that would generate sufficient revenues to offset the increased costs associated with other elements of the energy policy.

◆　◆　◆

So, is the preceding set of proposals politically feasible? We're optimistic that, yes, something along this line could work. The key would be to market the energy policy in such a way that every stakeholder sees himself or herself as gaining something. Yes, consumers might pay more per gallon of gasoline, but this could be phased in gradually as they found themselves using less and less of it. Business travelers could begin hopscotching between cities within a few hundred miles of one another by train without the hassle of dealing with airports (which are seldom located near city centers). Beleaguered airlines, in turn, could enter into agreements with rail transportation companies, or even create subsidiary rail services of their own. Oil companies could maintain their profits by moving into other forms of energy production, including synthetic fuels. Existing electric companies would recover their investments in new equipment through the reduction or even elimination of their fuel costs. Manufacturers and contractors would be handed an expanded domestic market for wind turbines and solar panels, and investors would have a broad menu of socially responsible businesses in which to park their money. Lacking the need to intervene in oil-related disputes, the federal government could drastically cut its military expenditures. Defense contractors could rechannel their resources away from creating agents of destruction in favor of building a sustainable infrastructure that enhances everyone's quality of life. Jobs would not be lost overall; only some job descriptions would change. The entire nation would be cleaner and greener.

And, yes, we would thereby be gifting the next generation with a much better world than the one we ourselves entered.

SOURCE NOTES

Chapter 1: The Well from Hell

Our account of the *Deepwater Horizon* spill is based on hundreds of news articles and telecasts that appeared during the months following the explosion. A nice summary of *"Deepwater Horizon's* Final Hours," by David Barstow, David Rohde, and Stephanie Saul, was published in the *New York Times* on December 26, 2010, and contains numerous other poignant human anecdotes that we did not include here. The background information and material on Billy Nungesser and Ivor van Heerden is based on our personal interviews, firsthand observations of the region, and van Heerden's book *The Storm* (Penguin, 2006).

BP's gag order was written right into its Regional Oil Spill Response Plan and, apparently, similar language was also included in its employment contracts:

> No statement shall be made containing any of the following: a) Speculations concerning liability for the spill or its legal consequences. b) Speculations regarding the cause of the spill. An extended inquiry may be needed to determine the actual cause, and legal liability could be affected by what is said. c) Estimates of damage and/or value expressed in dollars, production statistics, sales volume, or insurance coverage. d) Estimates of how long cleanup will take or cleanup costs. e) Promises that property, ecology, or anything else will be restored to normal. f) Do not release the name of injured or dead until next of kin have been notified.

The enforcement of the above policy was confirmed by numerous survivors of the disaster. By the end of 2010, many of them were talking to journalists nonetheless. We chose to not endanger any of those individuals' livelihoods by quoting them directly here.

On the size of the Macondo reservoir, published figures vary considerably, but the lowest estimate seems to be 50 million barrels, with the high running to several billion. The figure we quote (100 million barrels) seems to be credible and possibly even slightly conservative.

The data on the berms came from a series of major newspaper sources; some of our numbers differ slightly from the information blogged by Dr. Len Bahr, formerly associated with the Louisiana executive branch, who followed this subject diligently. Most of such minor numerical discrepancies seem to be related to the dynamic nature of the data (it changed from day to day). We stand by the validity of our general conclusions and comments.

Chapter 2: Black Gold

We wanted to limit the historical content in this chapter to the minimum we felt necessary to contextualize the current state of affairs. Considerably more material can easily be found in thousands of published books and articles. Drake's well, south of Titusville, Pennsylvania, is now the site of a museum and library; the grounds include a reconstruction of Drake's original well house and derrick. Samuel T. Pees, a retired petroleum geologist, has written a fascinating online work, *Oil History*, to which he adds new material from time to time. There is also a Petroleum History Institute that publishes a journal titled *Oil-Industry History*, which focuses on somewhat more obscure historical material.

The shenanigans of Louisiana's Judge Leander Perez are well documented in two old books: Glenn Jeansonne's *Leander Perez: Boss of the Delta* (Louisiana State University Press, 1977) and James Conaway's *Judge: The Life and Times of Leander Perez* (Knopf, 1973). Additional insights came from a 2003 personal interview with the former president of Plaquemines Parish and former protégé of Perez's, Luke Petrovich (since deceased).

Chapter 3: Onto the Shelves

Our description of the process of petroleum formation is based on the more technical explanations that can be found in most university geology textbooks. The meteorological information on Hurricane Audrey (1957) is mainly from National Oceanic and Atmospheric Administration (NOAA) records. The performance of the offshore oil companies during Audrey is based on industry sources, supplemented by several personal interviews with survivors who still live in that area.

The exemplary performance of offshore drillers during Camille (1969) is based mainly on two post-disaster technical reports prepared by the New Orleans and Mobile districts of the US Army Corps of Engineers (USACE). Information on the offshore devastation by Hurricanes Katrina and Rita in 2005 came from the US Minerals Management Service (MMS), later renamed the Bureau of Ocean Energy Management, Regulation, and Enforcement (BOEMRE).

Chapter 4: Oops—1980

Several pamphlets published regionally treat various aspects of the Lake Peigneur disaster. The curious reader can find a few videotapes of the actual waterfall and whirlpool online. One of us made several trips to Jefferson Island and its environs, talked to several locals who had witnessed the 1980 disaster, and made firsthand observations that are reflected in some of the descriptions in this chapter. The organization Save Lake Peigneur has collected and published online a considerable amount of additional information relating to the current controversy about natural gas storage at the site.

Chapter 5: More Oops—1969, 1979, and 1989

A great deal was written about the 1969 spill at the time of that disaster; a fairly complete story can be found in Robert Easton's *Black Tide: The Santa Barbara Oil Spill and Its Consequences* (Delacorte Press, 1972).

The 1979 *Ixtoc I* spill, although the largest ever until the *Deepwater Horizon*, received considerably less publicity. In 1981, Arne Jernelöv and Olaf Lindén published an article on behalf of the Royal Swedish Academy of Sciences with the title "A Case Study of the World's Largest Oil Spill." During the May–June 2010 US Congressional hearings on the ongoing *Deepwater Horizon* crisis, however, BP executives uniformly demonstrated total ignorance of the *Ixtoc I* spill. In July of 2010, *Scientific American* published a retrospective article by Mark Schrope on *Ixtoc I*: "The Lost Legacy of the Last Great Oil Spill."

Numerous books have, however, been written on the disaster of 1989. One that was particularly helpful to us was Sharon Bushell and Stan Jones, *The Spill: Personal Stories from the Exxon Valdez Disaster* (Epicenter Press, 2009). Dr. Riki Ott, a marine biologist and Cordova (Alaska) resident who experienced the unfolding events firsthand, has ever since been lecturing on the topic. Some of her perspectives, delivered in person at the Dixie Theater in Apalachicola in the summer of 2010, are also reflected in this chapter. Our sincere thanks go to Dr. Ott.

Chapter 6: Social Scruples Bedeviled

We supplemented the general material on the history of environmental initiatives with personal observations we've made during our experiences and travels nationwide. The data quoted are from the Louisiana State University Institute for Environmental Studies, the US Department of Commerce, the Louisiana Department of Environmental Quality, the Louisiana Workforce Commission (formerly the Louisiana Department of Labor), and the Louisiana Oil and Gas Association.

A great deal has been written and published about the Mississippi River Gulf Outlet (MRGO), including numerous articles in the New Orleans *Times-Picayune*, spanning the years 2005 to the present. Several scientists affiliated with the Louisiana State University Hurricane Center have conducted computer analyses (subsequently published in various scientific journals) relating to the MRGO's amplifying effects on storm surges. There exist numerous depositions and other legal exhibits relating to the lawsuits brought by Louisiana natives against the US Army Corps of Engineers (USACE), seeking redress for the damages they suffered from the MRGO flooding during Hurricane Katrina. The extent of the MRGO erosion can easily be verified through satellite images accessible online; one of us observed the damage directly from a series of points on the south bank of the canal. Although we requested that the USACE provide us a copy of the original MRGO cost-benefit analysis of 1955, Corps personnel ultimately responded that they were unable to find such a document in their archives. One reference they did supply, however, pegged the original cost-benefit ratio at about $1.50 to 1, without providing any supporting analysis. Even that small number, of course, was ultimately proven to be wildly inflated, insofar as the MRGO was a money loser from the onset. And then eventually it led to a huge amount of destruction as well as a loss of hundreds of lives.

Chapter 7: Chemical Voodoo

Numerous investigative reports and telecasts have explored the public health impacts of petrochemical pollution in Louisiana, and various documentaries have been aired by Public Radio International (*Human Rights in Cancer Alley*), CNN Health, Corpwatch, NOLA (an online New Orleans newspaper) (*LA Flunks at Enforcing Environmental Laws*, for instance), and many others. The Center for Disease Control's US Cancer Statistics Interactive Map graphically supports what we have said here on that topic. Even *Fortune* magazine published an article by Charles Mann on August 16, 2006, titled "How the Energy Business Is Drowning Louisiana."

Other material in this chapter originated with the industry sources we mentioned in the text, the Tulane Environmental Law Clinic's website, *Bloomberg Businessweek*, and various court filings relating to TELC and the Murphy Oil spill settlement.

Chapter 8: What Do the Simple Folk Do?

The explanation of the legal technicalities of mineral rights is based partly on a law review article in the *Louisiana Law Review* by Patrick Martin and J. Yeates, "Louisiana and Texas Oil and Gas Law: An Overview of the Differences," 52 *La L. Rev.* 769 (1992), in addition to Robert Theriot's law review article "Duty to Restore the Surface (Implied, Express, and Damages)," published by the Louisiana Mineral Law Institute in 2005 (see the institute's website). The oil and gas employment statistics came from the Louisiana Workforce Commission, whose representative kindly (but not completely successfully) attempted to resolve some of the inconsistencies we pointed out in that data—which we have also mentioned in our text. The information on oil executives' pay came mainly from the *Wall Street Journal Survey of CEO Compensation* (Hay Group, November 14,

2010). Our account of the Broussard family's struggle came from court documents and an article by Campbell Robertson, "Bitter Twist in Louisiana Family's Long Drilling Fight" (*New York Times*, December 29, 2011).

Chapter 9: Of Wisdom and Folly

The material on the individual politicians was drawn from their own websites, from state and other public information sources, and from Project Vote Smart, which cautions that some of the ratings may not be completely nonpartisan. The Louisiana legislature maintains a comprehensive listing of all legislative actions going back to 1999, so that is the date we chose to begin the narrative of specific examples of the oil/gas industry's influence on Louisiana lawmakers. In the interest of brevity, we suppressed the urge to give a year-by-year continuation of the list; however, we did confirm that 1999 was in no way unusual. The 2011 actions we included are quoted verbatim from Louisiana Mid-Continent Oil and Gas Association (LMOGA) sources and are therefore devoid of any outside bias. Data relating to the restoration program are from our own computations, the website of Louisiana's Oilfield Site Restoration (OSR) Program, and the *Daily Comet* of Lafourche Parish.

Our description of the William G. Corbello case is from the corresponding decision of the Supreme Court of Louisiana, No. 02-C-0826. Some of the pro-oil objections to the final decree are based on an article by William G. Davis of McGlinchey Stafford (a Louisiana law firm), "What Happens after the Well Runs Dry: Legacy Litigation in Louisiana."

Chapter 10: Drill, Baby, Drill

One of us is old enough to remember the oil crises of 1973 and 1979. Supplemental material was drawn from general sources and from President Jimmy Carter's 1977 Address to the Nation on the topic of energy. More detailed discussions of the threat of greenhouse gases and the workings of the IPCC and related matters are dealt with and documented in our book, *Global Climate Change* (Charlesbridge, 2011).

A great deal has been written about Dick Cheney's Energy Task Force; we have touched on only enough of the highlights here to clarify that the outcomes were heavily biased in favor of the petroleum interests. The *Report of the National Energy Policy Group* (May 2001) can be found online, as can the language of the decision *Cheney v. United States District Court*, 542 U.S. 367 (2004). An explosion of articles followed in the *New York Times, Washington Post, CNN Justice, Mother Jones*, and numerous other periodicals. Paul Roberts, for instance, wrote one in *Harper's*, "Last Stop Cheap Gas: Cheap Oil, the Only Oil That Matters, Is about Gone" (August 2004); and *CNN Money* published an article by Katie Brenner, "Lawmakers: Will We Run out of Oil?" (December

7, 2005). On April 23, 2009, Andrew C. Revkin reported in the *New York Times*, "Industry Ignored Its Scientists on Climate." Meanwhile, the Natural Arches dispute was also brewing: Paul Foy, writing in the *Seattle Times* on November 17, 2008, asked, "Natural Arches' New Neighbor: Drilling Platform?" As of this writing, that issue is still not definitively resolved.

Chapter 11: The Oil Industry's Gifts Keep Giving

Exxon Mobil's total evasion of federal income taxes in 2009 was examined by numerous writers, often with a slant: "As Exxon Pays Zero Taxes, Fox Host Defends Big Oil Subsidies" (John Romm of *Climate Progress*, April 10, 2011). On February 17, 2012, Peter Lehner reported for the National Resources Defense Council: "BP Hauls in $7.7 Billion in Profits, Gulf Fishermen Haul in Shrimp with No Eyes." Numerous other journalists simultaneously pointed out that Big Oil was posting record profits via high gas prices. The US Senate's rejection, on March 28, 2012, of an attempt to end Big Oil subsidies was also reported and commented on widely.

Literature on fracking has also been prolific, including Theo Colburn's "Natural Gas Operations from a Public Health Perspective," in *Human and Ecological Risk Assessment: An International Journal*, September 20, 2011; Steven Rosenfeld's "How an Anti-democratic, Corporate-Friendly Pennsylvania Law Has Elevated the Battle over Fracking to a Civil Rights Fight" (*AlterNet*, an online newspaper, March 13, 2012); and many dozens of others. The Halliburton loophole has also received a great deal of attention, including a *New York Times* editorial on November 2, 2009; "Protecting Health, Ensuring Accountability" (*Earthworks*, May 2, 2011); and Lena Groeger's "New York Court Affirms Towns' Powers to Ban Fracking" (*ProPublica—Journalism in the Public Interest*, February 22, 2012). The issue of offshore drilling in Florida has received a considerable amount of attention in Florida newspapers, including articles in the *Tampa Bay Times* on April 28, July 20, and October 12, 2010. Bill Frogamenti published "Don't Drill, Baby, Don't Drill" on Portfolio.com on May 21, 2010.

On October 4, 2011, the *Wall Street Journal* reported "Arctic Ocean Drilling Approved." On the same topic, there is Sara Reardon, "Shell Overcomes Legal Obstacles to Arctic Drilling" (*New Scientist*, March 30, 2012); Kiley Kroh and Michael Conathan, "The Department of Interior's Contradictory Policies on Arctic Drilling" (*Climate Progress*, March 29, 2012); Kim Murphy, "Arctic Ocean Drilling: Shell Launches Preemptive Legal Strike" (*Los Angeles Times*, February 29, 2012); and many others.

Chapter 12: Can America Learn?

Although most of this chapter consists of our own opinions, articles on various aspects of the energy independence issue have been written by many qualified economists, political scientists, physical scientists, and other thinkers. There do exist successful models to draw from. Norway's policies are one example; that small nation is the world's third to sixth largest oil exporter (depending on the year), has been energy independent itself for decades, and has a domestic program to curtail greenhouse gas emissions— capturing carbon dioxide on an industrial scale, for instance, since 1996. Petroleum there is treated as a national resource, and oil-related revenues are used to provide various social services and investments in infrastructure improvements. As a result, by almost all measures, Norwegians today enjoy the best quality of life on the planet.

We also recommend that interested US readers take a look at what happened in the state of Alaska. Oil companies conducting operations there pay hefty fees for that privilege. Most of this public revenue stream goes straight to the state government, which in turn does not levy a personal income tax. But a portion (25 percent) also goes into a fund that each year is distributed to all of Alaska's permanent residents. In recent decades, these payments have varied between about $1,000 and $3,000 per resident per year. Although this scheme falls considerably short of nationalization, it does spread the oil wealth around and prevents it from accumulating in the bank accounts of a small minority—as it has in Louisiana.

FURTHER READING

Bushell, Sharon, and Stan Jones. *The Spill: Personal Stories from the Exxon Valdez Disaster*. Epicenter Press, 2009.

Coll, Steve. *Private Empire: ExxonMobil and American Power*. Penguin Press, 2012.

Conaway, James. *Judge: The Life and Times of Leander Perez*. Knopf, 1973.

Cooper, Andrew Scott. *The Oil Kings: How the U.S., Iran, and Saudi Arabia Changed the Balance of Power in the Middle East*. Simon & Schuster, 2011.

Cooper, Christopher, and Robert Block. *Disaster: Hurricane Katrina and the Failure of Homeland Security*. Henry Holt and Company, 2006.

Jeansonne, Glen. *Leander Perez: Boss of the Delta*. Louisiana State University Press, 1977.

Lynas, Mark. *Six Degrees: Our Future on a Hotter Planet*. National Geographic Books, 2008.

Margonelli, Lisa. *Oil on the Brain: Petroleum's Long, Strange Trip to Your Tank*. Broadway Books, 2008.

Maugeri, Leonardo. *The Age of Oil: The Mythology, History, and Future of the World's Most Controversial Resource*. Praeger, 2006.

Misrach, Richard, and Kate Orff. *Petrochemical America*. New York: Aperature Foundation, 2012.

Mooney, Chris. *The Republican War on Science*. Basic Books, 2005.

Steinberg, Ted. *Acts of God: The Unnatural History of Natural Disaster in America*. Oxford University Press, 2000.

Tidwell, Mike. *Bayou Farewell: The Rich Life and Tragic Death of Louisiana's Cajun Coast*. Pantheon, 2003.

Van Heeren, Ivor, and Mike Bryan. *The Storm: What Went Wrong and Why during Hurricane Katrina—the Inside Story from One Louisiana Scientist*. Penguin, 2006.

White, Richard D. *Kingfish: The Reign of Huey P. Long*. Random House, 2006.

Yergin, David. *The Prize: The Epic Quest for Oil, Money, and Power*. Free Press, 2008.

Zebrowski, Ernest. *Global Climate Change: The Book of Essential Knowledge*. Charlesbridge, 2011.

INDEX